Letty's Story

Hell to Heaven

Letty's Story

LETICIA

TATE PUBLISHING
AND ENTERPRISES, LLC

Letty's Story
Copyright © 2014 by Leticia Lakusiewicz. All rights reserved.

No part of this publication may be reproduced, stored in a retrieval system or transmitted in any way by any means, electronic, mechanical, photocopy, recording or otherwise without the prior permission of the author except as provided by USA copyright law.

This book is designed to provide accurate and authoritative information with regard to the subject matter covered. This information is given with the understanding that neither the author nor Tate Publishing, LLC is engaged in rendering legal, professional advice. Since the details of your situation are fact dependent, you should additionally seek the services of a competent professional.

The opinions expressed by the author are not necessarily those of Tate Publishing, LLC.

Published by Tate Publishing & Enterprises, LLC
127 E. Trade Center Terrace | Mustang, Oklahoma 73064 USA
1.888.361.9473 | www.tatepublishing.com

Tate Publishing is committed to excellence in the publishing industry. The company reflects the philosophy established by the founders, based on Psalm 68:11,
"The Lord gave the word and great was the company of those who published it."

Book design copyright © 2014 by Tate Publishing, LLC. All rights reserved.
Cover design by Carlo Nino Suico
Interior design by Caypeeline Casas

Published in the United States of America

ISBN: 978-1-63306-756-1
1. Biography & Autobiography / General
2. Biography & Autobiography / Women
14.08.06

Contents

Preface 9
Prologue 11
A Little Girl's World Changes 13
Occupation 29
Life on the Farm 53
A New World Opens with School 77
The Americans Came Back 95
An Unhappy Odyssey Begins 111
A Flower Blooms 129
Purgatory Reclaimed 135
Coming Down to Earth 147
Choices 155
Leticia Runs For Her life 159
Two Worlds Collide 165
And Now, the Rest of the Story 169
Getting to Know You 175
The Ice Is Broken 183
Leticia Meets Stanley and the Blue Beetle 189
The Ride of a Lifetime 199
The Speakeasy 205
The Surprise 213

Time, Success, and Trouble 223
The Inheritance 227
A Price Too High to Pay 231
The Flame Goes Out 235
Dying 239
Depression 247
Sometimes a Bee Can Move an Ox 257
Through the Eyes of Leticia 261
The Struggle 269
Money 275
Leticia's Great Gamble—The WOW Finale 281
Epilogue 293

The true story of a little girl who overcame unbelievable obstacles in becoming a woman and who found love, happiness, and success in another world. Only the names have been changed to protect the innocent.

PREFACE

This story was told with great reluctance.

The events were of such painful enormity that there were times the heroine was unable to remember very personal details having blocked horrible occurrences from her conscious thoughts, forgetting people who were close to her, even family members temporarily.

The tears that accompanied the recollections, the long pauses of silence between haunting sentences so hard to form and utter, were all signs of how deeply the feelings ran.

Although intensely personal, this story is no different from the stories of other people everywhere who walk the path of hardship because of circumstances thrust upon them over which they have no control.

Like all others who have been an unwilling part of man's inhumanity to man and have survived, the survivor, when asked to relate the story, merely says a simple, "It was pretty rough," or in many cases, nothing at all, but always with a kind of blank, far-off, unwanted, recollected stare.

It is to all of you true heroes regardless of country or sex, that this *factual* book is dedicated: to those who had to carry a gun for your country and those who didn't, to women all over the world who had to keep alive and feed their starving and injured children by any means possible, so that they might survive to someday enjoy the blessings of a kinder, more peaceful world.

To all of you, my deepest and most profound respect.

Prologue

This is the *true story* of triumph over tragedy, of spirit over despair, and of a deep and abiding love that won out over all adversity. It is the story of a little girl from one world destined to survive and find happiness in another world—far away from the one into which she was born—and of a deep faith in herself and in God that enabled her to make a better life for herself and for those she loved. It is the story of a great love that is as alive and bright today as it was many years ago when this girl first learned to trust again. Lastly, it is the story of survival that strikes right at the heart of who we are as people and asks, "Who can say what you yourself would have done under similar circumstances to survive, and who is to judge what is right and wrong?" The ending of the story has yet to be written and judgment of a life rests in the hearts and minds of you, the reader.

A Little Girl's World Changes

It was nighttime and a little girl about five years old was sleeping peacefully in her bed, with gentle breezes from an open window caressing her smiling, angelic face. The night was warm, and all was quiet, giving way only to the chirping sounds of a tropical night, with myriads of birds and insects cavorting in their usual manner of mating.

The little girl lay in a deep, untroubled slumber, hugging a cherished old rag doll with a repaired tear in its head where the family dog had once tried to wrestle it from her arms. All seemed well on this quiet night on December 7, 1941, for an innocent little girl so unaware of the unstoppable events into which she would soon be plunged, sleeping away the last peaceful seconds of her young life.

Slowly and unrelentingly, all the intermittent chirping sounds of night became constant as if some large group of crickets were coming closer toward the little girl's window. Closer and closer the sounds came, growing ever louder and determined, causing the little girl in peaceful repose to begin tossing and turning in her bed.

Suddenly, the constant droning sound gave way, mingling with many high-pitched whistles that began to scream as they got even louder.

The startled little girl abruptly awoke and almost immediately was forcefully thrown from her bed as if by a huge unseen malevolent hand that entered her life with a loud, thunderous crash, followed by another and another, each violently shaking her house as the cool blackness and soft melodies of a serene night suddenly gave way to a deafening cacophony of sounds, accompanied by bright flashes that lit up her small room as brightly as daytime.

She froze in terror being unable to move—casting a wide-eyed stare out the open window fixated on the flashes now engulfing the homes of her neighbors and friends.

"My dolly, where's my dolly" she cried, frantically looking for the little cloth ragamuffin she loved. Finding the doll amid some debris now coming in through her window, she clutched the doll to her chest and began to *cry*.

The noises got still louder, the shaking of her house more violent making it impossible for her to stand, and amid her uncontrollable tears and sobbing, she pitifully cried, "Mama, make it stop! Please, Mama, make it stop! Stop it! Stop it! Please!"

But it didn't stop.

For a time interminable, each crash and rumble was followed by another, then another, and still another, as if all the anger of God in his heaven was being thunderously released upon the earth and now the earth was going to open and she would be gone forever.

Then the wall suddenly pushed into the room on top of her, part of it disappearing down into the street—the open window of her room now becoming a huge gaping hole looking into the street below, threatening to swallow her and her dolly.

"Mama, Mama!" she screamed, but Mama did not answer or come to her. Nobody came. Her arms and legs felt wet, as did her face, with the wetness beginning to flow over her eyes, more and more, sticky, warm, and red.

She pulled herself up into the room on the now slanting floor, her arms and legs staining the floor red, but numbed by fear, she did not seem to feel the pain. She looked for her dolly but couldn't find her, the large gaping hole having claimed her little friend.

She clung to a piece of wood jutting out of another smashed wall, the splintery wood being the only thing preventing her final journey into the ever devouring hole. It was here that she clung, and clung, and clung for a time so long, she forgot about that which she cried.

Then, just as suddenly as it all began, the deafening outbursts of thunder gave way to lessening crashes that seemed to be going someplace else. The little girl lifted her head from its huddled, contorted position and blankly stared into the huge gaping hole, which now seemed even bigger, with no wall remaining and the ceiling beginning to fold itself down into the monstrous gouged out opening, framing bright beams of light shining from many places on the ground up into a smoky black sky, further brightened into a reddish orange glow by many large fires. She could see silhouettes of airplanes in those light beams which were now themselves on fire with some beginning to fall lower and lower to meet the earth in a flaming orange ball.

The diminishing crashes began to now give way to the sounds of bells and sirens, automobile engines and horrible, horrible screams. Many names were being called out, but only the silence of no reply was coming back to the callers. Anguished cries and sobbing filled the night as well as smoke and ash, which made breathing and swallowing very difficult.

There she stayed, afraid to move for fear of falling through the hole down into the street and all the misery and rubble below.

"Mama, Mama," she kept calling now beginning to feel the pain from the splintery wood sticking into her hands, the bloody knees and elbows, and the cuts on her little face and head.

Without warning, there was noise and a pushing sound coming from the high slanted upper end of the room. Could this be someone coming for her? Had someone really heard her cries through all the noise and confusion?

"Leticia! Leticia!" A frantic, familiar voice was calling her name. How wonderful it sounded! The greatest, happiest sound in all the world—she could hear her name!

Then the wall again began to break apart, only this time by the axes of several men wearing firefighting clothes. "Mama, Mama!" she screamed again and again. Now she could see the faces of the men clearly and then—the most wonderful sight of all—her mother's face was behind those strong men. Yes, yes, her mama had heard her.

One of the men gradually lowered himself by rope to the little girl gently freeing her from her wooden perch and lifted her ever upward. She reached up to her mother's outstretched hand. Closer and closer, a distance so close yet so far away. Finally close enough, she grabbed with all her might, but the pain from the splinters and the bloody, slippery hand could not hold on. "Mama, Mama, don't let me go," she cried.

Then suddenly with a mighty lift—security! She was safe. How good it was to feel her mother's loving arms around her again in a hug so tight it drove the air out of her body. The pain, the blood, the terror were now all forgotten in those loving arms.

The next day arrived quietly, almost too quietly. The hot tropical noontime sun beat down mercilessly on the battered city. There were still some thinning clouds of gray-black smoke billowing from places where once beautiful buildings stood. And in the air, there was a strange smell which the little girl could not recognize—it was like nothing she had smelled before. She was hungry, but the smell made her a little sick to her stomach. She was now staying in her auntie's house which was not damaged but was quite close to her own.

She didn't mind the bandages on her arms and legs or even the funny round one on her head that her mama called Leticia's new hat, but her hands—oh, the pain when she tried to move her fingers made it impossible to hold anything or even go potty. The bleeding had stopped, but the swelling always made the bandages too tight. Daddy took her to the hospital, but there were too many people there who were very badly hurt, and the doctors couldn't get to her. She was happy that her daddy worked in the hospital and was able to get bandages for her.

She sat on the edge of the bed that she shared with her two younger sisters watching them play with a ball, and then suddenly, as if awakened from a dreamlike state, she said, "Where's my dolly?"

She went from room to room asking all her relatives if they had seen her dolly, but all either shook their head or said no. She *had* to find her ragamuffin friend. Now she remembered that dolly had fallen through that bad hole in her house and must be in the street somewhere. She was sure she could find her. She just had to go there and try.

It was now about midafternoon, and it would still be daylight for a while.

She slipped out of auntie's house and started to walk home but was able to only walk slowly, partly because her legs hurt and partly because there was scattered debris and crumbled houses everywhere and that smell which seemed to be getting stronger, a sort of heavy sweet smell that now was mixed with smells of ash and charred wood.

There were many of her neighbors milling around, some of whom had their faces locked in blank expressionless stares and who just gently pushed her aside when she asked them if they had seen her dolly, and still others who were crying and either didn't answer her or became *angry* with her when she asked.

It was the hottest part of the day, and her bandages were becoming more uncomfortable. She removed them and kept looking through the rubble for her treasured friend. The closer she got to her house, the stronger and more sickening the smells became, seemingly coming from everywhere and yet nowhere.

Then, she saw something shining through the haphazardly strewn boards and debris, the bright sun glittering in all directions off it. She moved the wood away and saw a beautiful golden bracelet on a woman's wrist that did not move. Somebody was in this large pile of wood! If she could get the woman out, maybe she would help her find her doll. Excited, she began to dig and move the debris, and then she grabbed the woman's hand—it was stiff and did not respond to her touch. She pulled harder, and suddenly the hand and bracelet were free, coming straight to the little girl and landing in her lap as she fell backward, winding up sitting on the ground. The little girl screamed incessantly, panic-stricken. There was no one attached to the hand! Her sobs were uncontrollable.

She fearfully pushed the hand away back into the woodpile and constantly withdrew backwards, scrambling on the ground until the wheel of a parked car blocked her movement. There she sat and cried, a frightened child caught up in confusion and despair, not understanding what was going on around her, not understanding death.

She then felt another hand on her shoulder. She instantly drew back, but this time, the hand moved and was accompanied by a young boy's voice.

"We better get out of here," the voice said. "The trucks will be coming." She didn't answer but stood up and followed him. As they walked a little farther not speaking a word, she saw some blue cloth on the ground that was just like the dress her dolly had. Her tears turned to joy! Now she would find her friend. She pulled on the boy's shirt so he would follow her across the street to explore, but he said no and shook his head in a most emphatic manner. But the little girl was determined. She was excited now, her heart filled with the expectation of seeing her doll again, her best friend in the whole world.

But just as suddenly, her joy turned to horror that made her feel cold all over even on this hot day, and she froze in terror. Now she knew where that sickening smell was coming from. There were people lying everywhere, very still, motionless, and silent.

Many were missing parts of their bodies, left only with huge, ragged, gaping bloody wounds; their faces were contorted in painful agonizing grimaces. Some had only the top half of their body with long, curly, yellow, sausage-like loops coming out, as if the lower half of their bodies had walked away on its own. The smell was overwhelming. The little girl vomited and retched until she was too weak to stand. Tears, vomit, and that horrible smell and sight, initiation of a type most fiendish for a little innocent girl to a cruel world of suffering and death.

Then, there's something worse—more terrible than what she had already seen.

It seemed like hell itself had suddenly spilled forth its devils that were now growling in fierce anger, barking, ripping away at one another and at the dead bodies that they had come to devour. Packs of big black dogs appeared almost out of nowhere, tearing apart and eating the flesh of all the dead people and fighting each other at the same time. They didn't care what they ate, and the little girl was right there amid this horrific violence. She wanted to run but couldn't. She knew if she moved that they would eat her too.

Suddenly, she heard it—the clanging of a bell, rolling wooden wheels on the street, and men yelling, "Over here!" A group of men with rag masks on their faces had come to remove the bodies. One of them snatched up the little girl, the rest driving the dogs away. She knew those eyes; she knew that soothing voice reassuring her that everything was alright. Daddy! It was her daddy! Fate had again taken a hand, and Leticia was safe once more. Her protector had arrived just in time.

But then, she thought, what of the night to come? *They come at night, and when they come, they hurt people, not caring who.*

I can't stop them, she thought. *But if I make the night not come, then they won't come. I will keep my light on all the time and hold back the terrible black of night, and then I'll be safe.*

Leticia never slept in a dark room again.

So it was, night after night—all the same, afraid during the day anticipating the night, and then, the twisting knot-like pains in the stomach, the weakness in her arms and legs as the little girl was again plunged into the deepest depths of fear as the ever-screaming bombs fell smashing everything. The little girl wondered if she too would be smashed and become just another piece of meat lying in the street for the dogs to rip apart.

The depth of her fear was immeasurable.

But sometimes in strange ways, God is merciful to those that are suffering greatly and gives a tiny bit of respite and peace to the minds of those who seemingly have no hope. For Leticia, an added problem brought some unexpected blessed relief.

Infection—a problem that, of itself, could snuff out her fragile life!

Her wounds had become badly infected when she handled the street debris and had fallen to the ground in fear of the horrors she saw.

Now her hands were severely swollen and painful, almost totally useless, and her legs and arms had open draining sores. Daddy couldn't get medicine from the hospital because it was all being used up by people who were badly hurt and needed it more. As the infection became worse, however, her daddy became desperate! It was now their neighbors' lives or that of his beloved Leticia—he had no choice. The thought drove a dagger through his heart. Surely God would understand. He *had* to do it! He couldn't sacrifice his little girl, even if it meant his own death as a looter and to be condemned to hell itself. He decided to steal the medications for her and risk everything. Yes, he knew it was a horrible thing to do, and he would be hurting others, but he couldn't bear losing his Leticia forever. The bullet that would enter his brain if he was caught would be less painful than having to live with the hurt of failing to have done all he could do to save his little girl.

Leticia was now almost delirious with fever.

The dark-brown liquid daddy put on all her wounds burned terribly, but she knew he was trying to help her. The tears that streamed down her face came from forgiving eyes that looked at her father, and she never complained.

Day after day, it was the same brown liquid, the same pain, then the forceful opening of her wounds to drain the pus, but she never pulled away. She allowed herself to scream and cry every time Daddy would say to her, "Okay, Leticia, this is going to hurt a little."

The fever persisted, the treatments continued, and a little girl slipped into the uncaring corner of the mind governed by delirium. It did not matter anymore, the pain of her arms and legs. It did not matter anymore, the bombs screaming and shaking the house with their thunderous presence. She had now entered a place where only some lucky people go to get relief; blessed relief from all the pain, fear, and anguish; the blessed relief of almost not being there any more; blessed relief that only God in his infinite mercy could grant.

She did not know how long she was in this place of the mind and complete detachment, nor did she care. She only felt that she was almost happy there. There, protectors weren't necessary. No one was there to hurt her. She could almost feel the warm, loving presence of God. How good it was to be there!

The end came gradually. Not the end of her life, but the end of this place of the mind where she had been. Faintly, she began to hear voices, voices that gradually became louder, voices that were familiar to her, which later were accompanied by the distant sounds of explosions.

Her legs and arms didn't hurt as much anymore, and she was beginning to move her fingers. As she slowly opened her eyes, she began to see blurry faces that became ever clearer until she could recognize the smiling faces of her mama and daddy who were both crying and smiling at the same time. She didn't know why.

All the hugs felt good, so very good, but it was hard for her to keep her eyes open, and the little girl now fell into a deep sleep going to another place of the mind and body where God lets all people renew.

She had survived but had no understanding of what, how, or why.

She only knew that it was good to be back, back to a world with all its troubles, back to the people she loved.

She never wanted to leave again, but right now, it was time to just sleep.

Over the following days, memory and reality became one with a disappointing sadness. Leticia was happy to be back, but she was back to the same hardship she had left. Her arms and legs felt better, but she was still greatly troubled by the sights and sounds going on all around her.

She remembered that in days past, she never heard her parents fight or argue. If a serious discussion or disagreement arose, her parents would disappear and "go hide" in another room away from her and her brother and sisters. There they would settle the difficulties, and when they returned, all would be well although they usually would then not be talkative at all.

But now, auntie's house was overcrowded, and there was no place for the adults to "go hide." All troubles and worries were discussed openly, but the manner was fearful, not calm. To see the adults upset increased the little girl's fear; then, she herself would find a place to hide, although there was none, so she overheard all the worries of others.

Things that she had taken for granted before were now scarce and considered luxuries—and the adults were now rationing everything. The biggest problem was food and water, but the adults were most concerned about the water. The water supply had been damaged by the bombing, and all the water had to be boiled before anybody could drink it.

Bathing consisted of running outside in the rain without any clothes on. Leticia was not yet aware of the differences between boys and girls and was ecstatic about being able to do her "rain dances." Rainy days became a special occasions holiday because in addition to getting clean water to drink and getting herself clean at the same time, she was feeling heavenly while doing it *and* planes couldn't fly in the rain, so no bombs would fall! Everyone frequently prayed that it would rain every day, but of course, it didn't.

Food was obtainable as farmers somehow managed to get their supplies of meat, fruit, and vegetables into Manila between the bombing raids, but paying for the food was another matter. The destruction caused by the bombs had wiped out the ability of many people to earn a living, so nobody had any money. Bartering became the way of life, but it was still necessary to have something with which to trade.

Leticia was more fortunate than others. Her daddy still worked at the hospital, which the Japanese were careful to avoid in their attacks, so he was still able to provide for her and for all those at auntie's house. Although everything that Daddy brought home was strictly rationed, they all appreciated whatever they got, no matter how small the portion. There were many moments of quiet as Letty, and the others looked at the sparsely covered plates in front of them at supper time, hearing only the sounds of the rumblings in their stomachs, but no one complained. Only prayers were said, giving thanks to God for allowing them to eat while they knew others were much less fortunate. Nothing was ever wasted or thrown away.

As the bombing continued, the amount of destruction increased and massive piles of debris began to collect in the city. It was impossible to remove it. Leticia and her mama went out one morning to walk to a spot where a vendor usually waited with his cart full of vegetables to sell. They were able to get a few ears of corn and started walking back to auntie's house. They passed buildings partially knocked down with complete sides missing so Leticia *could* see inside them *and look into* many rooms all at once, rooms where her neighbors had once happily lived. A few of the rooms still had personal pictures on what remained of the walls, and in some rooms, pictures of a sorrowful Jesus stared back at her.

The huge piles of rubble alongside these building openings were far too big and too many for easy removal so these piles of rubble lingered for many days. Under these piles were dead people; Leticia was sure because her nose was never wrong. These people hadn't been dug out—an inviting meal for hungry rats.

Leticia didn't really understand what a rat was and tugged at her mama's dress to stop walking so she could watch all the brown, furry animals darting in and out of the deep spaces in the woodpiles and debris. She wondered if they might like to play with her. Mama grabbed Leticia's hand and pulled her close. "You must never go near them. They will bite you," Mama said. Leticia didn't quite understand why, but she did understand the fearful tone of mama's voice, so she started to walk faster with her mother still holding her hand tightly.

That night, when all the adults got together to talk, Mama told them what she had seen.

Leticia added, "And they were big too!"

As they discussed the problem, everyone began to contribute similar observations, and they began to realize that they were starting to become overrun with rats. It wouldn't be long before the rats would become bolder and begin entering their homes or biting children in the streets.

"How do we get rid of them?" Leticia heard one man say.

Leticia's daddy then answered, "We burn them all out."

"That's too dangerous," was the reply.

But her daddy persisted. "Maybe we can get an added benefit."

"What do you mean?" another asked.

"I mean that maybe we can move the bombing away from us."

"What?"

"How?" Questions filled the room.

Then Leticia's daddy revealed his bold plan. It was dangerous and daring, but it might succeed. And why not? Leticia knew her daddy was very smart and knew everything.

Daddy said that they would mark where the rats were, have cans filled with gasoline and coal oil ready, then when the planes started bombing, they would wait until just the right moment, then set big fires *on* all the places the rats were, and hope they could fool the Japanese into thinking that the bombing had done more damage than it really did, so that next time, they wouldn't waste bombs covering the same area again.

A man jumped up and said, "But we risk burning down our own homes—all of Manila!"

Daddy answered, "That's true, but right now, if the bombs don't get us, the rats eventually will, so I think it's worth the gamble."

Several other men then all agreed. "This must be done. It's a brilliant plan! If it works, we might get the bombs off our heads if just for a little while."

The men and women all worked together and when the time came during the next bombing raid, they took their lives in their hands, and brave Filipinos ran with filled gasoline cans into the fiery maelstrom. So much fire, so much light, that the night became day!

The next day, Leticia went outside with her mama. She couldn't see any rats, and the bad smell she had been forced to live with and had come to hate was also gone.

The rats were gone! And something else good had happened: the huge fires had not only killed the rats but had become a funeral pyre for all those poor dead people.

That night, the bombs fell in a distant place; the plan had worked beyond their greatest hopes! It seemed like all evening, other happy Filipinos came to auntie's house to congratulate daddy on his brilliant plan. He was now a hero. And they were right. Both the man *and* his plan were brilliant, but Leticia always knew that. *After all*, she thought, her chest bursting with pride, *he's my daddy!*

Sometime after mid-December, Leticia watched the nervousness and worry of the adults increase. She also noted that there was a noticeable decrease in *familiar* faces of men, but no new men were arriving. She knew that they had not all been killed because the adults were always talking about "reports" from them. She constantly heard everyone talking about a place called Bataan.

"We should not worry," her daddy said. "General MacArthur is still at the Manila Hotel."

Then someone interrupted, "But the Japanese have already landed at Lingayen Gulf!"

And still another said fearfully, "And also at Lamon Bay!" There was a great deal of nervous, confused shouting, and then followed by a strange silence.

"What should we do?" she heard, but no one seemed to know. The men all began to leave the room after her daddy said, "Let's wait and see what MacArthur does."

It wasn't a solution, but it was an answer that offered some hope.

For Leticia, in a few days, it would be Christmas, and she eagerly anticipated Santa Claus. She remembered last Christmas with all the presents and lights; people singing songs and telling her stories about baby Jesus. She just couldn't wait!

Leticia had already written her letter to Santa. She had only one thing on it, a new dolly. The stores weren't open, but that was okay. Leticia knew that Santa Claus didn't need stores—he came from far away on his sled with reindeer just loaded with presents. But Santa always came at midnight. Could his reindeer outrun the planes dropping bombs? Sure he could. He was Santa Claus, and like her daddy, he could do anything. Santa *always* came on Christmas!

She hoped and dreamed and added a few more little things to Santa's letter.

She also worked on the presents that she was going to give others, a Christmas card she had drawn with pencil for her mama, a few pieces of sugar cane she had gotten in one of her very "clever" barter arrangements for her shoes that used to hurt because they were way too tight, and some other things she was still working on for her auntie and her sisters.

Christmas Eve! She awoke with her eyes open as wide as saucers in the joyful anticipation of what was to come.

Uh-oh, she thought, *my gifts for the others still aren't finished.*

All through the day she toiled away. She just *had* to be ready for Santa. She had a surprise present for him too!

Leticia didn't even notice that this day was different from other days. No men were at the house; no men were anywhere to be seen in the streets. There were lots of cars and trucks in the streets, all jammed up, but the very few men she did see were the drivers.

Gee, everyone must be rushing to do their Christmas shopping, she thought.

Quite hurriedly, her daddy came rushing into the house.

He must have presents under his shirt, she thought. *I'll go see.*

But daddy's face wasn't happy. He nervously gathered all the women and children into one room. "What's wrong, Daddy, what's wrong?" Leticia asked.

Daddy answered her and all the women in the room at the same time, "General MacArthur left Manila and has gone to Corregidor to fight for the Philippines. He has declared Manila a defenseless city."

"Oh my god no, no!" the women screamed, and they began to cry hysterically.

Leticia walked over to her daddy, tugged on his shirt sleeve, and looked up into her daddy's face as innocently as only a child can. She asked, "But, Daddy, who will protect us here?"

Daddy answered, "It's all right, Leticia. Since the general declared Manila a defenseless city, the Japanese have no reason to bomb us anymore. Secretary of Justice Laurel is telling all Filipinos to cooperate with the Japanese who will now come, and everyone will be all right."

But the look on daddy's face did not look as reassuring as his words. Leticia knew her daddy would never lie, but somehow, she felt that daddy himself did not believe what he was saying.

Leticia was confused, but she was happy that the bombing would stop! For sure Santa would get through now!

She continued to prepare for his arrival, a child immersed in the warm, wonderful innocent thoughts of all children everywhere, at this holiest time of the year.

As everyone in the room settled about the table for Christmas Eve supper, singing softly the gentle, familiar refrains of "Silent Night"—the singing became punctuated by the too familiar sounds of many long screams followed by sudden crashes of thunder that knocked things off the walls. *They* were bombing us! The women began to scream, "But they were supposed to stop!"

Everyone looked at Daddy whose surprised face turned very angry.

"God send them all to hell for this!" he yelled.

Leticia thought, *But this is Christmas. How can all this be?*

She was right. It was Christmas 1941, and somehow for the first and only time in her short memories of all her Christmases past, Santa didn't get through.

Occupation

The bombings continued for several days, and then suddenly, without warning, it stopped. No bombing, no one in the streets, almost no sound at all. A strange eerie quiet settled over them that was almost as terrifying as the bombing.

"You are not to go outside," daddy told us.

"Stay inside, the Japanese will be coming soon," he said, in an even more forceful tone.

"Who are they?" Leticia asked. "What do they look like?"

"Hush now, you will know soon enough," Mama said.

But nothing happened. Maybe Daddy was wrong. Maybe nobody was coming.

They waited. The silence and the waiting made each fearful minute seem like hours.

How would they treat us? Leticia thought and wondered. *They had been bombing us and hurting my friends and neighbors. They probably were going to hurt us more. What are we going to do? Will they hurt my mama and daddy?*

The more she thought, the more fearful she became.

And the silence, making things so much worse.

Even when one of the older women farted, it wasn't funny anymore and sounded like a small bomb going off in the distance.

Leticia kept asking Daddy, "When will the silence end?"

Daddy answered, "Too soon, Leticia, I'm afraid it will be all too soon."

And daddy was right.

Auntie was looking out the window when suddenly, she got excited and yelled, "Look! It's snowing!"

"What?" everyone exclaimed.

It was true, except the snowflakes were thousands of white leaflets being dropped by planes on Manila. One of the women ran outside to get one. The leaflets were written in Tagalog and said the Japanese army would be entering the city later in the day. The leaflets contained the "Rules of Behavior" for all inhabitants of the city. No sooner than the snowstorm of leaflets had fluttered down on the city, a loudspeaker was heard speaking in Tagalog telling all inhabitants of Manila the same information that was written on the leaflets. For several hours following, the loudspeakers blared out the same message:

> The invincible Japanese Army, the Asian Brothers of all Filipinos, has come to liberate the Philippines from the decadent white foreigners who have been stealing away the wealth of all Filipinos. All inhabitants of the city will line the streets and receive all Japanese soldiers with great respect. You will be given flags to honor Japan and they should be waved with enthusiasm shouting "Banzai!" continuously as the Japanese soldiers march by, especially the children. All liberated inhabitants of Manila are to bow when greeting or passing a Japanese soldier at all times. Any troublemakers who fail to follow these rules or offer any resistance of any kind will be considered as traitors and dealt with immediately in the harshest of ways.
>
> Long live Japan and our glorious Emperor Hirohito. Banzai!

Over and over again, it was the same message.

"Well, at least, they are not going to shoot us," auntie said.

Leticia's daddy was silent, for he knew well that "liberation" by the *Japanese* meant subjugation, but he also wanted to protect all the women and children in the house, so Daddy said, "Do exactly what they are telling us to do. This is not the time to be brave. This is the time to do what is necessary to survive."

And so everyone waited, waited for the Japanese to march into the city. All of them wondered what would happen now, waiting in fearful anticipation. Their whole world was about to be changed for them right before their eyes, and they were powerless to do anything about it.

Soon in the distance, Leticia could hear a lot of shouting with one word resounding clearly over everything else *that* was going on, "Banzai! Banzai!"

She didn't know what it meant, but it must be important though because everyone was shouting it.

As the cheering got closer, it was accompanied by the trudge, trudge, trudge of marching feet. Many people lined the street in front of her auntie's house all waving white flags with a big red ball in the middle. Leticia had one too, but she was so small she couldn't see anything except the backs of all the cheering people.

Trudge, trudge, trudge—the sound was louder now as the long wide column of soldiers was marching by. Being very inquisitive, the little girl decided that if she couldn't see above or around the people, maybe she could see more from down below. She got on her hands and knees and began crawling through the forest of "trees" in front of her, "trees" that wore shoes.

Finally, she got close enough to see what was going on. Being a little girl and shielded by a line of "trees," she was able to watch and still feel safe. Trudge, trudge, trudge—a sound made by the canvas covered legs of the marching Japanese soldiers. She saw many pass and thought, "Gee, they all look like us Filipinos, but their faces scare me."

The faces were stern and unsmiling. Along both sides of the wide marching column, Leticia could see two lines of separate soldiers who were not marching like the others. These separated soldiers were walking along with the marching column and kept urging the Filipino people to cheer. Each time they cheered, other men with moving picture cameras mounted on trucks would take pictures of the people.

It all seemed to Leticia to be just a big parade like the ones that she had seen her own people do on holidays. Everybody had lots of fun at those parades.

Then Leticia saw a soldier riding on horseback. He was in front of the next group of soldiers in the wide column and had a pretty uniform with a lot of shiny medals on it.

He stopped the column because of a disturbance in the crowd. An old man who Leticia had seen many times in the neighborhood, but did not know well, had come to watch the parade.

Two Japanese soldiers were shouting at him, but he just looked at them and kept smiling. The soldiers got very angry and began to slap him on the top of his head. The man continued to stand there looking at the soldiers but now did not smile anymore.

The two soldiers struck the backs of his knees with their rifle butts, and the old man was forced to kneel on the street, but he still kept looking straight into their angry faces. The old man looked confused and turned his hands palms up as if to ask what they wanted. The soldiers were now so furious that the horseback soldier got off his horse and walked over to them. He yelled at the old man who now looked terrified.

Leticia wondered why these soldiers were yelling so much at an old man who was deaf and couldn't speak.

Suddenly, the two soldiers bent the old man forward while he was kneeling down. The horseback soldier raised a long, sunlight-flashing sword slowly above his head and, with one swipe at the old man's neck—and a dull *ffifttt*—*cut off his head!*

Thud!

The head hit the street and rolled down the little slope of bricks, spewing a spray of blood as it turned over and over, coming to rest right in front of Leticia, looking directly into her face.

She was terrified, but unable to scream. The scream seemed to be stuck in her throat and wouldn't come out. She wasn't even able to cry.

The shocked and horrified crowd that had been a cheering crowd was now silent. Japanese soldiers were pushing back the crowd with their rifles.

Then there was an undercurrent of murmuring in the crowd.

Someone was talking over a loudspeaker in Tagalog saying that it was the old man's fault for insulting a Japanese soldier by refusing to bow in respect and that he deserved the punishment.

The crowd continued to grumble and stopped only when the soldiers pointed their rifles into the crowd in menacing fashion.

The grumbling stopped, but so did the cheering, and the flag waving.

Leticia later asked her daddy, "Why did the Japanese officer hurt an old deaf man who could not speak?"

Her daddy sadly replied, "To set an example and teach us a lesson, baby."

The Filipino education of Japanese "liberation" had begun, and before it was over, many, many hard lessons would be learned and never forgotten.

What she had seen had a deep and profound effect on Leticia. At the time, even she did not realize just how deep. She just could not forget it, just couldn't let it go.

She could not forget looking into the face of a head that was no longer attached to a body, to a person who had been a neighbor. She could not forget the leaky red tubes that continued to slowly drain. She remembered that just a minute before it happened, the old man was just watching the parade, alive and smiling. Then, the change of a smiling face to a look of questioning disbelief and finally, to total and absolute fear, and the horrible sound of the sword cutting through the flesh and bone of his neck.

She would remember all this forever, playing and replaying the gruesome scene over and over again in her mind.

Mama noticed a worrisome change taking place in Leticia that she discussed with her daddy on many occasions. The little girl had become withdrawn and far less outgoing.

She seemed always preoccupied with something she refused to talk about and was far less affectionate to those around her. Whenever anything she was doing was interrupted, she would become very irritable and jumpy, alternating between very quiet one minute and jumpy the next. Mama was deeply concerned.

During the day, Leticia would not want to go with her mama to the vendors to buy food anymore. Mama would find caches of food leftover from previous supper meals that Leticia had hidden around the house, sometimes bug infested.

She would not go outside the house to play anymore, and when she did, she did so reluctantly and then only with her daddy.

When Japanese soldiers were around, she would immediately disappear to be found later hiding away from everyone.

However, the nights were by far the worst for Leticia. She refused to ever be in a room unless the light was on and would never sleep in a dark room. Mama observed her little girl sleeping, sometimes with tears streaming down her face in a profuse night sweat, then slowly begin whimpering, crying out loud, and then waking up with a startled look on her face, eyes wild and very wide in fear, from some terrifying nightmare that would not let go of her little girl. Mama would hold Leticia on nights like this, the little girl holding on with all her might. She would try to calm her down by saying, "Shhh, it's okay, baby, shhh, everything is all right, Mama's here," but nothing ever seemed to work. Her little girl would continue to cry uncontrollably, until by sheer, utter exhaustion, she would fall off back to sleep to confront her private demons once more.

No one really understood post-traumatic stress syndrome in 1941, but a little Filipino girl had experienced it firsthand at only the beginning of several years of a war that would leave deep emotional scars.

She had experienced death up front and personal and would keep replaying it over and over again in her mind for a very long time afterward.

Leticia's neighbors had changed too.

Publicly, they were unenthusiastically polite and obedient to the Japanese-imposed martial law. Privately, they were hostile, and many wanted to join other Filipinos on Bataan or just get out of the city to some rural place that the Japanese did not go.

Above all, they avoided giving direct opposition in the city because of fear for their families.

There were, of course, also those that favored collaboration; many of them were from the wealthy and elite. It was even heard that many of the collaborators were to go to Japan to learn the ways of the Japanese so that they could properly teach all other Filipinos to become a partner in the glorious destiny of Japan.

During her time in the Manila occupation, Leticia doesn't remember the Japanese soldiers abusing her personally. She would overhear her daddy and mama talking about beatings that others had received, and people just disappearing, but during this phase of the war, the Japanese were winning and seemed to be most concerned about getting Filipinos to cooperate.

The Japanese propaganda was constant:

- Filipinos on Bataan were all sick and dying of malaria and dysentery in the worst possible way.
- MacArthur and the white foreigners were losing and couldn't protect Filipinos.
- MacAthur was running away in the face of the invincible Japanese army just like he ran away from Manila.
- Their only hope for the future was to join their Japanese brothers in their divine crusade to drive the white foreigners out of Asia and become part of the Greater East Asia Co-Prosperity Sphere. Asia was for Asians, and the white despoiler did not belong there.

Leticia's daddy and mama had to make many difficult decisions for a defenseless family under the heel of a conqueror. Cooperate and maybe survive; resist and maybe just disappear like the others or be killed.

One night when the family was eating supper, Leticia asked her daddy a difficult and confusing question, "Are the Japanese really our brothers and friends?"

Daddy made no reply.

She persisted, "They look just like us, don't they?'

Her daddy remained silent. Then as if trying hard to figure out the answer to her own question, she said, "Friends don't bomb and hurt their friends, do they, Daddy?"

Her daddy finally broke his silence and said, "No, Leticia, they don't."

That evening, Leticia's daddy began thinking, trying to come up with some plan to deal with their problem. Several days later, he made his intentions known in the most serious and concerned of tones.

"We are going to leave Manila," he said. "I will work out the details later, but I think this is best for all of us, and this is what I have decided."

This fateful decision was going to change everyone's life—forever.

Leticia's auntie was a very pretty girl.

Being pretty is a blessing, but there are times when being pretty can bring on troubles through no fault of the one so attractive, and so it was with Leticia's auntie.

She purposely did things to avoid attracting attention to herself. She dressed very plainly in loose fitting clothes, never wore makeup, and avoided groups when she was at the vendors for food. But beauty is in the eye of the beholder, and with Leticia's auntie, there was a lot to behold. Somehow, she had caught the eyes of the Japanese soldiers.

Leticia was home one day doing her chores. As she was sweeping the floor, she heard a knocking at the front door, and the little girl went to see who was there. Since it was morning and the adults had gone out, she was the only one at home.

She thought to herself, *Maybe that's Mama with food in her arms, and she can't open the door.* So with broom in hand, but not able to see outside to make sure who was knocking, and still being cautious, she asked in her little squeaky voice, "Who is it?"

The reply came instantly, "Japanese soldier. Open door, please."

Leticia was panicky! The words alone made her cold all over with fear. She didn't know what to do. She absolutely froze with terror; visions of a severed head running through her mind. The broom was now almost a part of her hand with her blanched fingers squeezing it so tightly. There was no place to hide. She *had* to face them!

She then reluctantly, ever so slowly, began to grasp the door lock, when the voice outside said in an even louder tone, "Japanese soldier. Open door, now!"

She immediately pulled her hand away from the door lock at the sound of the stern voice, but she remembered her daddy had said not to resist or do anything to make the Japanese angry, so Leticia slowly opened the door.

Frightened before, she was now completely scared out of her wits because standing there were three Japanese soldiers looking directly at her, and she was all alone!

The soldiers were speaking to her, but she couldn't hear them, her mind now off in another place out of fear. She felt completely weak all over, and then she felt a warm, wet feeling in her panties that now ran down her legs to her feet and the floor, making a puddle under her. She thought she was going to fall down. The Japanese soldiers kept talking to her, but she was now dumbfounded with fear.

Since *she* looked very frightened and did not respond, the Japanese soldiers stopped talking. One of the soldiers nudged the arm of the soldier next to him and pointed to the puddle on the floor and remarked on the odor now starting to taint the air. All three soldiers then looked at the puddle and began to smile. Their voices softened as one of them patted Leticia on the head saying words she still could not listen to.

Finally, the three soldiers realized that no one else was home and left.

Leticia just stood in the doorway, staring blankly into the street as the soldiers walked away. How long, she could not remember.

Sometime afterward, Mama was saying, "Leticia, get up. Are you all right? You smell terrible."

That evening at supper, Mama told the others how she had come home and found Leticia lying on the floor. The little girl was extremely quiet.

Daddy said, "What happened, baby? Tell your daddy."

After many such requests, Leticia finally said, "Japanese soldiers came to the house."

All the people in the room began to look at each other in a fearfully concerned way. "Did they hurt you?" asked her daddy.

"No," Leticia said.

"What did they want?' her mama asked.

Leticia looked blankly at everyone, glancing from face to face and said, "I don't know."

They were all to find out very soon.

∽

A couple of days passed, and nothing happened.

Then early one evening, when everyone had finished supper, the knock on the door was heard again. This time, Daddy answered the door as Leticia ran to a corner of the room and cowered there in fear.

When Daddy opened the door, Leticia could see the same three Japanese soldiers standing there that she had met before. To everyone's surprise, their manner was quite cordial. They told Daddy that they wanted to talk to the pretty girl that they had seen enter the house earlier and even apologized for scaring the little girl who had spoken to them a few days earlier. Because of their demeanor and because Daddy really had no choice, they were invited in, and Daddy asked Leticia to get her auntie who was hiding in the bedroom after she had heard what the Japanese soldiers wanted—they wanted *her*!

Before Leticia went to get her auntie, however, she stood staring at the soldiers in a curious manner, somewhat less afraid now. One of the soldiers who was quiet and not speaking much looked funny. While the other two soldiers were trim and looked like soldiers, this third one looked very fat and bulged all over. He even walked funny because of his shape. Leticia couldn't get over his strange appearance which reminded her of a clown she had once seen in a circus before the war.

As Leticia turned and was about to go fetch her auntie, the soldier who did most of the talking and appeared to be in charge said, "Stop." He motioned for Leticia to come over to him, and immediately, the little girl's fear returned.

But this time, Daddy was saying, "It's okay, Leticia. Don't be afraid." She very slowly made her way across the room, each step hard to take, each foot feeling like it was stuck in molasses. Finally, she was right in front of the soldier confronting her fear face-to-face, not knowing what to expect, her only assurance being her daddy's voice.

The talking soldier then asked the funny fat soldier to step closer to him. The talking soldier then reached inside the fat soldier's shirt and pulled out a huge orange. He slowly turned, bent slightly forward toward Leticia, and extended his hand with the orange in it to the little girl. Leticia just stood there, not moving.

She looked to her daddy who said, "It's okay, Leticia. You can take it." She slowly reached out, and the Japanese soldier handed the orange to her. She stood there, just staring in disbelief at the fruit. What a beautiful orange it was, so big and ripe! She was still very hungry because supper had been only a small bowl of rice that evening. What a treasure, and it was all hers!

But as she turned again to go to the bedroom where Auntie was hiding, the soldier said, "Stop."

Uh-oh, he wants the orange back, she thought. Leticia again walked toward the soldier with her arm outstretched, holding the orange up toward the soldier to give it back, but instead of taking Leticia's orange, the soldier again reached into the fat soldier's shirt and took out another orange and handed the second orange to Leticia, saying, "For the pretty girl."

Leticia was now standing there, holding a huge beautiful orange in each hand. She looked at the fruit, then at her daddy and mama, then at the fruit again. The soldier who had given the fruit to Leticia then said something in Japanese to the fat soldier who then walked over to the dinner table and suddenly began to *deflate*!

Oranges and apples seemed to come from everywhere—his pockets, inside his shirt, his small knapsack, everywhere, until there was a very large pile of fruit on the table, and a very skinny, deflated Japanese soldier standing next to it with a big smile on his face. No one in the room could believe it. They were all very hungry, but no one could believe what they were getting to eat. Ohs and ahs filled the room. Leticia ran into the bedroom to get her auntie.

"Look! Look!" she said excitedly to her auntie. "Come and see what we have."

Auntie was afraid, but she was hungry too. She slowly emerged from the room with Leticia holding her hand leading her out. This delighted the Japanese soldiers who then pointed to all the fruit on the table and said, "For you."

The soldiers politely asked her name and then introduced themselves. The tension in the room had eased considerably. Two of the Japanese soldiers politely left the house to wait outside for their companion, while the third soldier remained inside to talk with Auntie and Leticia's family.

For Leticia, the visit lasted until she slowly devoured every last bit of her wonderful orange, delightfully savoring every last mouthful. Her stomach didn't hurt anymore, her daddy was with her, and everyone was calm. With her hunger satisfied, she slowly fell asleep in her little corner of the room.

It was the first night in a long time that she didn't go to sleep hungry.

For the most part, these Japanese soldiers were nice to Auntie and continued to bring her food and even some candy. But there were others who would follow her home, sometimes in a drunken mood, who were not nice and whose advances really scared her.

And now, there was an additional problem. Auntie was becoming too visible and known to the Japanese, and to her own people, for being too friendly with the conquerors.

Her Filipino neighbors, who were faring less well, began to wonder if she was a collaborator. She was beginning to get strange sideways looks from her neighbors, and she had heard that there was a lot of "talk." No one ever said anything to her face.

Regardless of how nice some of the Japanese soldiers were and the fact that she was truly grateful for the food, she was very fearful of the relationship. Many people were going hungry, and she knew all too well that feeling of hunger, but what terrified her the most was that she had heard of the "comfort houses" that were being set up for the Japanese soldiers and was afraid of being sent there to a life she thought that she would not be able to endure. She was a pretty, single, unprotected, young girl, and she knew all too well her extreme vulnerability. Additionally, her own people were beginning to shun her, and they were becoming resentful of the food she had and they could not get.

What was she to do?

The man she truly loved was away from Manila fighting somewhere with the loosely organized Filipino guerillas. She did not know when she would see him again, if ever. She had to deal with the problem all alone. It was too much for her. She knew she was caught between the rock and the hard place and was being slowly squeezed unmercifully. She was a loyal Filipino who was being pushed to the brink from both sides. Finally, she couldn't stand it anymore. She approached Leticia's daddy one evening and totally broke down, sobbing uncontrollably.

Leticia heard, "What will I do? What will I do?" She kept saying between the sobs, "I can not go on like this."

At first, Daddy did not know what to say or do, so he kept trying to soothe Auntie by putting his arms around her and trying to reassure her. Daddy said, "It's okay. Our own people understand." But all his soft, kind words didn't work. Auntie did not believe Daddy, and in his heart, Daddy didn't really believe himself. He tried to offer some comfort, but he was failing. He kept searching his brain for an answer.

And then it struck him!

It was just a thought, but if Auntie were married, the Japanese might leave her alone *and* her own people would view her totally differently. It might work. Yes, yes, it might work! Leticia's daddy knew the man who Auntie really loved, and what's more, he knew how to reach him. Daddy might even be able to help by getting Auntie's true love a job in the hospital as cover for his return to Manila. The hospital was always short of help. Yes, indeed, it just might work! To make Auntie feel better, he told her what he thought he would do. She gradually stopped crying as she listened intently to his words, hanging on every one.

When Daddy finished explaining, Auntie had totally stopped crying and had a new hopeful look on her face and even a little smile. "Can this really work for me?" Auntie asked Daddy.

"Yes, I think it can," Daddy replied. Auntie threw her arms around Leticia's daddy and began kissing and kissing him in gratitude. She then got up and went to her bedroom to think all about this new happy turn her life was going to take, for Daddy had given her hope, something that had been missing now for quite awhile, not only from Auntie's life, but from the lives of all the others too.

As Leticia's daddy just sat there after Auntie left, Leticia could see that he was still deep in thought. The little girl could sense that there was still more on his mind besides Auntie's boyfriend coming back to Manila.

Then, Leticia heard her daddy say. "You know, *that* might work too!"

"What else might work too?" Leticia asked. Daddy didn't answer her directly but kept softly mumbling to himself. All Leticia could make out of the mumbling was "honeymoon to farm, honeymoon to farm" and "everybody goes, everybody goes." Although Daddy's mind was totally preoccupied with these mumbling thoughts, Leticia sensed something important was happening. Daddy was going to help Auntie and then some. He was formulating another of his plans, and Leticia knew Daddy's plans *always* worked. After all, he was her daddy!

The following evening after supper, Daddy gathered all the family at the table and said, "I have something very important to tell you." He paused a moment, then continued, "It is becoming increasingly dangerous for us to stay in Manila. Auntie is beginning to get into trouble because of all the visits by the Japanese soldiers to the house. My dear little Leticia is suffering the mental anguish of what happened to her, constantly being forced to relive the events every time she sees a Japanese soldier, and just walking in the streets during daytime to the vendors for food has become too dangerous for Mama. Increasing stories of bad things happening to our neighbors can't be overlooked because it may not be long before the same things happen to our family too. So

I have finally decided the best way to get all of you out of the city at the same time."

Daddy had everyone's full attention. Each of the family members had his or her own private thoughts about what this announcement meant specifically to each individual.

In full uninterrupted silence, they listened. All sounds were blotted out except for daddy's voice. He began by saying, "I am going to bring Uncle home so he can help and protect Auntie. They are going to be married in our church in open ceremony with all the neighbors invited." Auntie now had a big smile on her face. "Leticia will be the flower girl, and all of us will actively take part in the ceremony for all to see. I will give the bride away. After the wedding, a reception will be held in the house. The bride and groom will announce that for their honeymoon, they will be going to the farm of Grandma Basilia and Grandpa Candido near Alcala and because their joy is so great, they wish to show their gratitude to our family, by inviting all the children, along with Mama and Daddy to vacation for a while at the farm for some rest. All of them will then have an excuse to leave the city at the same time that no one, even the Japanese will question.

"Since uncle is with the guerillas, their little party will be all protected all the way to the farm and while they stay there. They will then all remain on the farm for as long as they can in the hope that the Japanese will forget about them in all the confusion that now exists in Manila. After all, who is going to miss a family that stays to itself most of the time anyway and rarely goes out of the house? And since we are leaving for very good explainable reasons, are not considered insurrectionists by the Japanese, and have no part in Japanese affairs, we might not even be missed. If we let some of our homeless neighbors use our house in Manila while we are away, our neighbors may even want us to remain a long time away on the farm."

Daddy's plan sounded great!

He had thought it through very well. Letty's family had an excuse and reason for everything *and*, by being gracious to their neighbors, who had no homes because of the prior bombings, the very people who looked upon Auntie before with suspicion, would now look at her with favor, *and* the neighbor's help would be unknowingly enlisted in their cause since it would be to their benefit to have Letty's family stay away a longer time.

It was another of Daddy's brilliant plans, but this time, it was a plan sent to him from heaven. Everyone was going to get something special and personal from it, but most importantly, they would all be a lot safer.

Leticia always trusted her daddy in everything, and she just knew that he was the smartest Daddy ever. When Daddy had finished talking, everyone was in excited, joyous agreement with his plan. Leticia just looked at all of them, and with a very special gleam and twinkle in her eyes, she said, "Told ya."

In the days following, Daddy would tell Mama that it would be necessary for him to be away "here and there." He was always careful not to tell Mama where he didn't want her to know. He didn't want to put others at risk. For those periods, Daddy wouldn't come home.

Then one evening, Daddy came home, and he was not alone—Uncle was with him. There was great rejoicing in the house, and especially happy, of course, was Auntie. Everyone talked and talked for a long time, and then Auntie and Uncle retreated to a place to be by themselves.

Uncle was fully aware of Daddy's plan and was enthusiastically in favor of it. The next day, Daddy was going to take Uncle to the hospital where he was sure Uncle would get a job. Everyone was happy because they knew what Uncle's arrival meant—a chance for a better life amid the conditions of war.

Uncle did get the job, and things seemed to be going as planned, until one day, while everyone was at home having supper, a familiar knock was heard at the door.

Daddy opened the door. There stood the Japanese soldier who had come so many times before to see Auntie. The room fell silent. He was invited in, and as usual, he had brought some fruit. As he gazed about the room, his eyes searching for Auntie, he saw Uncle. At the same time, Auntie, who had temporarily been out of the room, returned and began to speak to the Japanese soldier. At first smiling, the soldier's face now became expressionless as Auntie continued to speak, explaining that she had been betrothed a long time ago to Uncle who she thought was dead and who now had returned. The Japanese soldier did not get angry, but he seemed more sad than anything else.

"Let me see your papers," he said to Uncle. Uncle showed his papers to the soldier. They were in order. The soldier then returned the papers to Uncle, looked at Auntie once more, and then said to all, "I must be going" and quietly left. So far, so good. It appeared that at least for now, they had "pulled it off," but everyone knew that they had to get the wedding done quickly because time offered too many opportunities for something to go wrong.

In all haste, plans for the wedding were made, the church was reserved, and as many of their neighbors as they could think of were invited, being sure to invite the ones most needy of a home.

The big day finally arrived!

Everyone was happy and in a festive mood. The groom was very handsome, and the bride appeared absolutely radiant in her wedding dress. For the first time, Auntie did dress up, put makeup on, and wanted to look beautiful. And boy did she ever! Truly, Uncle was a very lucky man.

In the middle of all the gaiety, there was little Leticia. She had on a beautiful little pure white dress, was holding her floral bouquet, and looked totally angelic.

Daddy couldn't take his eyes off Leticia. The bride was radiant, and everyone else in the wedding party looked beautiful including Mama, but it was Leticia who completely captivated his attention.

Finally, the entrance to the church, the procession to the altar, and the solemn ceremony. Everything about the wedding was beautiful, but to Daddy, it merely formed a backdrop against which his beloved Leticia shined the brightest of all. The pride he felt for Leticia welled up inside of him, a pride that only a father can feel for his little girl. His thoughts drifted away to another place and another time.

Someday, he mused, he would see his own Leticia marry, and he would be so proud to give her away at her wedding—so proud, yet a little sad too. Someday, he too would feel the great pride and joy so many other fathers had felt for eons…someday.

Daddy's dreamy mind was then brought back to reality as the wedding march began to triumphantly play. The ceremony was over, the wedding was done, and Auntie and Uncle were married.

Everyone was now going to Auntie's house for the wedding reception and celebration and food! The mood was very festive and gay, and there were so many people. During the reception, small gifts were presented to the bride and groom by many people.

After she received the last gift, Auntie stood up and said, "My husband and I are very grateful for all the kindness we have been shown and would like to return some of this outpouring of affection." She then chose a family who had suffered the most and had no place of their own to live, and to them, she said, "My husband and I want you to live in our house while we are away on our honeymoon for as long as we are gone and consider our house to be your home."

A huge ovation and cheering broke out! The response to this gesture to cover their leaving was way beyond their expectations, so much so that they couldn't get anybody to leave the reception. The festivities continued. The house door and windows were open to help cool the house, and many people were milling around having fun.

Suddenly, the laughter and noise calmed down, and everyone became silent, staring at the front door. There stood a Japanese soldier in a resplendent uniform, all by himself. He walked slowly across the room, not saying a word; the people were moving to create a path for him directly to the bride and the groom. As he got closer, Auntie recognized him as the soldier who had come to the house many times before.

She smiled and said to him, "Welcome." He returned the smile and took out a small decoratively wrapped box from the pocket of his uniform. He extended his arm, holding the small box out toward Auntie, and said softly, "For the bride."

Auntie smiled and accepted the gift, saying, "Thank you very much. Won't you please stay and have something to eat with us?"

The Japanese soldier courteously replied, "I am very sorry, but I cannot stay." He took a long, last look at Auntie, then slowly turned and left the room.

The celebrating resumed, lasting awhile longer. Then, their neighbors began to tire and finally left in small groups.

They had done it! Pulled it off! It was time now to make their escape.

Daddy gathered everyone together, making sure they were carrying with them as few things as possible so as not to make anyone suspicious. Then, all of them left.

The journey may have been long on the bus, Leticia didn't remember. She just slept peacefully, all the way to Grandma and Grandpa's farm.

The first couple of days at the farm were the happiest that Leticia had experienced in a long time. Grandma and Grandpa were wonderful. Leticia liked Grandma Basilia immediately, but although Grandpa Candido was always very nice to her, she had heard that he was very strict and that a lot of people were afraid of him. When she first saw him, she understood why.

Grandpa stood ramrod straight and was much taller than the average Filipino which immediately commanded attention. He also had a very commanding way about him too that automatically demanded respect, almost a military bearing, although he was not in the army. But when he spoke to Leticia, the fearsome appearance seemed to melt away, letting her see through to his heart which was soft and kind, especially to her.

But the happiest thing about the farm, the one thing that made her heart sing with joy, was the fact that Daddy and Mama were with her all the time. They weren't rushing off to work or constantly shopping for food. They were there with her, and she reveled in their attention, especially her daddy's. Where Daddy was, you would always find Leticia tagging right along, even when he was doing something that didn't involve her at all.

Leticia would play all kinds of games with her daddy and immensely enjoyed the animals when Daddy would catch them for her and safely let her pet them. It was almost idyllic. Leticia now had some friends, and it didn't matter that some of them had more than two legs. The frogs at the pond, the chickens, the dogs, the caribou, and she was gaining new friends almost every day!

So it was for almost two weeks, the happiest two weeks of her entire life!

Then one day, Leticia heard Daddy and Mama talking over what sounded to her like serious matters, matters of great concern. They were not arguing, but Leticia could tell that neither of them was very happy. The little girl walked into the room and tugged at her daddy's pants saying, "Daddy, what's wrong?"

Her daddy didn't answer her right away and just said, "Go outside and play, Leticia. Your mama and I have important things to talk about." From the tone of daddy's voice, Leticia knew that those important things were not good things.

Later in the afternoon, while Leticia was washing some dishes, Daddy walked into the kitchen, carrying his canvas travel bag. Mama followed behind him and was crying.

"Daddy, where are you going?" Leticia said in a manner reflecting much alarm. Her Daddy put down his bag, smiled, and said to Leticia, "Come outside with me, baby. I'll help you feed your doggie." The two of them took some table scraps and a bowl of water outside to feed their farmhouse pet.

"Leticia, I have something to tell you," Daddy began. Leticia's innocent eyes now grew fearful as she looked at her daddy's serious face. He paused a few moments as if searching his mind for the right words to say and then said, "Leticia, Daddy has to leave the farm and go away for a little while."

Now alarmed, the little girl said, "Why, Daddy? Aren't you happy here? Did I do something wrong?"

"No, baby, you didn't do anything wrong, and I love being here all the time with you," her daddy answered.

"Why then?" she persisted.

"Because I've been away from the hospital a long time, and if I don't go back to at least show myself, the Japanese will get suspicious and come here looking for me. If they do, all of us will be in trouble and maybe even call guerillas. I cannot let that happen. I must go back now."

"I don't want you to leave, Daddy. I'm afraid for you," she said.

"I don't want to go, baby, but I have to go," Daddy said. "I want you to be a big girl now and help your mama while I'm away. Will you do that for Daddy?" he asked.

Tears began to fill her eyes as she said, "Yes, Daddy, I will."

"And remember, it's only for a little while. I'll be back as soon as I can, and we will play your favorite games again," daddy said.

"How soon? When?" Leticia asked.

"I don't know, baby. I'm not sure, but it won't be too long," he said, trying to reassure her.

Then they both went back into the house to get his bag. Leticia and the whole family accompanied him as they walked down the path from the farmhouse to the bus stop, which was on the little dirt road that would eventually lead to the city.

After a short while, the bus came and stopped, opening its door to let Daddy on. He turned and began to hug and kiss everyone good-bye. Leticia came last as if her daddy had purposely saved her the last turn.

He looked at her and said, "You're going to help Mama for me, aren't you?"

"Yes, I will, Daddy. I promise," she answered.

Then, she jumped into her daddy's arms and hugged and kissed him with all her might.

She didn't want to let go. Finally, Daddy slowly put her feet on the ground and released her. As he began to step up onto the bus, Leticia ran to him, holding onto his clothing for dear life.

"Don't go! Don't go, Daddy, please!" she cried.

He couldn't say anything. The words were all choked up in his throat, and he was now fighting back tears himself. He looked back toward Mama with a look that implored her to help. Mama picked up Leticia and moved back away from the bus. Her daddy got inside, and the bus slowly began to pull away.

Leticia fought her way out of her mama's grip and broke free. She began running after the bus, which was now gaining speed and raising a cloud of red dust behind it from the dirt road.

"Daddy! Daddy, come back!" she screamed. She was running as fast as she could. She stumbled and fell but immediately got up and started to run again. "Daddy!" she shrieked. But the bus kept moving farther away. She kept calling, "Daddy, please come back!"

She couldn't breathe; the dust of the road was choking off every gulp of air she took to run. Her legs were aching so badly that she could hardly lift them, and yet she wouldn't quit. She then gave her mightiest effort, the very last ounce of her strength, and fell, unable to get up from the exhaustion.

She stretched out her hands, reaching for the unreachable, and weakly cried out, "Daddy!"

With her little heart beating wildly, completely breathless, and with her legs now so weak that she was unable to get up to run again, she sat in the red powdery dirt of the road, watching the bus move farther and farther away.

The tears streaming down her face now mixed with the dust and dirt irritating her eyes, forcing them to close and making her lose sight of the bus with its precious cargo.

She frantically wiped her face, trying to clear her eyes to see the bus just once more.

As her sight came back, the bus now was far off in the distance.

It was late afternoon, the sun was beginning to set, and as Leticia strained to see her daddy's bus just one last time, the red-orange glow of the setting sun settled down on the earth. The bus now appeared to her as a tiny reddish dot of dust, slowly disappearing completely and forever over the horizon.

It was over. He was gone.

Leticia lay in the dirt, all curled up into a ball just like a baby, sobbing uncontrollably. Nothing could ease her pain, nothing.

All she knew was that the person she loved the most in the whole world was gone.

And what was worse, she knew that she would never see him again.

LIFE ON THE FARM

For a long time, there was no consoling Leticia.

Her mama and grandma tried everything, but to no avail. A huge part of her heart was gone which had left a void so large that it seemed impossible to fill.

She was losing weight because she refused to eat. She did not even put up a fuss when her sister would take her food from her plate. Mama would make special treats that she knew Leticia liked, but the little girl would not touch them. She was now silent at all times, never speaking to anyone and only appearing to half-hear what other people said to her.

She did not seem to care about her special things that her sisters would take and not return. She just did not seem to care about anything. She would not do her chores, but Mama didn't have the heart to spank her.

Leticia would sit with her doggie on the porch for hours, just silently stroking the dog's head but never saying a word. The dog just sat there obediently content as if knowing of the torment the little girl was feeling.

During the day, it was becoming increasingly difficult to find her when she went outside. Leticia would disappear for hours, never answering her name when called. Then like magic, she would miraculously appear late in the afternoon toward sunset, run down the path to the bus stop, and wait for the bus. When it would arrive and open its door, Leticia scrutinized each face that got off the bus, looking for that one special face that never came.

Then as always, she would walk back up the path in a slow, sad, dejected manner with her head down and crying.

Day after day, week after week, it was always the same.

One day, Mama decided to find out where Leticia disappeared to during the day. She waited until her little girl went outside and then decided to follow her. She did not have to go very far.

Leticia went out the front door, down the steps, and crawled under the porch to sit in the dirt. She had withdrawn into herself and to her "special" place where her fragile little world came to peace with her mind. She would stay there until sunset and then come out to meet the bus. Even when it rained, she was there.

Both Mama and Grandma began to feel that Leticia was losing her mind, until one day something strange happened.

One of Candido's older children brought home an old magazine that he absent-mindedly left on one of the kitchen chairs. That night at supper, Leticia was brought to the table to eat, and this magazine was on the chair. At first, she paid no attention to it, and she just sat on it; but as the meal progressed with Leticia just staring at her vegetables, she began to get restless because the magazine was causing some discomfort. She picked it up and began looking at it.

She was only five years old and couldn't read yet, but the pictures held her attention. The magazine had lots of pictures in it of Manila, some of which she recognized. She became increasingly interested and ignored everyone in the room as she poured through the magazine. Both Basilia and Mama noticed this, and when Candido's boy returned to get the magazine, they stopped him and told him to go away. Leticia kept going through the magazine front to back and back to front and wouldn't stop.

She began to gaze more at the pictures of people, especially the photos of more mature people in the magazine. Then something must have clicked! She remembered that her daddy had gone back to the big city—to Manila, and there were people there just like the people whose pictures were in the magazine. Maybe they knew about her daddy and could help bring him home. When she left the table, she took the magazine to her room, looking at it over and over again.

At last! Something was getting to Leticia and arousing her interest.

She wanted to talk to these people in the pictures, but she didn't know how. She knew they were saying something because there was writing next to each picture—maybe what they were saying was about Daddy and maybe it was good news because all the people in the pictures were smiling, and they all looked happy, even the ones that weren't Filipino. Yes, that's it! Somehow she would talk to them.

It was then she realized she couldn't read! She hadn't yet learned how.

Almost overnight, she transformed from a little girl who seemed totally lost, moping around all day, to a little girl who became very active, constantly searching everywhere trying to find more magazines. She became determined to read because now she was a little girl with a purpose. She began to speak again and to interact with people. She would wait for Grandpa Candido to come in at night from the fields and mercilessly pester him to teach her to read until he agreed. Actually, he was very happy to see this change in Leticia and was doubly pleased because the point of all her activity was now focused on something so constructive.

Nobody he knew had a child so young that was not only asking to be taught how to read, and, in addition, was so enthusiastic about it. Deep down, he was thrilled. So were Mama and Basilia. Leticia's salvation had come in the form of an old, worn-out magazine!

Leticia did all the chores expected of her during the days but couldn't wait for the evenings to come.

She would climb up onto Grandpa Candido's lap eagerly anticipating all that he would teach her. He started with the

ABCs and was astonished at how fast Leticia learned. Her lessons in numbers followed quickly. Candido had no simple readers like *Dick and Jane* or *Run Spot Run* for Leticia, so he decided to start with something that he thought was very important, that Leticia already knew, but did not yet recognize in its printed form. He decided to first teach her the Lord's Prayer.

This was absolutely the right choice. Leticia liked learning to read the prayer because not only was she learning to read it, but she was talking to God at the same time. She practiced it until she could now always recognize the words in other printed works too. She was progressing so fast that Candido was running out of things to use as teaching material. On his trips into Alcala, he would always make sure to bring back home something in print to the eagerly awaiting Leticia. She was absolutely voracious and could not get enough of Candido's teaching.

Her intense desire to read and the large amount of attention being given to her by her Grandpa had a downside too. Her younger sisters were becoming jealous of all the attention being focused on Leticia and began to gripe. At their young age, it was difficult to explain why Leticia was getting all this extra time spent with her.

However, the seeds of jealousy had unfortunately been sown and would, years later, be harvested as bitter fruit.

From the time Leticia had arrived at the farm, doing assigned chores was a normal and expected thing. One of the chores assigned to her was to feed the animals, except the pigs, which was considered far too dangerous for a little girl five years old.

Of all the animals she had to feed, none scared her more than the guard dogs. One dog in particular, a huge coal black brute of a dog that only Candido could control, was kept tied down at all times except at night.

For many months, Leticia would always bring this monster his food, being careful to stay just beyond the full stretch of his tether rope and pushing his bowl of food to him with a stick. All this time, she would always calmly talk to the dog as she gave him food, but the dog always growled and barked at her as he charged at her, straining the rope to its limit. As time passed and the routine became commonplace to both the dog and the girl, Leticia noticed the dog's barking and growling had become less.

So she started to hand throw the meat scraps to him before setting down the bowl. The dog would immediately go to the thrown scraps and sniff at them for a long time before devouring them. He then began to walk slowly to the bowl of food Leticia had set down and continue to eat.

One day, when Leticia brought the food, her mind was preoccupied with other things, and she wasn't paying too much attention to the dog. She walked to the place from which she always fed him, picked out several large meat scraps, and threw them to the dog. The dog did not make a sound. He went to the scraps as always and began his usual routine of sniffing and eating.

Leticia was now fully lost in a daydream as she knelt down on the ground with the food bowl, adding a little water to the bowl. As she did this, out of the corner of her eye, she noticed a black shape next to her. As she slowly lifted her eyes, she saw a dangling rope. Her eyes followed the rope from the ground as it rose. She slowly lifted her head to find the rope's end. Its end was attached to the collar of a huge black monster whose face was so close to hers that she could feel each of his hot, panting breaths on her neck.

Somehow, the dog had gotten free!

She froze in fear, not making a sound. She was kneeling down, and he seemed to be massively towering above her. At first, she looked straight into his face, but his two amber eyes burning out of his jet-black face only terrified the little girl even more. It was too late for anyone to help her.

She shut her eyes tightly and began to whimper, a little girl resigned to what she surely thought was going to be a horrible fate. She imagined his huge fangs sinking deeply into her neck and then lifting her off the ground like a doll and violently shaking her, thrashing his head from side to side as she had seen the farm dogs do before when they were fighting mad. She waited, whimpered, and tensed up even more.

Nothing happened.

Then she felt a wet nose sniffing at her hand—the hand that had thrown the meat scraps to him. He began to lick her hand. She opened her eyes and stopped crying. She still could not move. The dog then lifted his head and looked directly into Leticia's face.

He slowly began licking her cheek as he wagged his tail. Leticia realized he wasn't going to hurt her! He liked her!

Somehow, over the many months that this tiny little girl had come to him every day, not to beat or tease him, but to always bring him food, she had bonded herself to him.

Leticia then began to move her hand to pet him. The dog's tail wagged even faster.

To Leticia had come a very special and rare thing, she had been blessed with a "forever friendship." In the coming days, Leticia was able to do things with her big, black friend that nobody, even Candido, had ever been able to do.

After she would feed him, she would loosen his rope from its tether and use it as a leash to have him walk with her anywhere. As anyone else approached them, the dog would stop, hunker down, and growl. Leticia would then speak to him saying, "Aso, okay. Aso, okay," then nudge him, and they would continue on their way. Aso was no longer a mean, vicious, guard dog; he was Leticia's special personal protector.

When she would crawl under the porch to be alone to read, Aso would be there at her side. Wherever she went, Aso would go, the two of them together.

As time went on, his leash became unnecessary. Leticia's voice was all it took for complete control. As time passed, reading became her passion an obsession. She would look everywhere for things to read. On one occasion, the obsession got her into trouble.

Candido's fifteen-year-old son had several books from school. Leticia had seen one that she liked and began reading it at the kitchen table. It was much too advanced for her, but she enjoyed looking through it anyway.

Suddenly, this boy came up behind her and put his hands over her eyes as if playing hide and seek. At first, Leticia just thought he was playing a game, but slowly and steadily, there was a severe burning and pain in both of her eyes. It was the worst thing she had ever felt in her life. She began screaming, rubbing her eyes, and blinking wildly. Her eyes began to tear profusely. She couldn't see! Realizing what had happened, Basilia rushed Leticia over to the kitchen sink. Taking water from a nearby bucket, she poured it on the little girl's face and eyes. The burning and pain was intense, and Leticia was almost hysterical. Basilia kept washing out the little girl's eyes, over and over again, but the burning felt like it would never stop.

After what seemed like an eternity, the burning and pain began to slowly subside.

When Basilia looked at Leticia's eyes, they were very red and grossly swollen, almost swollen shut. She could not see very well at all. Grandma then put wet compresses on her eyes, and Leticia rested that way for the remainder of the evening.

Why? What happened? She wasn't bothering anyone; she wasn't being bad.

Grandma later explained to her that she should never touch the books of this boy again. Basilia explained that the rest of the children were envious of the time and attention Candido was giving to her and that this envy was turning to resentment. The boy, who really did not like Leticia and viewed her as a usurper of affection and as an unwelcome visitor, had squeezed the juice from several tiny very hot peppers between his hands and then rubbed their juice into Leticia's eyes.

Leticia never forgot the pain of this event or the hard lesson that she had learned.

What's more, through no fault of her own, she had made her first family member enemy—and she would never forget him either.

After a few days, her eyes began to feel normal again.

The incident had not dimmed her desire to read, but now Grandma and Grandpa had to help Leticia in other ways. She needed a new source of reading material and a place where she could get it without being hurt.

Candido knew of a neighbor who lived about one mile away on the next farm nearest to them who had been a teacher and would have books at her house. He was not a person who asked for favors, but he needed some help for Leticia, and he decided to approach the woman. To his great joy and peace of mind, the neighbor graciously agreed to loan Leticia some books, but wanted to meet the little girl.

One mile was a long way to go, and the farms were only connected by a dirt road. There was no transportation except caribou driven work carts, and they were always being used for work.

No one had the time to take Leticia to the neighbor's house and back, and the road was not without danger because of its extremely rural location, and a war was on, but Leticia would not let any of this deter her. She persuaded the adults that she could walk this distance and back after her chores were done, and that if Aso went with her, she would be safe. They somewhat reluctantly agreed, and thus, a great adventure was about to begin.

When the neighbor met Leticia for the first time, it was obvious to her how enthusiastic Leticia was and how much the little girl wanted to read.

It was raining that day, and the little girl showed up at the neighbor's front door soaking wet, with an equally wet big, black dog that Leticia had tied to the porch railing. The neighbor realized that this little girl had just walked one mile in the rain to borrow a book! This amazed her. What determination for a little girl!

They talked for a long while getting to know each other, and finally, they settled on a little book of fairy tales that Leticia was happy to borrow.

Finally, off she went after the rain stopped to make the long trek home.

It wasn't long afterward that Leticia returned to the neighbor's house again, book in hand, dog in tow, and a request to borrow another book.

This scenario was repeated again and again until the neighbor was running out of simple children's books to loan to Leticia. When she saw how determined and persistent the little girl was, she offered to teach Leticia to read the more advanced books and the ever important magazines.

Leticia could not believe her good fortune.

It meant a lot more walking, almost every day, but she didn't care.

She was going to really learn to read!

Over the course of the following year, there were many, many, one-mile walks to and from her benevolent neighbor's house. The more she walked, the more she learned.

She began to look at the walk as sort of a "price of admission" to pay in order to learn more, a price she was only too happy to pay.

She began to look forward to the walks which were getting easier as she was getting bigger and stronger. The most amazing thing about the walks was that she was never hurt by anyone or anything on these walks during those dangerous times.

Aso was undoubtedly a great asset, but Leticia always felt that God was with her, and she was never afraid. Leticia's grandparents were religious people, and Grandpa Candido had even been an altar boy in his youth. Both of them made a great impression on this little girl instilling in her a reverence and faith in God which served her well all through her life.

After two reading lessons, Leticia would return to the farm; and as soon as she was able, she would take her book and crawl under the porch and read for as long as she could. Her reading sessions under the porch were very special sessions to her because they offered her more than just an opportunity to read.

They offered her an opportunity to travel!

An amazing thing was happening to Leticia.

As her proficiency at reading grew, she actually began putting herself mentally into the stories, magazine articles, and pictures.

Reading now offered a fantastic way to escape—to go anywhere in the world she wanted to go. Her imagination became unbounded. If an article or story was about Texas or Paris, she was able to go there.

She had a free, irrevocable passport to go anywhere in the world at anytime.

It was wonderful!

She had developed a cycle of read more, go somewhere new and exciting, read more to go to another new place. She loved it and couldn't get enough. She had created a whole new wonderful world that she could make and fashion any way she wanted, and the best part of all, it was all hers!

But for Leticia, life was not to be all fun and mental trips to Rome and beautiful beaches. There was a real life, and she was very much a part of it.

Because nobody had much money, she would help her mama pick vegetables and fruit grown on the farm, which they would then take to Alcala to trade for other things they needed. They would travel by cart or wagon drawn by caribou, and Leticia was usually excited about going.

However, the Japanese were now in Alcala, and although she was excited to see the other things that they could trade for, she was always fearful of the soldiers when they were around, because on one of their trips, Japanese soldiers had slapped her mama for not bowing low enough to suit them.

At this time, the conduct of the Japanese soldiers was controlled by the local field commander. How the Japanese soldiers behaved depended on how the local field commander enforced discipline. If discipline was lax, the treatment of civilians in the rural provinces could be harsh.

With all that was going on around her, Leticia was going to face even more sadness. Leticia was beginning to see less and less of her mama.

At first, it was the many trips that mama made to Alcala trading vegetables.

Later, Mama was making trips to Manila and told Leticia that she was helping at the hospital there. Leticia thought that was wonderful because she could now find out about her daddy, but each time that she asked her mama about daddy, she only heard silence or an "I don't know."

Not only was she now seeing much less of Mama, but when she did see her, Mama was somehow very distant. Something had happened to Mama, and Leticia did not understand what, but whatever it was, the little girl didn't like it.

She loved her mama but had somehow lost the closeness to her. Soon, Mama was staying away at very long intervals in Manila. Leticia now rarely saw her mama. She had become almost estranged.

At about the same time, Auntie had also changed, but from Leticia's standpoint, not for the better. Although she had never *really been close to* her Auntie, her aunt had always treated her well even during those tough times in Manila, but after Auntie's baby was born, Auntie began to treat Leticia very harshly, almost like a servant. As was the custom in her culture, children were brought up well disciplined and taught never to answer adults back or ever be sassy. For this reason, Leticia did everything Auntie told her to do and never complained or whined.

Auntie had changed Leticia's chores into a nightmare. In addition to always feeding all the animals, Leticia was made to carry heavy buckets of water from the well to the farmhouse. When they were in Alcala, she had to make multiple trips from one of the town's two water supply areas to Candido's house which was six houses away, a chore far too heavy for a little girl six years old.

She was made to carry all the wood for cooking, and if she put the thin end of a piece of wood into the fire instead of the thick end, she was beaten. Washing all the dishes was also her chore, and if ever a dish was broken, Leticia was severely beaten. The beatings became routine for trivial things, and it seemed to Leticia that she could not get out of her auntie's way.

Each day, it seemed that Auntie added a new chore for Leticia to do. Although she always did what was asked of her, it seemed that Leticia could not please her aunt. Leticia just continued enduring the abuse.

She would lay down to rest, but her aunt would get her up immediately to do something else after berating her for being "lazy."

Finally, Grandma Basilia could not stand the abuse anymore and stepped in to protect the little girl. From that point on, Basilia assumed the role of surrogate mother to Leticia who appreciated and loved her grandma very much. Her beloved father seemed to be lost to her forever. Her mama was never there to help her. She was a little girl so very, very much alone.

Basilia's face with its gentle eyes, framed by beautiful thick snowy white hair, was the only kind, sympathetic face she saw.

She grew to love Basilia more and more as time passed, and she became closer to Basilia than she was to her own mother. She even called Basilia *Inang Baket* (old mama) out of great love and respect.

Many factors were beginning to shape Leticia's life and character. Some she understood; others, she did not. Regardless of the fact that Basilia was now protecting Leticia, the little girl still had to deal with her aunt on a daily basis.

The problem was that Basilia was Grandpa Candido's second wife.

Grandpa had remarried after his first wife died. Grandpa's children (Leticia's aunts and uncles) apparently did not fully accept Basilia, and they were constantly arguing with her. Basilia had come from Zambales, another province, and did not have any children of her own. The problems that existed between Basilia and Candido's children were either not fully appreciated by Candido or ignored, Leticia did not know which. Since Grandpa's children held influence with Grandpa, it was sometimes hard for Basilia to protect Leticia.

Although Grandma could not read herself, she encouraged Leticia in her passion to read. Auntie would constantly take Leticia's books away, removing from her her one true enjoyment. Auntie wanted Leticia to work even more.

When Leticia would tell Basilia about her missing treasure, her grandma would always get it back for her amid much furor. And it wasn't just the books that were taken. Whenever Basilia gave something special intended just for Leticia, it was always sure to disappear. Because of this, Leticia became like a little pack rat, trying to hide away anything she valued, but many times to no avail.

In spite of all that she was forced to put up with, however, she did not complain because although she didn't like what was going on, abusive hard work and almost a condition of servitude, it was still far better than having the horrible bombs falling all around her.

Leticia's world was already getting a little brighter because now she had a loving ally. Basilia saw Leticia as the child of her own that she had never had, and she showed it, constantly fussing over the little girl to make up for the hurt and injustices of others. Leticia both felt and returned the affection and saw her grandma as a substitute mama—a beautiful, small, dainty, and classy lady who never raised her voice to the little girl.

The bond between them became very strong. Leticia knew that she could always depend on Grandma no matter what, and she behaved accordingly. Anything Basilia needed or wanted, Leticia would literally run to get.

If Leticia was with Grandma in Alcala and looked at something in a store window, simply saying to Grandma, "Those are beautiful shoes, aren't they, Grandma?" before long, those very shoes would be hers, given by a beaming old woman.

So it was that the bond between them grew stronger and stronger and would last throughout their entire lives.

One day, while Leticia was reading a borrowed magazine, she became struck by two things. It was an American magazine with two features that transfixed her.

The first was a picture and article about a man called John Wayne. He was so big!

He had a cowboy hat, two guns, and even a horse in some pictures, and different clothes of a hard working man and a soldier in others. The article said how big and tough he was and that nobody pushed him around. And he was strong and good-looking too!

She became enamored of this man whose picture in a magazine was her only link to him. A real American hero!

I'll bet if he came to the Philippines, he could throw out all the bad guys, she mused. *Yes, that's what we need, John Wayne and no bad guys. That would make everyone happy. I'll bet he could even help General MacArthur.*

The second magazine feature convinced her that she was right.

It was an article about children just like her, but there was a big difference. All the American children in the pictures were all smiling and looked like they were having fun. No matter which picture she looked at, and no matter what they were doing, they all looked very happy doing it.

They all lived in nice places, beautiful houses that actually had water that ran into their houses to sinks and toilets. No buckets of water to carry, no outhouses to go to on rainy days. Wow, that was terrific! Their daddies and mamas were with them, and they were all smiling too. She was amazed! What a great place they must live in.

Leticia also noticed that all their houses were undamaged and that there were no bomb craters in their streets. She was now very sure John Wayne had done a great job.

He was their protector and would beat up anybody who tried to hurt them; that's why they were all so happy. There weren't any bad guys to hurt them. Then reality struck her mind.

Why couldn't it be like that in the Philippines too?

If the bad guys would leave, Filipinos could be happy too.

She now was very, very sure the answer was John Wayne.

If he could come to help General MacArthur, they could make the bad guys go away.

So she decided that she would work very hard to do her part, and every night, she would pray for God to send John Wayne because she knew in her heart that God was the only one who could do it.

At this time, Leticia's independence and creativeness were beginning to show themselves, first being manifested in the activities she devised for amusement. She didn't have any games or toys like the American kids had, so she made her own.

An old rag became a doll. She got some straw and then went to Grandma to show Basilia her "new" doll. She put the straw into the rag, gathered it together in one or two areas, and said, "See, Grandma, here's dolly's head and waist." But the straw kept falling out, and Leticia couldn't maintain dolly's figure.

Realizing what was going on in Leticia's mind, Basilia said, "Let me show you how to make your dolly's head stay on."

With a needle and thread, she sewed around Leticia's selected neck area for the doll and—presto!—dolly had a stay-on head.

Leticia got so excited she wanted to learn to sew too. She kept entreating Grandma to show her, which Basilia was happy to do.

Leticia sewed the waist. By the time the little girl had finished putting in the last stitch at the foot area of the doll to trap all the straw inside, Leticia could sew. Her imagination was making it possible for Leticia to learn new and exciting things. She could now make stuff!

Leticia created very unusual games for a child, especially a little girl. One of her most unusual was the spider fight. Uncharacteristically for a girl, Leticia would catch spiders and put them in matchboxes. Then she would get a stick, attach a string to the stick's middle, and suspend the combination so that the stick hung in balance. She would then get two of her match boxes and, very carefully, release the spiders, putting one spider on each end of the stick. Leticia would watch intently as the two spiders advanced toward each other and began to fight. The winner would always cover the loser with a white web.

Leticia would then collect the winner and put him back into his match box for the next fight. His reward would be a dragonfly that Leticia would love to run after and catch. Sometimes, she would just play with the dragonflies, catch them, and release them.

But there were times when her games would get her into trouble. As much as she enjoyed walking with Aso, she equally enjoyed climbing. She was the only girl always in a tree but usually with a purpose. Guavas. Leticia loved guavas, and so did the other kids from the neighboring farms. However, the other kids didn't want to climb the tree to get the fruit.

Although it didn't take much encouragement, Leticia always made them feel that she was doing them a great big favor to climb the trees to get fruit for them (and as always, for herself).

When Leticia obliged, they would stand at the base of the tree and catch the fruit that was being thrown down. One day, the fruit-gathering stick with sharp pointed end slipped from Leticia's hand as she was reaching for a guava and fell vertically downward, pointed end first, just like a spear. Leticia heard a faint little "Ouch!"

She looked down toward the other children and noticed one little girl standing there crying, with the sharp end of the wooden dart stuck into her head, and the other end pointing vertically upward toward the sky. The other girl really wasn't hurt much but was more scared than anything else.

The problem was that she looked so comical standing there with the dart sticking out of her head that when Leticia got down from the tree, she began laughing hysterically. The other girl walked home, dart and all. Leticia took her guavas and ran home. No sooner had she gotten home, someone was knocking on the door. An angry mother with a little girl in tow, dart and all, was outside demanding satisfaction. Leticia knew she was going to get it!

After the woman had stated her case to Basilia, she left with reassurance that Leticia would be punished.

Basilia was angry and tried to catch Leticia to punish her, but Leticia was too elusive, constantly running around and hiding in and behind her grandma's large, full-length, puffy skirt. Finally, after many exhausting efforts, Basilia gave up. Leticia crept out from under her grandma's skirt. She had gotten away with it, she thought, but that night, Leticia went to bed without supper. That was the first and last time Basilia ever tried to spank Leticia.

Leticia's independence and reasons for doing things always seemed justified.

She was beginning to get into a lot of fights because she was now standing up for herself. The problem was that she was little and everyone else was bigger, so she was the one always getting beaten up. Some of those beatings were administered by Candido's children when Leticia demanded her stolen personal things back. But her perception of self-worth was slowly, almost imperceptibly, starting to change in Leticia's psyche.

Life has a tendency to either grind you down like sandstone or polish you up like a diamond, depending upon that of which you are made. Leticia was a diamond!

One day, Leticia was playing marbles with several of the neighborhood children. Not surprisingly, all the other children were boys. Leticia was very good at games like this and was winning quite handily. This embarrassed one of the bigger boys who was now being made fun of by the other boys because he was being beaten by a girl. The boy then began to cheat and to take advantage of Leticia. When she accused him of cheating, he got angry and pushed the little girl down on the ground calling her names. She didn't cry and wasn't afraid—she was mad!

She picked herself up off the ground and, with a full fist, lunged at the boy, swinging with all her might at the same time. She connected flush on the nose of the very surprised boy, who began to gush blood from his nose that ran down over and into his mouth, down his chin and onto his shirt. He was a very startling sight to behold, so much so, that the other boys just stood perfectly still, with very wide eyes and mouths open. The bleeding boy started to cry and began to half stumble and half run in his panic to get home. Leticia turned to the other boys and just squinted at them. Nobody said a word.

After a few seconds, Leticia began to walk away. As she was leaving the previously silent boys, she heard one boy say to another, "Did you see that!"

For once in her life, she had delivered justified punishment and had not been beaten up herself. It felt good; it felt very, very good!

She walked home slowly, just daydreaming and relishing her victory. She now knew what it was like not to let others push her around, and she liked it. A seed of pride and self-respect had been planted in a very deserving little girl.

When she finally got home, she scarcely had time to find Grandma. Then a knock on the door was heard. Leticia answered the door with Grandma. Standing there was a boy holding a blood-soaked towel to his nose, pointing to Leticia, saying, "That's her, Mama, that's her!"

The irate mother then launched a tirade into Basilia, screaming about how little Leticia had beaten the crap out of her bigger son for no reason. Basilia looked puzzled but was a very perceptive grandma.

She looked down at Leticia, then up at the bigger boy, and then down at little Leticia again. She then said to the angry mother in a very stern tone of voice, "Please leave. I'll take care of this." She slowly closed the door.

She looked at Leticia, smiled, and said, "When I clap my hands, you cry very loud."

Upon hearing what sounded like a really good beating of Leticia, the mother and son walked home happy and smiling. Both Leticia and Basilia also got a good laugh out of the act.

When the bully and his mother were far enough away, the act stopped, and Basilia looked proudly and kindly at Leticia, saying, "Good for you, baby. I'm so proud of you!"

In addition to her burgeoning independence and creativity, Leticia became a very enterprising little girl. Her first experience with enterprise presented itself in a very unexpected way.

One day while out walking near her farm, Aso was not with her. It was a nice, sunny day that was not too hot, and she had finished her morning chores. She was walking along the roadside, which was scarcely more than a wide path, not going anywhere in particular, just daydreaming. Suddenly, she heard some movement in the foliage a little way off the side of the road. She stopped to look and up popped the heads of two Japanese soldiers. The soldiers, who had been crouching down among the plants began to stand up. They looked directly at Leticia who became quite fearful. Aso was not there to protect her!

She began to hesitatingly back away. The two soldiers started walking toward Leticia. She was about to turn and run when the soldiers called out repeatedly, "No be afraid, not hurt you." They were smiling. Something about their attitude halted Leticia's impending flight.

As they came closer, she noticed that they were not officers, but just average soldiers. She also noticed that they were carrying some leaves in each of their hands. As they walked up to Leticia, she bowed deeply as she had been taught. The soldiers kept smiling and started talking to her. They asked her where she lived, and Leticia pointed to the nearby farm.

They told her that they were in the woods looking for special plants, but they were not having good luck finding any except the ones that they had in their hands. They raised up their hand held leaves for Leticia to see. Leticia recognized the leaves immediately as tea leaves. *The* soldiers then asked Leticia if she knew where they could find some.

Leticia said that she wasn't sure, but that she would ask her grandma who might know. The soldiers seemed delighted with the response. She asked the soldiers how many leaves they wanted, and they responded, "All we can get, and we will give you one centavo for the leaves if you pick them for us."

Since Leticia's family had very little money, this sounded like a lot. Leticia then asked them if the one centavo was for the number of leaves that they were now holding. The soldiers replied, "Yes, if you bring us this many, we will give you one centavo." Unbelievably, with the innocence of youth that allows children to say things that adults would fear to say, Leticia then asked, "If I bring you twice that many, will you give me two centavos?"

"Yes," the Japanese soldiers replied.

She boldly continued further, "And if I bring you three times that number, will you give me three centavos?"

The soldiers then looked at each other, amazed at the audacious little girl, and smiling very deeply said, "Yes, if you bring us leaves of good quality of the type and number that we hold in our hands, we will pay you one centavo for every multiple."

Leticia then counted every leave the soldiers were holding.

One soldier then said to the other, "Smart little girl."

When finished counting, Leticia said, "Okay, I will ask Grandma, and then I will look and be back here the same time tomorrow." The soldiers were pleased and agreed to meet her.

Something incredible had happened!

Leticia had haggled with the Japanese army and the little girl had come out on top because she already knew where huge numbers of the tea plants grew!

Better yet, she was aware that the Japanese liked the Filipinos to serve them, and that if she took advantage of this by meeting them away from the farm, her aunt wouldn't know about the money and wouldn't be able to take it away from her like she took away all her other things. She knew that this was very important to do because all the arguments between the older family members were *always* about money.

Leticia had developed street-smarts. Leticia had no idea at the time, but she had just come into her own as a businesswoman. She had just started her own little "black market."

The next day, Leticia told Grandma in front of Auntie that she was going to take the long walk to return a book.

She left the farm but was careful to hide a small sack under her dress.

Leticia then went straight to the tea plants and gathered many leaves, stuffing them all inside the sack. Although the sack became quite full, the leaves were light, and Leticia was able to carry the sack without too much difficulty.

Remembering how she had been cheated at marbles, she carefully counted every leaf. Nobody was going to cheat her again. The Japanese soldiers were waiting exactly where they said they would be and were absolutely delighted when they saw the little girl approaching with the sack.

Leticia bowed and placed the sack at their feet. She then said that she had brought ten times the number of tea leaves they wanted, and that *they* should count the leaves to be sure that she wasn't cheating them.

The soldiers roared with laughter. They couldn't help admire the courage of this little girl. When the soldiers opened the sack and saw the excellent quality of the leaves Leticia had brought to them and considered the size of the sack, they happily gave Leticia ten centavos without even counting the leaves and asked her when she could bring more.

To Leticia, she had just made a fortune, and the soldiers were willing to give her even more money for more tea leaves.

Amazing!

She was in business all by herself and wasn't even in school yet!

As with many people, success often brings problems of its own. Leticia now had a source of money, but it didn't matter if she couldn't keep it. Everything she had was being taken by others, especially her aunt. She knew that if she had hidden the money, chances were that it would be found and taken away.

Something else had to be done.

Leticia decided that she would give the money to Basilia because her grandma was the only one that she trusted. Basilia was astounded, not only at the fact that Leticia had the money, but whom she had gotten it from.

At first, she thought that Leticia's vivid imagination had made up the whole story of Japanese soldiers giving her the money and surmised that Leticia had stolen it, but from who and where? No one else had any money to steal.

Then as the little girl went on and on with detail after plausible detail of her venture, Basilia began to believe her. However, as she came to believe Leticia, she also became very fearful. What if this favored treatment fell sour and these men hurt Leticia? Japanese treatment of others was simply to take what they wanted. Why would it be any different with Leticia?

But Leticia went on and on all excited about the venture and told her grandma that the Japanese soldiers were nice to her and didn't seem to mean her any harm, and after all, they had actually given her the money—which was unheard of!

So with a great deal of trepidation and some reluctance, Basilia agreed to become Leticia's business partner.

For quite a while, Leticia's little tea business worked out fine. Both she and Basilia were ecstatic. Basilia was able to pass money back to Leticia mostly in the form of necessities that the little girl had been lacking without arousing family suspicion, although Basilia's constant, focused attention on Leticia always produced jealousy in the others. When speaking to Basilia about Leticia, the little girl became "your favorite granddaughter" or "the little Queen of Sheba."

Then one day, as Leticia arrived at her usual spot to meet the Japanese, she noticed that they were not there yet. At first, thinking that they were just late, she sat down at roadside and waited. Time passed, and still they hadn't come.

It was getting late, and Leticia had to get back to do afternoon chores or endure the expected beating. She decided to hide the sack far off the roadside among the bushes and return the next day. The following day she returned and waited, but the Japanese soldiers did not come.

She kept coming back day after day, but the soldiers never returned. Sadly, she realized her tea leaves business was over. But maybe, not totally over.

Leticia had tasted success, and she wanted more. She didn't quite understand money, but she knew it was important because it was what her aunts and uncles always fought over. She also knew that you couldn't get much or do anything without it.

So the next time Grandma took her to Alcala, she took a small amount of the tea leaves with her to sell.

The Japanese soldiers in the town, however, were different than the ones that she had traded with on the farm. When she bowed and approached them to trade, they simply took her leaves, laughing at her requests to be paid, and walked away.

Her era of Japanese trading had now truly ended.

So it was in 1943, Leticia was on the threshold of starting school.

In a very short lifespan, extraordinary events had shaped the character of this little girl:

- *independence*—forged by loneliness and the lack of even ordinary things
- *imagination and creativity*—forged by the strong desire to escape to something better
- *enterprise*—forged by the realization of how important money was, so vividly shown to her by the unhappiness at home all rooted in money and want
- *determination*—forged by her newly found sense of pride and her will not to give up

All of these traits were fused into Leticia, a true child of circumstance.

She had these strong building blocks upon which to grow, acquired from hardship, but blocks that were her very own and could not be taken away.

Leticia was now ready for school!

Completely unknown to Leticia, a half a world away in an entirely different culture, a little boy in a small New Jersey town was also about to start school, but he would go to school under totally different conditions.

If Leticia could have seen him at that time, he would have embodied one of those smiling American boys that she once saw in a magazine, for his life was vastly different and much happier than her own. *Many years later, fate would determine that this little boy was to have a profound effect on Leticia's life.*

A New World Opens with School

School! The very word brought excitement to Leticia.

It meant many things to her.

It meant that she would be going to a place where she could read all the time, and not only that, but she would be encouraged to read and not have to hide to do it. She would be making new friends and be able to learn new things. Best of all, she would be out from under the taskmaster's eyes because being at school, her aunt would not have her available to do the always added-on chores. She relished the thought of school and couldn't wait to start.

School meant freedom!

When her day of registration came, her grandma took Leticia to school; but when she got there, it seemed that her day of freedom would turn into a day of disappointment.

Basilia produced all the necessary papers for Leticia to be registered appropriately, but the school officials at first refused to believe that Leticia's papers were truly hers.

Leticia was the required seven years of age to start school, but she was very tiny, and the school officials felt that Basilia was presenting someone else's papers just to get Leticia in. For quite some time, the school officials kept interrogating Grandma, but no resolution to the impasse could be found.

Finally, an unbelievable thing happened. An older school matron entered the discussion and calmed everyone down. As

Basilia insisted that the papers were truly Leticia's, the matron stated that they would resolve the problem in a most unusual way. The matron, who seemed to hold considerable influence and importance in school matters, told everyone that in her experience, all children seven years or older, would be able to perform an "ear touch" maneuver, and if Leticia could do it, the school officials should register her. Neither Basilia nor Leticia had any idea what the matron was talking about, so the older lady went on to explain further.

Leticia would be asked to extend her right arm fully, straight up above her head.

She would then have to bend her elbow so that her forearm touched the top of her head while resting across it, and in that position, she would then be required to touch her left ear as far down as the earlobe with the fingers of her right hand.

This "registration test" did not seem to make any sense to Basilia or Leticia, but the fact of the matter was that Leticia was not going to be allowed to register if she couldn't do what was asked.

Leticia thought, *If I can't do this, they won't let me in school for a long time, and I'll never get away from my aunt.* She began thinking, *My neck is too long. If I could make it shorter, maybe I could do this test.*

And so, with all the eyes of the school officials watching, Leticia extended her right arm straight up, stretching mightily to reach the ceiling. She then bent her elbow, at the same time, hunkering down her head as much as she could.

Then she pushed her arm as far over as she could, extending her fingers to the limit, but she was still just a little short, she just could not touch her ear beyond its very top. She began to panic. She reached and reached but to no avail. She just couldn't reach beyond the upper rim of the ear. She was now desperate.

She looked at the faces of the school officials who were beginning to downcast their eyes. Suddenly it came to her! No one had said that she couldn't tilt her head. One last time, she hunkered down and stretched and reached but this time tilting her head to the right.

Success! She reached the earlobe and held the ear. She had done it! Everyone smiled, and the elderly school matron said, "Register this girl." It was her first triumph at school and it felt wonderful; she felt the joy of acceptance! Grandma was also very happy for Leticia and was grinning from ear to ear.

Basilia said, "You will like going to school here. I must leave you now and go home, but I will pick you up later this afternoon when school is over."

Confident in her new success and in knowing that Grandma would come for her, she eagerly looked forward to her first day at school, although with the same uncertainty of anybody who has started any kind of new venture never attempted before.

Regardless of all else, Leticia realized that she was now in school for real, and she was determined to make the most of it. When she got to her classroom, she was happy to see all the other children who were now going to be her new classmates; maybe some of them would even be her new friends too. After she had been seated, she looked toward the front of the room and noticed two people.

The first of the two to speak was a woman who introduced herself as Mrs. Daradar, a Filipino, who said she was going to be one of Leticia's teachers. Because the children were from many different areas where many different dialects were spoken, Mrs. Daradar spoke in Tagalog, the national common language of the Philippines, and said that she would be teaching their lessons in Tagalog.

Leticia was very lucky. Since Grandma and Grandpa were from different provinces, they had spoken Tagalog for many years after they met, so Leticia already spoke Tagalog. Mrs. Daradar then introduced the other adult at the front of the room who was a Japanese man. She told the students that he was also going to be their teacher and was there to teach them how to speak, read, and write in Japanese and that he would also be in charge of their physical fitness and indoctrination.

Mrs. Daradar then told all the students how lucky they were to have two teachers and that they were going to learn many new and wonderful things. The Japanese teacher did not say much that first day of school, but he did teach all the students their first Japanese school lesson, how to bow. Bowing, they were told, was a sign of ultimate respect, and all Filipinos had to bow to all Japanese at all times.

Leticia had learned her first lesson in the new school order.

As her first year of schooling progressed, Leticia enjoyed all that Mrs. Daradar taught, and the teacher quickly observed that Leticia was an exceptional student. The little girl's reading skill in particular was far advanced beyond the level of the class that she was in and Leticia picked up writing and arithmetic like a sponge.

And she was popular too. She got along well with all the other children who seemed to always follow what Leticia said to do because, in spite of her small size, her knowledge especially in reading skills was prodigious. She would bring in magazines obtained from her neighbor and, during free recess time, read the stories to the other children who all listened intently.

This worked out fine until it came to the attention of the Japanese teacher who forbade Leticia to bring in any more decadent western magazines and punished her with a cane stick beating across her bottom so severe that she could not sit comfortably for days afterward.

There were, however, the approved textbooks that Mrs. Daradar used to teach, and both the teacher and Leticia put her reading ability to good use. As it was, Mrs. Daradar was an older woman and was in poor health, often missing class time. With the war ongoing, teachers were scarce, so she handled a heavy load of classes. Mrs. Daradar developed a close relationship with her new outstanding pupil, and on many occasions when she felt too ill to teach, she would actually let Leticia teach the reading classes.

In point of fact, Leticia was a great gift to Mrs. Daradar, and it bothered her greatly when Leticia's natural independence clashed with the Japanese way of doing things and got her punished. Leticia worked hard learning the Japanese script and language and actually enjoyed being shown something new that she viewed as challenging.

She didn't mind the gymnastics and calisthenics because it was fun and a big game to do them, especially the stick battle competitions. Even the rigid rules of conduct and obedience to the Japanese teacher weren't that bad because children her age needed guidelines anyway.

All the bowing all the time, bowing to the east at sunrise and every time the emperor's name was mentioned, wasn't that bad for a girl of seven who didn't realize the difference between a gesture of respect and a bow of conquered subservience as an inferior people.

It was, however, the indoctrination rituals that always got her into trouble in spite of the fact that she was obedient and not trying to cause any trouble.

She was a Filipino Catholic who loved her country and both loved and respected her God.

She found herself always at odds with the indoctrination forced upon her by the Japanese to remold her and her people into the Japanese image. She had a sense of who she was even at this early age and didn't want to be remade into something she wasn't and didn't want to be. Some of her worst punishment came from clashes of ideology brought about by her innocence and her naturally inquisitive mind.

Unfortunately for Leticia, her questioning of the Japanese ideology, always without intent, took place in front of the entire class and produced a situation which no oriental, particularly the Japanese, could tolerate—loss of face!

One incident came about in complete innocence with Leticia not even realizing the trouble she was getting into as it happened. On this occasion, the Japanese teacher was imparting to the children that Filipinos and Japanese shared a common heritage: that they were both Asian and of the same race. He then stated that Japan wanted to "protect" the Philippines and join with her as an economic partner for the greater good.

This union, with Japan at its center, would be called the Greater East Asia Co-Prosperity Sphere. Leticia and all the children were listening intently when trouble came.

The Japanese teacher began to very enthusiastically explain that it was the divine mission of Japan to bring the "eight corners of the world" under one roof and shouted, "Hakko Ichiu!"

Upon hearing the phrase "Hakko Ichiu" so loudly said by the Japanese teacher in such an enthusiastic way, Leticia responded, "God bless you!" thinking that the teacher had sneezed.

The Japanese teacher became infuriated! He approached Leticia and struck her in the face extremely hard. The little girl fell to the floor in great pain feeling as though her eye was going to pop out of her head. She began crying which even increased the anger of the teacher. With three innocent words meant to compliment, she had insulted the divine edict of the emperor, made fun of a sacred Japanese mission and belief, and produced loss of face for the Japanese teacher as the other students laughed at what Leticia had innocently said.

She could not have said anything worse because on top of everything else, the Japanese were anti-Christian and Leticia had invoked God to bless the Japanese teacher using a Christian phrase.

As Leticia continued to cower on the floor and cry, it was only the quick thinking of Mrs. Daradar that saved Leticia from a further beating. As the Japanese teacher went to get his cane pole and then began approaching Leticia again with the infuriated look still on his face, Mrs. Daradar put her arms around Leticia saying to the Japanese teacher, "Please forgive her. She has not yet had the proper religious instruction of Japan and does not understand what she said. I will personally correct this."

For a moment, Mrs. Daradar did not think her intercession would work. Then miraculously, the Japanese teacher got control of his anger and said to all the children, "We Japanese are a loving and protective people. Our tolerance is strained by disrespect. We will not hesitate to punish all those who show lack of respect for the emperor."

All were then made to face the east and bow deeply for half a minute in reverence.

For Leticia, this was an incident that she would not easily forget.

Later that afternoon, when Grandma came to pick her up, Basilia was startled by the huge swelling of Leticia's face, with her left eye completely swollen shut and black and blue. Her nose had long since stopped bleeding and only the crusty remnants of blood on her upper lip gave testament to the extent of Leticia's suffering.

The little girl's head was still throbbing a lot, and she began to cry when she saw Basilia. After explaining to Basilia what had happened, Basilia became very angry, but of course, there was nothing she could do. When they got home, Leticia did not do chores that night.

Basilia's anger looked like it would pour over onto a demanding aunt, so Auntie had the good sense not to bother Leticia. As her grandma applied cool, moist compresses to Leticia's face and swollen eye, Leticia began to talk softly.

"Grandma, the Japanese tell us that our God is not the true God and that we must look to Japan for the correct religion," she said half crying and half talking. "They teach us that only their emperor is descended from the true Japanese gods and only he is divine." Then Leticia asked her grandma, "Is the emperor really Jesus's son?"

Her grandma answered softly, "No, he's not, Leticia."

Leticia then asked her final question, "*Grandma, how many Japanese emperors came back from the dead like Jesus did?*"

Her grandma looked Leticia straight in her only open eye that she could see out of, smiled a big, broad Basilia smile and said, "*None of them, baby, not a one of them!*"

⁂

A few weeks later, Leticia was walking to school.

It was a beautiful, clear, sunny day, and she loved to walk.

She began to hear a faint buzzing sound coming from behind her that she initially paid no attention to. As she continued to walk, however, the buzzing became louder and changed to a *droning* sound that was all too familiar to her. She turned around looking skyward, and in the distance, she could see many planes approaching in tight formation.

She panicked! To Leticia, planes meant bombs!

They were coming straight towards her, and there was no place to hide. She frantically looked for some kind of cover, but there was none. She ran off the side of the road and tried to take shelter behind a large tree as the droning got ever louder. Closer and closer it came until the sound was almost on top of her, seemingly everywhere.

She curled up into a ball, tucking her head under her arms, waiting for the inevitable screaming of the bombs—that terrifying, ear-splitting, high-pitched "wee" as the bombs fell to earth. Her heart was beating wildly as she braced herself, vividly reliving in her mind all the bombings and death in Manila.

It was going to happen all over again, she was no longer safe, and now she was going to become like one of those dead people she remembered, who had been eaten by dogs and rats. There was no place to hide, nothing she could do. She felt cold inside with fear, the fear of being totally helpless before inevitable death.

But there were no bombs, nothing happened.

All that she could hear was the constant, deafeningly loud, droning of the airplane engines.

No explosions!

She slowly lifted her head and looked into the sky. She could clearly see many, many planes flying in V formations. The planes all had large red balls painted on their wings and fuselages, and all were flying in the same direction, but they weren't dropping bombs on her.

She watched in dumbfounded silence, her mind now completely empty of thought, as wave after wave, formation after formation passed overhead. It seemed like forever before they would pass; there were so many.

Then the droning gradually lessened, as the last planes passed overhead. Leticia continued to watch them, a human statue frozen by the enormity of the event and the unwelcome memories that it brought back. Finally, the droning faded into just a faint buzzing as the last of the planes became as many flat, pointy-topped shapes gradually diminishing far off in the distance, now looking, to Leticia, like a huge swarm of flying insects.

She picked herself up off the ground. Her dress was dirty, but she didn't seem to notice. The sense of relief that no bombs had fallen left her with a feeling of being totally drained of energy. She continued on her way to school as if a little girl in a stupor.

Later that evening, she told her grandma what she had seen. Basilia answered her by saying that she had seen the planes too.

"They were flying to fight a battle somewhere," she said to Leticia.

"Will the planes come back?" asked the little girl.

"Some of them will," Basilia said.

After that day, Leticia saw many similar flights, and it seemed that it was just as Grandma said: when the planes returned, there always seemed to be fewer than had flown out.

Something seemed to be slowly changing.

The Japanese who came to the farm were now much less friendly and, instead of trading for vegetables and other foodstuffs, now began to just take what they wanted.

In spite of the hardships in the past, Leticia always had food to eat because Candido grew the food on his farm, but the Japanese were now taking large portions of the farm produce for themselves.

In addition, many Filipino farms were being forced to plant cotton to be shipped to Japan because of shortages there, in place of sugar cane and other food staples. This was creating Filipino food shortages, and the hunger in Manila was beginning to visit Leticia on the farm.

To the Filipinos, coprosperity with Japan meant Japan prospered; Filipinos were forced to do all the work. Many of the workers on Candido's farm just disappeared, making the work even harder. And for Leticia, a difficult life only got harder and more hungry.

But Leticia was a very resourceful little girl. She made a decision for herself that nobody was going to take everything from her, not the Japanese, not her aunts and uncles, not anybody. She was determined not to starve, and like her daddy, Leticia's mind was very creative, especially when forced by circumstances.

She knew that on Candido's farm, there were places with lots of snakes. As her grandpa had always told her, "If you leave them alone, they will leave you alone." Since they helped control the rats and mice, Grandpa did not mind, and even welcomed the snakes that lived on his farm. To outsiders who didn't understand the relationship, especially the Japanese, the snake areas were to be avoided. So Leticia reasoned this would be a great place to hide stuff if you knew how, and she knew how!

Constant confiscation of her things by her aunt had taught her well! Leticia set about to find a tin can of appropriate size that could be sealed tight. It took her a long time, but one day, on a trip to Alcala with her grandma, she found what she was looking for, and the irony was exquisite, for she had rummaged out from a pile of throwaways, an empty discarded Japanese ammunition box. She carried the box all the way home and began making her plan.

Leticia knew that she had to do many chores all the time, and now she saw a definite advantage to her labor. She was going to use the chores to get what she wanted.

All the Japanese, her aunts, and uncles would see is a little girl doing what she was told. She even had a trusty, silent helper in Aso. It was perfect!

Every morning before going to school and before the Japanese came, she did her job of letting the chickens out of the coop to feed them and to collect the eggs. *Leticia had decided to charge a silent tax for her labor.* Every time she collected the eggs, the collections were two or three eggs short, which were concealed in her dress. No one missed the eggs, and if anything was said, Leticia just replied, "Lazy rooster."

Then before starting off to school, she and Aso went to the snake area.

Aso was a big help because he always cleared a safe path for her and stayed around her while she was there to keep the snakes away. She had found a small out of sight place behind a bush to keep her ammo can and, each time, would place her precious treasure in the can and seal it tight.

She now had food *and* something to trade in Alcala with the city people for other items that she wanted. It was a wonderful system and worked beautifully.

She had been in her own little tea leaf "black market" business, and now was in the "food tax" business. She saw no difference between the "black market" business and the "tax" business.

After all, she thought, people in the government did it all the time to get rich. Leticia decided to do it to keep from going hungry. Leticia took advantage of every opportunity, even storms. Windy rain storms always knocked down mangoes from the trees. After a storm was over, she would go out and be the first to get the best fruit lying on the ground. Depending on timing, she would then either take the fruit to school and trade for other things that she wanted or go with her grandma to Alcala to trade her fruit along with her ammo box treasure and just about anything else she had scrounged from the farm.

She bartered in the streets routinely and got quite good at it.

As always, success attracts attention; sometimes good and sometimes bad.

The good attention first came from Grandma who noticed right away that Leticia had things to sell that Basilia herself had not packed on their cart. She watched in amazement as the little girl developed almost a regular clientele, some of whom traded with Leticia because they wanted what she had, and others, because she was just an adorable, cute, little girl, and they just liked her.

Finally one day, Basilia asked Leticia where she got all the things that she was trading and selling. Leticia looked at her grandma warmly and said, "I tax the Japanese, Grandma."

Basilia was speechless! Finally, Basilia said, "What?"

Leticia did not explain her little "tax and trade" business to her grandma but just said, "Would you help me by keeping my centavos like you did from my tea leaf business so that Auntie won't take my money again? I'll take care of you too, Grandma," the little girl said.

Grandma agreed as she looked at Leticia in loving admiration.

Afterward, Grandma always got an extra egg to eat after the Japanese confiscators left the farm each day.

Leticia was now very popular at school, especially with the boys. She was smart, cute, could hold her own in any games they played, and wouldn't take crap from anybody. What boy wouldn't like her? Some of the other children at school came from farms that were faring worse than on Candido's farm. They were always hungry too and noticed that Leticia always had food to trade.

She promised that she would bring eggs in for them if they would help her get fruit like guavas that weren't on her farm.

They agreed, and the first Filipino child's coop was formed, beating the pants off the Japanese Greater East Asia Co-Prosperity Sphere.

Leticia would climb trees and throw fruit down to the boys who waited below.

Everybody scrounged and ate, traded different fruit for eggs, and did it very quietly so as not to attract too much attention to themselves because the Japanese were now taking more and more from the Filipinos almost on a daily basis, literally taking the food out of their mouths.

But unfortunately, there was the bad attention too, attention that Leticia could not hope to avoid forever.

Her aunt had begun to notice things like Grandma having extra eggs to eat, Leticia with a new dress for school that Grandma made for her with new fabric that she bought, and little ribbons in Leticia's hair that Basilia had also made.

Although her aunt began interrogating Leticia without end, the little girl would not divulge her secret and took many severe beatings to protect her grandma and her way of getting food. Her aunt was both jealous and greedy—jealous of the attention and the close bond between Leticia and her grandma, which was above all other family members, and greedy because she always wanted and took the money, Leticia's own earned money, that Basilia gave back to her for school expenses and lunch food that she couldn't trade for. Leticia was essentially paying her own way and was being robbed of the "privilege."

Leticia went to bed hungry many nights because she refused her aunt's demands for her school money. Over time, her dislike for her aunt only grew. While all these things were going on in Leticia's personal world, other things on a much larger scale were going on around her and were going to shape her world anew.

To an ignorant little farm girl, it seemed to Leticia that there were an awful lot of Japanese soldiers in the Philippines, and they all needed to eat; but if they didn't have enough food to eat and were taking food away from all Filipinos, how was their coprosperity deal going to work?

Something was wrong.

In spite of all the Japanese propaganda being told to the Filipinos, all the glorious victories the Filipinos were being told about didn't match up with what Leticia was seeing. If things were going so well, why were the Japanese becoming ever more aggressive in their confiscations of Filipino foodstuffs and being so tense and so much more overbearing?

Leticia began hearing words that she had never heard before: *Coral Sea* and *Midway*. Although the Japanese were claiming victories in these areas, they were not behaving like winners. Why not?

One day, while Leticia and Basilia were riding in their vegetable cart on their way to Alcala, they heard the droning sound of aircraft that they had become accustomed to. Since these planes were always Japanese and no longer bombed them, they both only casually glanced up as the planes flew by. However, this day was different.

After the planes had flown by and were somewhat off in the distance, the tight V-shaped formations began to change into disarray with planes flying in every which way directions.

They could hear the crackling sound of gunfire and began to see some of the planes trailing black smoke as they headed downward toward the earth. It was a sight that Leticia had never seen before. As the planes moved all over the sky, Leticia saw that some of them looked and sounded different than the Japanese planes that she was accustomed to seeing.

These different planes had funny bent wings and made a high-pitched whistling sound as they flew. These funny-looking planes that were chasing the Japanese planes had stars on their wings.

Everyone was shooting at everybody else, and the whole scene was one of total chaos and confusion. Leticia and her grandma watched as though in hypnotized amazement.

Planes were falling to earth everywhere. Occasionally, they would see a white parachute slowly float to earth and then disappear among the jungle trees on the ground.

They watched as planes with red balls on their wings sometimes disappeared in midair in a large orange-yellow cloud of flames that made a strange sound of "poof!"

Others streaked to earth like a comet with a long black tail, going further and further downward until the planes with the red balls became all orange-black with the sound of that of a bomb exploding to be recognized only by a large billowing black cloud rising from the spot that they touched the earth.

The scene was repeated over and over again until a small remaining group of planes, some of them trailing thin vapors of smoke, with red balls on their wings flew in an opposite direction from the small group of bent wing planes which themselves flew the opposite way. As the two groups of planes separated, no further sound was heard except the fading drone of the planes' engines, occasionally sputtering, as each group disappeared as dots on the horizon, far away.

Leticia had seen her first aerial dogfight.

One night, sometime later, something strange happened. Leticia had finished her homework and went to sleep as usual. She was very tired and slept a deep, sound, restful sleep. She awoke the next morning because her pillow had gotten bumpy, and some of the bumps were pressing on the side of her face.

She opened her eyes and slowly began to focus on small, round, brown objects all over her pillow that had broken through an opening in a little cloth package wrapping that was lying on the side of the pillow. She immediately sat up to take notice of the surprise.

It was a whole bagful of nuts! This was wonderful! She loved nuts. But who was her Santa Claus? It wasn't Christmas yet for a while. She knew it wouldn't be her aunt because her aunt never gave her anything—she just took. It must be Grandma, that's right. Grandma always did nice things for her.

She scrambled around looking for a place to hide her present so it would not be taken away, and after finding just the right place, she hid the nuts there and went off to talk to Grandma.

Leticia said to Grandma, "Thank you for all those nuts you gave me. Where did you get them all?"

Basilia warmly smiled and replied, "I didn't give you those nuts, Leticia."

Leticia was puzzled. "Where did they come from?" she asked. Grandma didn't answer. As she pondered the mystery, Leticia noticed that the others had nuts too. She immediately ran to her hiding place to see if her nuts had already been stolen.

No, her nuts were still there untouched. What was going on?

She went back to her grandma and pleaded with Basilia to tell her how the nuts got onto her pillow. Finally, Basilia took Leticia aside and said to her, "I will tell you, but only if you promise not to tell anyone, because very bad things will happen if you do."

Leticia anxiously said, "I promise, Grandma, I promise!"

Basilia, convinced that Leticia would keep her word as they already had many secrets between them said, "Uncle Genecio brought them for you."

Leticia was stunned. She loved her uncle Genecio who was much older than all her other aunts and uncles, but she had not seen him for a very long time, ever since he had joined the Filipino Scouts to help General MacArthur long before the Battle of Bataan. But how? When?

Leticia was full of questions, but Basilia would not give her any more answers. With happy thoughts now in mind, thinking that she would soon see her brave uncle Genecio, Leticia went to her room to enjoy her wonderful present and to dream of nice things.

But in the days, weeks, and months following, Leticia was not able to see her uncle because he always came in the dead of night, and try as hard as she could, she could never stay awake long enough, and she never knew the exact night that he would come.

She began leaving him little thank-you notes, and on some mornings, she would find a little note saying, "You're welcome," along with her new presents which were now candy, chewing gum, and different kinds of fruit which her family couldn't get, in addition to the nuts.

On one special occasion, Uncle Genecio had even left her a new dress. It was wonderful. She now had one other kind benefactor besides her grandma, and she couldn't wait to see him. Apparently, Grandma had seen and talked with him because she always had special news after his visits. He had told her that the reason that the Japanese were now scrounging aggressively for food was because their supply ships were constantly being sunk by American submarines and very little was getting through. He also told Grandma to have hope because the Americans were coming back soon, and the Japanese would be driven out. To Leticia and her family, this was great news!

Genecio also told Grandma of a big battle that had been fought at a place called Midway and that the Japanese had been badly beaten. The Americans were now winning battles on other islands too and that all the Japanese propaganda about the invincibility of their army and navy was a lie. Soon, the Philippines would be free again and out from under the conqueror's heel.

It was important to be patient, wait, and to do the best they could for right now.

Genecio assured Basilia that he had the information on good authority that General MacArthur was indeed coming back very soon! Then on one of his nightly visits, Genecio brought news that was very moving: Admiral Yamamoto had been killed!

Genecio told Grandma that the rumor was true and that Yamamoto was killed when American fighter planes shot down the bomber he was using to inspect his front line troops. This news was not only monumental, but it was devastating to the Japanese because it meant that their best leader of war strategy was gone.

For Americans and Filipinos, this was great news, but for the Japanese, the news of Yamamoto's death could not be worse or have more dire import. For the Japanese, it was like their divine wind of Japan was now blowing the wrong way—against them!

The fortunes of war were now changing.

For the Japanese, the desperate days had begun!

The Americans Came Back

And so they waited and waited, listening for any news of the anticipated American invasion and trying to make sense of the increasing confusion around them watching the skies, and always looking toward the sea.

They knew that Genecio would only tell them that which was true, but waiting and enduring made time seem to pass so slowly as 1943 had long since passed and 1944 was dragging onward.

Japanese propaganda continued to tell of great victories by their air force and of far away battles on islands that Leticia had never heard of. But as the Japanese talked of the great glory of their pilots, Leticia watched the skies and noted that the planes flying overhead again and again were becoming fewer and fewer.

As she waited for Genecio's prediction of an American invasion to come to pass, it wasn't the Americans that came but more Japanese. In fact, the Japanese propaganda was now almost delirious with joy in their news broadcasts because General Yamashita, their finest army general, their "Tiger of Malaya," had arrived in the Philippines to throw back into the sea any Americans foolish enough to attempt coming back to the Philippines. The propaganda went on about how Yamashita looked forward to crushing General MacArthur.

Truly, these were very confusing times for everyone, but especially for a little girl caught up in a war that she didn't understand. Things were very hard on the farm at this time also, because almost all of Candido's workers had either disappeared or just ran away, leaving a tremendous work burden on Candido and all the family members.

All the adults, including Grandma, were now constantly in the fields.

Since she was too small for all the heavier work that the farm demanded, Leticia had to do all the cooking for everyone's meals just like her grandma had taught her. Everyone and every hour was pressed into the effort. Sometimes, she missed school days because of the added workload, but she never stopped her little "tax the Japanese" business because what she was scrounging now was of life-and-death importance due to the ever-increasing Japanese total confiscation of everything.

As the year progressed, Leticia also noticed changes at school.

At first, the Japanese teachers were "changing off" so that she was starting to see new instructors replacing the ones that she had had, but now, there were days on which no Japanese instructors came at all. Then finally, Mrs. Daradar was doing all the teaching again by herself because the Japanese teachers didn't come lack at all.

In fact, Mrs. Daradar was not teaching any of the Japanese curriculum, and school was now totally taught in Tagalog, and they were learning all about their own Filipino heroes again like Jose Rizal.

When Leticia asked Mrs. Daradar where the Japanese teachers were, Mrs. Daradar simply responded, "I don't know."

The children never pursued the subject because they all were happy that the Japanese teachers were gone. They were happy to be allowed to be Filipino once again! During this time of confusing change, Leticia did not see her mama and did not know where she was.

She was totally bonded to Basilia now as her Inang Baket and depended on her for everything. Luckily for the little girl, her grandma loved her very much and was the best surrogate mother that she could be under the circumstances. Even so, Leticia was very lonely and missed her daddy above all else. She had not seen or heard from him after that terrible day when he had left on the bus for Manila. It seemed like the world had just completely swallowed him up.

Now that things were changing, maybe he would come back for her, she thought. She had learned to write in school, and she thought that if she wrote to him, he would understand how bad things had gotten and how much she missed him. Leticia set about writing a long letter to her daddy. She poured out her heart telling him how much she loved him and missed him. She implored him to come back for her, to help make things right on the farm again, and to help her embattled Grandma who was the only one who truly cared about her. She finished her letter signed with her name and three little hearts and *X*s, put the letter in an envelope, and was ready to mail it.

Her aunt had stamps but felt that putting a good stamp on Leticia's little letter was a waste of money, so she gave the little girl a used stamp and told her to go mail it. Leticia was happy to get the stamp and glued it on the letter very carefully. Maybe her aunt wasn't so bad after all, she thought.

It was her first letter, and she did not understand that the cancelled stamp was useless. It was a cruel joke to play on a trusting little girl who had just poured out her whole heart into a letter to someone she deeply loved. With a bright, innocent smile on her face and eyes wide open in anticipation of doing something wonderful for someone she loved, she ran off to the post office.

After waiting a long time in line to give her letter to the postmaster to mail, her eyes began to fill with tears as she listened to him say that her letter was no good to mail. She pleaded with him, trying to explain that her aunt had said the stamp was okay, but he just kept saying that the stamp was no good to send the letter.

What was worse, he would not give her letter back to her.

Tears streamed down her face as she begged for her precious letter, but nothing made a difference. The postmaster was a Japanese replacement worker, not a Filipino. The Japanese postmaster now demanded that Leticia go home and bring her aunt back to the post office. Leticia ran all the way home, hoping that her aunt could help get her letter back. Instead, her aunt became angry that she had to go to the post office with Leticia and blamed the little girl for the trouble that was being caused.

When they got to the post office, the angry postmaster delivered a lecture to Leticia's aunt that she was unpleasantly forced to endure. Upon finishing his tirade, the postmaster was in the process of giving Leticia's letter back to her aunt who said in a haughty tone, "Just throw it away. I don't want it!"

Grabbing Leticia by the hand, she dragged the little girl out of the post office and, when outside, beat her for causing the trouble. For a long time, Leticia had heard the depressed expression of other adult Filipinos: *"No mama, no papa, no Uncle Sam."*

She had never felt it so deeply or really identified with it until now.

As the days wore on, days turned into weeks and weeks into months, but nothing happened. The anticipated good news of an American invasion began to turn into despair among the Filipinos. They had patiently waited, suffered, and waited some more, but it was always the same—nothing happened.

Then, on a day like any other day, in *October, 1944—Leyte!*

The beginning of the end for the Japanese was heralded by great thunderous rumblings in the heavens far off. What uncle Genecio had predicted was now coming true, the Americans were landing on Leyte island. The news spread quickly as to the meaning of the explosions. The Japanese in the Alcala area began mobilizing and great troop movements were hurrying off everywhere.

Although the Americans were invading in the Visayan area of the Philippines, it would be only a matter of time before they would come to Luzon also, Leticia thought. The months that followed were marked by great confusion, anxious anticipation, and much misinformation. As Christmas 1944 approached, Genecio came to visit again with his usual sack of goodies. These presents now had a special meaning because of the time of year and the fact that the war was turning in favor of the Americans.

He told Basilia that a great battle would now be fought all over the Philippines and that it would be a very dangerous time. He warned against any unnecessary travel. That night around Christmas, Genecio stayed a little longer to enjoy the warm holiday thoughts with family. Once again, it was late, and Leticia did not see him.

The following morning, she awakened to find an early Christmas present from Genecio and looked forward to seeing him soon. However, unknown to Leticia, this was to be Genecio's last visit, forever.

On January, 1945, the great American invasion landed on Luzon.

Very fierce fighting took place with an enemy that lived and was equally prepared to die by the code of bushido. This fighting seemed to be everywhere after the Americans moved inland, and the Filipino Scouts were in the thick of the battle. It was after the battles of this time that Genecio's next promised visit never occurred.

Leticia waited anxiously to finally meet her benevolent uncle, but for the little girl of so many hardships and disappointments, this greatly anticipated meeting would never take place, for after the battle became so severe that General Yamashita was forced to leave Manila and withdraw into the mountains, Uncle Genecio was never heard from again. Sadly, Leticia realized that another person whom she loved was lost to her forever and that she would never even know what Genecio looked like. He would go on living in her heart and distant memories as a loving phantom who took out time from the horrors of war to make a little girl happy.

Even though she had never seen him or gotten the chance to know him, she would miss him deeply because he was a large part of her memory of the dwindling few people who really cared about her.

Leticia's world had once again been brutalized. In spite of all that was happening, farm chores went on through the chaos and confusion. Then one day, Leticia went to the chicken coop to collect the eggs as was her routine; only this morning, it took her a lot longer. As she walked about the different hen nests, she quickly became aware of the rooster who, on this particular morning, did not remain outside in the chicken yard. This hen-protecting rooster began chasing Leticia, pecking her legs and, as roosters often tend to do, tried to peck her on the forehead between her eyes.

The battle of the chicken coop was on! Leticia looked for some way to get rid of the rooster, but he was very pesky and didn't give her a moment's peace.

Finally, she grabbed a straw broom that was leaning against one of the hen stalls and started swinging away at her pesky nemesis. She hit him several times and finally was able to half push and half lift him out of the doorway of the coop.

She dragged the flat bamboo door across the entrance of the chicken coop as she kept swinging the broom at the rooster. Then she ducked inside the coop and blocked the entrance with the flat, homemade door of bamboo.

Whew! She was finally inside and her noisy, cackling, feathered tormentor was outside the coop on the other side of her bamboo shield. She sat on the ground and rested a few minutes, gathered herself, and began picking up eggs from under the noisy, cackling hens that were still on their nests. As she gathered the eggs, carefully placing them in a small basket, she heard a commotion outside.

There were sounds of shouting in Japanese mixed with many booted feet running outside, some of which were running right next to the chicken coop.

Leticia peered through one of the cracks in the bamboo door and saw many Japanese soldiers running everywhere—some were going inside the other buildings on the farm, some were rapidly disappearing into the cornfield, and still others were crouching down behind anything that offered cover or a place to hide.

After a few minutes, a lot of shooting and explosions erupted. Leticia didn't know what to do. She was trapped in the chicken coop but didn't know where else to go to safety. The shooting and chaos had started so suddenly that the little girl had forgotten to put down the two eggs she had collected and just stood behind the bamboo door holding one egg in each hand.

She heard *ratatattattat*, then *buda buda buda* constantly and erratically, sometimes interrupted by a small, loud, muffled explosion sounding like it had occurred under some sort of a lid or inside a house. She peered outside again through the crack in the door and could still see Japanese soldiers running around, but this time, some of them had large red stains on their uniforms.

Leticia couldn't see who was shooting at them yet, but she had a good view of the rest of the farm. Then the Japanese soldiers began to leave their places on the farm and ran into the cornfields, disappearing from sight as the tall, leafy, corn plants swallowed them up, some of them turning to deliver a short *ratatattat* from their guns as they disappeared.

Then as she looked in the opposite direction, she could see soldiers in different kinds of uniforms slowly advancing onto the farm. Their guns even sounded different. As they advanced, they would approach each cover area cautiously with protective fire from their guns—*buda buda buda*—and one of the slower Japanese soldiers to leave then fell to the ground and did not move anymore.

As these different soldiers advanced farther and came closer to the small hutches and farm buildings, they would throw something into each hutch that exploded with the same muffled sound she had heard before. It then occurred to Leticia they were advancing right toward her chicken coop and were throwing hand grenades into each hutch!

They were going to do the same thing to her!

She frantically looked for another way out, but there was none—no windows, no back door, nothing. She couldn't dig her way out through the dirt floor under the coop wall because she had no time; the soldiers would be upon her in seconds! If she opened the bamboo door, she would almost certainly be shot, being mistaken for a Japanese soldier. She backed away from the door in panic—the racks of hen nests preventing her from going any farther.

She was trapped! She was going to die!

Leticia heard running footsteps coming closer and closer; then the footsteps were right outside the door. She held her breath in terror!

Suddenly, the bamboo door was torn away and flung open! Bright sunlight instantly streamed in, and she knew what would come next—the hand grenade and death. She would be completely blown apart! At the top of her lungs, she let out a loud shrill scream, over and over again, screaming in total panic for her life, waiting for death to be thrown through the doorway, exploding at her out of the sunlight.

As she screamed, she shut her eyes as tight as she could and made her whole body rigid so as to make death somehow less painful.

There she stood in the sunlit coop, screaming hysterically, totally unprotected, totally vulnerable, waiting for the "plop" of the hand grenade as it hit the dirt and the explosion that she would never hear.

But there was no "plop"; there was no explosion.

Slowly, the sunlight began to disappear until it was almost all gone. Leticia was now sobbing uncontrollably. She slowly opened her eyes and found herself staring into a huge black shadowy form that towered above her and was almost totally blocking out the sunlight as it took up almost the entire doorway.

Leticia's mind was numb with fear—she couldn't think, didn't know what to do, and then out of pure reflex, again shut her eyes as tightly as she could, stiffened her whole body, her face grimacing and contorted at the expectation of death to come, and raised up both arms as high and straight as she could, each hand holding an egg that now was crushed, the yolk and other parts flowing through her fingers, out of her hands and down her forearms. She just stood there, a little girl hysterically awaiting her final moment.

The black shadow did not move. Leticia did not move. Time did not move.

No sound from the black shadow. No sound from Leticia.

The world stood still—

Then slowly, the grimace on her face eased up, and two terrified little almond eyes gradually, ever so gradually, opened. Her frightened gaze travelled from the bottom of the shadow on the dirt floor, slowly and steadily upward, until its upper limit seemed to rest on the ceiling of the coop.

She tried to swallow, but there was nothing wet left in her mouth to swallow down. Suddenly, as her eyes remained fixated on the very top of the black shadow, she began to see flashes of white. The white then became both wide and constant almost at the same time. Leticia then heard a loud, booming laugh. The black shadow then spoke saying, "Well, ah'l be a. What ya'll doin' here? It's okay, little girl. Ya'll come with me."

Leticia couldn't speak; she was still very much afraid. At first she couldn't move, but a really large, brawny arm took hold of her and, in gentle manner, started leading her out into the sunshine.

As she got outside, the black shadow turned into the biggest soldier that she had ever seen.

The shooting had stopped, the confusion had calmed down, and large groups of other big soldiers just like the black shadow soldier were positioning around the farmhouse and hutches and beginning to smoke cigarettes as others stood guard. The black shadow soldier led Leticia to a large rock and sat down. As he removed his helmet, Leticia could see that he had blond, wavy hair, and when he looked at her, he had the only blue eyes that she had ever seen in her whole life. The only thing that she could understand about his uniform was something she had seen a long time ago in a borrowed magazine, USMC was written on it. She then realized that this soldier wasn't just an ordinary soldier—he was an American Marine!

Leticia didn't speak for a long time and just kept looking at this big, smiling man. He didn't seem to mean her any harm, she thought. Actually, he was quite nice. Poor Leticia. She had cried so much that her tears and drainage from her nose now mixed together, making her an awful messy sight. In addition, in her abject fear, she had pooped in her pants and really smelled bad. But nothing about the way Leticia looked or smelled seemed to bother this marine.

Leticia tried to wipe her nose in her sleeve, but things only got worse because now she wiped the eggs on her forearm over her face, making an even bigger mess than before. The marine only laughed harder.

Another soldier with USMC on his uniform came by and started to talk with her blue-eyed marine and said, "Boy, she sure stinks."

Leticia's blue-eyed marine said, "Yep, pooped in her drawers, po' little kid. She's scared stiff." The blue-eyed marine tried to talk to Leticia, but she couldn't quite understand all he said because of the way he talked. She could understand and speak English, but he spoke funny. He kept talking to Leticia, trying to put her at ease by reassuring her. He seemed nice, and Leticia did calm down even though she felt uncomfortable because of the mushy feeling in her pants, and she smelled so bad.

The marine gave Leticia a chocolate bar and put her on his lap, continuing to talk to her in a reassuring tone, although in an English that she couldn't understand. The chocolate was the best that she had ever tasted. Finally, the little girl got up enough courage to speak.

She looked into his blue eyes and said, with all the innocence of childhood, "Are you John Wayne?"

The marine smiled broadly and said, "No, dahlin', I'm not, but me an' all ma buddies here are real good friends o' his, an' we come here to help ya'll an' make things right." That was all Leticia had to hear.

She thought, *Oh boy, John Wayne's friends! Things will surely be okay now!*

The marine then noticed the eggshells, some of which Leticia was still holding. He then said to her, "Do ya'll live here abouts?"

Leticia answered, "Yes."

The marine then said, "Do ya'll know where to get mo' o' these eggs?"

Leticia again answered, "Yes."

The marine asked her, "Would ya'll be willin' to trade some eggs fo' some chocolate bars and good food that we brought with us in cans?" Leticia liked the chocolate bar a lot, and if the marine had more good food in cans like that, she would be happy to trade, so she said, "Yes."

The marine said, "Great! Ah'l work out a good deal fo' ya'll an' help yo' family too."

Leticia liked the idea a lot. She agreed to meet the marine for an exchange the next day, but there was something that she just had to do first. Leticia knew that she had to get cleaned up fast because there was no way she was going to go through life smelling that bad. No, siree, not when she was going to help John Wayne's friends!

The next day, bright and early, an excited Leticia hurriedly went about her chores being sure to collect six extra eggs for her exchange. She put them in a small straw basket and then covered them with some loose straw. She put the basket aside in the hen house and kept doing other little odd jobs, waiting for the marine that she knew. She could hear the sound of gunfire off in the distance, but it did not seem threatening to her.

Finally after some time had passed, the blue-eyed marine came back and had several other marines with him. He carried a small sack and smiled when he saw Leticia.

"How are ya', dahlin? Boy, yo' sho look different. Smell better too," he said.

Leticia's face was clean and bright and had a huge smile for someone she viewed as a friend.

"I have some eggs for you," she said.

The marines all looked at one another and smiled. The blue-eyed marine answered by saying, "Ah have some good things fo' ya'll too." Opening the sack, he showed Leticia chocolate bars and cans of C rations with all sorts of things like fruitcake, peaches, spam, and plum pudding inside. Her eyes became big as saucers. She knew that she only had six eggs which weren't nearly enough to trade for all the things the marines had brought.

Since she was trading good food for good food, she decided to do something that would probably get her into trouble with Grandpa. She ran back into the chicken coop and took some of the eggs from her collection that were supposed to be for the family and decided to add these to the six eggs that she already had for the marines. She filled two small baskets with about eight eggs each and, with one basket in each hand, carried them outside of the coop to the waiting marines. They all looked attentively as Leticia slowly approached them.

She put the baskets on the ground and moved back the straw, revealing the beautiful eggs. The marines all broke out with big, broad smiles on their faces, some of them saying, "Aaall right!" They were more than just happy to trade.

It was on that particular morning that Leticia learned just how much the marines loved fresh eggs. She realized that she was swapping one treasure for another treasure and feeling good about it. Plus, the marines were very nice to her.

The blue-eyed marine sat down on one of the caribou carts with Leticia and, taking out some chewing gum from his pocket, gave the gum to her, saying, "Boy, yo' sho look prettier than yesterday. Smell better too." Both of them laughed.

The marine then said, "Think if ah or one o' ma buddies came 'roun' every couple o' days or so, that ya'll can trade some mo' eggs fo' the stuff we bring?"

Oh boy, could she! Leticia happily said, "I will give you all that I am able to."

The marine said, "Fair 'nuff."

The blue-eyed marine then said, "If it's one o' ma buddies that comes in place o' me, ah'l tell him to ask fo' ma little girl friend, okay?"

Leticia was now beaming and said, "Okay."

"What's yo' name?" the marine asked.

"Leticia," she said.

The marine looked at her and smiled in a gentle way, saying, "Leticia sho is a pretty name." He then added, "Remember now, if it's one o' ma buddies, they're goin' to ask fo' Leticia, ma little egg girl, an' they won't trade with nobody else."

Leticia felt ten feet tall!

As the marine left, she carried the sack into the coop and there, examined all the wonderful things inside. This was a wonderful situation, but she realized that she now had two problems to solve. Knowing that her aunt always stole things from her, she decided to keep a few C ration cans for herself in her special hiding place with the snakes. That problem was easy to solve; the other would be a lot tougher.

Leticia had to convince Candido to let her continue to trade with the marines. This worried her because he might say no and ruin everything. She gathered up all the cans and candy bars, put them into the sack, and trudged off to the farm house. She sought out her grandma first and showed her privately the sack and what it contained. Grandma was very pleased, and what was more important, Leticia had someone to help plead her case to Grandpa.

However, when Grandpa saw what Leticia had gotten for the eggs, all her worries vanished. Candido was also very pleased and marveled at the good deal Leticia had made. No money changed hands, but they all had some good things to eat, some of which they had never had before or even heard about. Candido spent a long time talking to Leticia about her trade and was worried for her safety, but Leticia convinced him that the marines were nice to her and that she didn't feel threatened by them. As a matter of fact, she said that she liked them a lot.

After he was convinced that Leticia was telling the truth as best as she knew it, Candido gave Leticia his permission to trade with the marines but allowed her a maximum number of eggs to trade each day, as the family needed eggs too.

What was more important, he instructed all the aunts and uncles to leave Leticia alone in her trading and gave the little girl free reign to deal with the Americans, which was probably inspired by Leticia telling him—*with great emphasis*—that her blue-eyed marine had said that he only wanted to trade with her. Candido also realized that if the marines wanted to just take the eggs or anything else for that matter, they could do it over any objection he might make.

He sensed a good deal—a good relationship—and had the good sense not to interfere. After giving the entire sack of food to Candido and the family, Leticia went outside to contemplate her sudden good fortune. She was a remarkably resourceful little girl of considerable enterprise.

She had been in the tea leaf "black market" business with the Japanese, she had bravely "taxed" the Japanese by concealing and trading food, and now was voluntarily exchanging eggs for food in fair trade with the Americans to help herself and her family.

Leticia thought, *Gee, if I just can find things that people want, and get myself paid as much as I can, then I will be okay.*

She had learned many hard lessons of life, and in the future, she would learn many more, but she had learned the most important lesson of all very well: *she had learned how to survive.*

Leticia was back in business!

An Unhappy Odyssey Begins

Another year passed, and now, the war was over.

The inexorable movement of time had turned 1943 into 1946. During all that time, Leticia had never seen her father or mother. Although she had been very lonely because of their absence, she knew that the war had separated many people and that other children had not seen their parents either, so she looked forward to being with her parents again now that the terrible strains of war were a thing of the past, or so she thought.

She asked Basilia many times to take her to Manila so that she could see her parents, but her grandma always had some excuse to avoid the trip. In the meantime, Leticia had done very well by her family with all the trading and marine friends that she had made for them.

In fact, all the farms were beginning to recover, and Leticia was having fun with other children again and trading with them too. They would even go to Alcala in little groups by themselves to swap fruit and sugar cane for other items the city people had that the children had experienced from their contact with the Americans during the war.

They loved candy and chocolate. But Leticia's relationship with the other children was beginning to change, especially with the boys. It was a slow change and not really noticeable to her yet, but it was real. She was older, and although she still competed with the boys at their own games, they were beginning to look at her differently. Now when Leticia would climb trees to get fruit, all the boys would gather together in a tight group at the base of the tree looking up.

Being the impish creature that she was, Leticia always took a bite out of each piece of fruit before throwing it down to the waiting boys below. She thought it was funny that some of the boys would always take their first bite of the fruit exactly out of her bite gouge.

One day, Leticia was talking to Basilia about these events and lots more. Basilia listened intently. She was a wise old woman, and that evening after supper, she gathered together some nice soft material, a little bit of lace, a needle and thread, and sewed for about one hour.

The next morning before Leticia had gotten dressed for school, her grandma said to her, "I have a present for you."

Leticia smiled in surprise because it wasn't her birthday and Christmas was still far off. She said to Basilia, "Thank you very much, Grandma," and gave Basilia a big hug and kiss. "Why are you giving me these beautiful shorts?" Leticia asked.

Grandma answered, "They are not shorts, Leticia. They are bloomers."

Leticia said, "Oh?"

After thinking for a moment, Leticia continued, "What are bloomers for, Grandma?"

Basilia smiled and softly answered, "All girls, when they grow up to become big girls, wear bloomers. You are getting to be a big girl now, so I made your first beautiful, special bloomers because you're grandma's special big girl. It would make me very happy if you would wear my present all the time, and I will even make you more.

Leticia loved her grandma very much and was thrilled to get a present that Grandma had made all by herself just for her and said, "I love the bloomers, Grandma."

Leticia then got dressed for school, but before she did anything else, she put on her beautiful present. From that day forward, bloomers were always a part of Leticia's wardrobe. It made her grandma very happy but undoubtedly disappointed many little boys.

Leticia was growing, and although she was not tall and still quite petite, she was growing in other ways. She was also becoming uncomfortable. When she told her grandma that all her blouses were getting tight, and her top buttons were always opening, Basilia realized that she had more sewing to do. As usual, the boys were beginning to notice the changes, and Leticia was feeling increasingly more self-conscious around them.

She was blossoming early into a pretty young girl, and Basilia knew that now it wouldn't be long until she would have to help Leticia deal with the bleeding that was to regularly come and to explain to her that it was all a normal part of growing up for every young girl.

Leticia's mind, however, had had a long headstart at growing up before her body began to mature. Although she enjoyed playing games with all the other children, the prior years of early reading had advanced her mind to a plane of thinking well above that of children her own age. She was quite mentally precocious and was starting to realize that she was finding conversation with anyone older than she was to be much more interesting than her peers. Leticia would spend a lot of extra time talking with her teachers at school and, because of her excellent grades, found herself a favorite with all her instructors. She naturally seemed to seek out older people to talk to and felt very comfortable with them as opposed to her peers.

She would take many walks to her neighbor's house and enjoyed talking at length about many things with this nice lady who once had loaned her innumerable books and magazines, and had made it possible for her to enrich her mind during the worst of times.

At eleven years of age, Leticia was a true 'tweener. She was 'tween the age of innocence as a child and physical entrance into puberty, and 'tween her chronological age and the mental age of an older, more mature child. Indeed, Leticia was now older and becoming more inquisitive by the day. She and Basilia would talk about many things, and her grandma would always answer all her questions—except one. Every time Leticia would ask anything about her father and mother, Basilia would either not answer at all or just say, "I don't know, Leticia."

But three years had passed since she last saw or even heard from her parents, so Grandma's silence made Leticia feel that there was some secret that she was not being told. She knew that her grandma loved her and would never do anything to hurt her, so Leticia kept persisting in frequently asking her grandma the same question, "When are Daddy and Mama coming for me?"

At length, Basilia felt that she could no longer protect Leticia but did not have the heart to tell her the truth. Basilia approached Candido, who was the father of Leticia's mother, feeling that as Candido's second wife, she did not have the right to intervene on her own. Both Candido and Basilia decided to summon Leticia's mama to Alcala for a serious family meeting as the farm was undergoing post-war repairs.

Leticia's mother did come to Alcala and, after three years of not seeing Leticia and her sisters, saw Leticia for all of one day only! Leticia was ecstatic to see her mother. She ran to her giving her a great big hug, but although her mother put her arms around the little girl, the hug did not feel as warm or as tight. There was something different about her mother. Even her face looked different. The warm smile for Leticia that she remembered for all the past three years was now cooler.

Leticia asked, "Where's Daddy? Didn't he come for me too?"

At that question, Leticia's mother said to the little girl, "I have to talk to your grandpa and grandma now," and went inside their house.

Normally. it was not the custom for children to sit in on adult meetings, and this particular meeting was no exception. Leticia just waited outside playing. The meeting lasted a long time, and being just outside the house, Leticia could hear loud voices, but not clearly enough to understand what they were saying. Then the talking quieted down.

The door opened, and Basilia came outside, asking Leticia to go to the store for her.

The store was fifteen minutes walking distance from their house, and Leticia really didn't want to leave, but she always did what her grandma asked of her, so away she went, hurrying off so that she might be back all the sooner. When she got back, she excitedly went about the house looking for her mother, but her mother was not there.

"Grandma," she asked, "where's Mama?"

Basilia took Leticia by the hand and sat down with her on a large rattan chair. Grandma's eyes were red and watery. Leticia saw that her grandma had been crying and said, "What's wrong, Grandma? What's wrong?"

Basilia could not answer. Finally, in a voice choked with emotion, she managed to say, "Your mama's not here, baby."

Leticia furrowed her brow and, in a quizzical voice of disbelief, said, "What do you mean?"

Grandma answered sadly, "She's gone, Leticia. She already left."

"But that can't be, Grandma. She came for me," Leticia said. Leticia pulled her hand away from her grandma and began running from room to room frantically looking for her mother. "Mama, Mama!" she kept calling, but no reply was heard.

She slowly came back into the room where Basilia was and approached her grandma. "Why, Grandma, why?" Leticia asked over and over again.

Basilia fought back hard against the tears that were welling up in her eyes and against giving Leticia the answer that she wanted. "I don't know, Leticia," Grandma said.

Leticia kept asking, "Why didn't Mama wait? What did I do wrong to make her mad? I always did all my chores. I shared my food. What did I do wrong?" Leticia began sobbing so hard that she almost couldn't catch her breath. Basilia could no longer hold back and also began to softly weep, cradling Leticia in her arms as both shared the same sorrow.

After a long while, Leticia stopped crying and pitifully looked at her grandma, asking, "Why doesn't Mama want me anymore? I'm a good girl."

Basilia had no answer; she just hugged her little granddaughter even harder. Leticia then stood up and, looking into her grandma's face in a forlorn manner, said, "*She never even said* goodbye."

Several months passed in silence with no word from her mama or dad.

Leticia was now in the fifth grade and walked the one mile distance each day from the farm to school in the city of Alcala. She loved to walk because it was a time when she could shut out her family sorrow and let her mind wander to happier places in her solitude. It felt good to walk, and for Leticia, it was a sort of walk to freedom. The freedom, however, was short-lived.

Leticia's aunt had had a second baby and decided to move from the farm to live in Alcala. Upon arriving in the city, she sent for Leticia. The little girl was told that her new chore, added to all the other chores, would be to take constant care of the new baby. Essentially, this decision reduced Leticia to a full-time house servant, beaten for every little incident that her aunt perceived as disobedience, especially when the little girl tried to do her homework for school which meant that she would not be working around the house. Her aunt was totally unconcerned with Leticia's schooling and viewed the little girl's main function as servant to the house. Worse yet, Basilia was not there to protect Leticia.

Finally one day, Basilia came to visit. Leticia ran to her grandma, and each participated in a gigantic bear hug that seemed as if it would never end. During this visit, a dejected, tearful Leticia related the circumstances of her life in Alcala to her grandma who became very angry. Basilia took Leticia back to the farm. She loved the little girl and could not bear to see her exploited in such a manner, worst of all, by her own family.

After a long talk with Candido, Basilia tried to do her best for Leticia. Her mother and father did not seem to want her, and the abuse by her aunt was not tolerable. In an attempt to make life better for Leticia, Basilia sent the little girl to Zambales to live with Ernesta, her father's sister who was a nurse, hoping that this more educated aunt would help the little girl. But Ernesta's feelings toward Leticia were cool because she knew the true story, the actual events surrounding the mystery of what had happened to her parents and also knew the whereabouts of Leticia's father. After only a few days, Leticia was shuttled to another uncle named Lazaro who was brother to her father.

Lazaro was a very good, kind man whose wife, Marta, was also a nurse. From their first meeting, Leticia liked both of them, and the feeling was mutual. Aunt Marta realized immediately how intelligent Leticia was and the keen interest she had in everything, soaking up like a sponge, all things happening about her.

It was at this time that Leticia became interested in nursing, constantly asking Marta about her work. At last! Someone the little girl could talk to who was not only intelligent and interested in the same things, but who actually took an interest in her. For the first time since she had been given books and magazines as a tiny girl on the farm, she felt her mind and imagination reawaken, and it felt wonderful!

Leticia had found something in life that she loved to do over and over again, never tiring of it and always wanting to learn more. It seemed that the more she learned, the more she forgot about the problems and unhappiness of her own life.

Marta could hardly keep up with Leticia's voracious appetite for knowledge. Every spare minute the little girl had was spent pleading with Marta to show her something more. Marta loved it. The two became very close, sharing a deep interest in nursing and the care of others who were suffering.

This relationship was one of the major turning points in Leticia's life.

She was extremely mature at age eleven and had found something that she wanted to always do; she wanted to be a nurse just like Aunt Marta.

But as with all things, the bitter comes with the sweet.

Raul was Marta's son and had always been a discipline problem. He resented Leticia as an intruder when she first arrived. With the blossoming of her knowledge and talents leading to a close relationship with his mother, Raul's resentment, now coupled with an intense jealousy, grew to epic proportions. He began causing so much trouble at home that Lazaro and Marta could not control him. Finally, after thinking that she had found a place for herself after six months of happiness and learning, the situation got so bad that Leticia, seeing the sadness Raul was heaping onto Marta, requested a reluctant Marta to send her back to Ernesta.

Leticia had given up something that meant a great deal to her. Compared to the bright and shiny attitude of Marta, Ernesta was discouraging. Knowing that Ernesta was also a nurse, Leticia tried to show her all the things she had learned and talked to her about healing sick people, but to no avail. Instead of being supportive, Ernesta even tried to discourage Leticia about nursing telling the little girl, "So you think nursing is so noble and glamorous, don't you? Wait until you have to clean up all their vomit, feces, and urine without so much as a thank you. Tell me how you'll feel then,"

Leticia did not know what to say, but she did know how she felt. She knew that deep inside, nursing made her feel very good and gave her a self-worth that was all new to her, a feeling of usefulness that nothing else seemed to give. The talks Leticia had with Ernesta about nursing seemed to bring about a melancholy in Ernesta. Whether nursing brought back memories of failure or broken relationships was unclear. Something had soured Ernesta on nursing, and Leticia began to realize that she didn't feel that way nor did she want to be talked into feeling that way. It seemed Ernesta's problem was only magnified by the undiminished attitude and freshness Leticia had about all things regardless of the sadness of the little girl's family circumstances.

Leticia's stay with Ernesta was once again only a matter of days. Suddenly, after a particularly deep melancholy, Ernesta said to Leticia, "I know where your father is, and I'm going to tell you how to get there."

Leticia was thrilled! At last, she would be able to see her daddy. "How soon? When?" she asked her aunt.

"You can go tomorrow, if you wish," Ernesta said.

"Yes, yes, please tell me how to go. I'll go right away," Leticia said with glee.

"Your father is in Pampanga, and I will write down the directions to get you there tomorrow," was Ernesta's reply.

Leticia was so happy she felt like she could walk on air. For the rest of the day and night, she sang. All she could think about was tomorrow.

Tomorrow I'll see my daddy, tomorrow!

The day began full of promise and expectations of a wonderful happening.

The sun was shining, and all seemed right with the world. Leticia had gotten up early, but in fact, she had hardly slept at all during the prior night, too excited to allow the peacefulness of sleep to close her eyes. All she could think about was that she was going to see her daddy.

As soon as Ernesta awoke and was up and about, Leticia was asking her for the directions to her father's house that she had promised.

Leticia gathered her meager things together, dressed, and, with directions in hand, went off to catch the bus to Pampanga. She could hardly catch her breath as she got on the bus, squeezing herself into an empty seat. It was a long ride to Pampanga—hot and quite dusty—but Leticia didn't mind because something special was at the end of her trip. Throughout the entire journey, Leticia's mind drifted back in time to when she was a little girl during the war, thinking of her father and wistfully thinking about what he might look like after all the years that had passed. She tried very hard to remember but could just not picture his face in her mind. She thought about the good and the bad things that had happened during the war and was happy to realize that the bad times were over. Everything was going to be fine now because she was going to be with her daddy, and he would take care of her. The world was very big, and she was only eleven. The bad treatment that she had received from selfish, uncaring, and at times cruel relatives now would be a thing of the past. She couldn't wait to see her daddy.

The bus pulled up to the station, and Leticia got off with her little suitcase in hand. She looked around, feeling completely lost in this new place. She strained her neck, looking for her daddy, but he was nowhere to be seen. She looked and looked, then waited and waited, but her father did not come. Could he have gotten the time or bus number wrong? Surely, he could not have forgotten.

People were busy, but a kind attendant looked at the piece of paper with directions Leticia showed him and was able to tell her how to get to her father's house.

"It's a long walk," he said.

But Leticia just smiled and answered, "That's okay."

After walking for some time, Leticia began to realize that the attendant was right. It was a long walk, a very long walk. The sun was quite hot and high in the afternoon sky, and she hadn't had anything to drink since she had left Ernesta. Blisters on her feet began to hurt and make each successive step harder to take. She sat down by the side of the dusty road on her travel bag wondering how far she still had to go.

People were milling around everywhere, but none seemed to pay any attention to her. It was as if she didn't exist. She got up and resumed her journey. Finally, after walking about another hour, she saw a small white house that matched the number and description written in her directions. A great feeling of relief came over her because now her feet were bloody from the blisters, and she knew that she wouldn't be able to go on much farther. In spite of the pain, she joyfully ran up to the front door and knocked.

No answer. She knocked and then knocked again. Still, no answer. Leticia began to worry. What if nobody was at home or if her daddy was out looking for her? She knocked even harder. This time, she heard a latch being undone, and the door slowly opened.

A young woman, who appeared partially asleep, looked out at Leticia through her slightly ajar door. "What do you want?" she said.

"I've come to see my daddy," Leticia replied.

At first, there was silence. Then the woman said, "Who are you?"

"My name is Leticia Pampo," was replied in a soft, respectful voice.

Without closing the door, the woman turned her face and called out, "Felix! Felix!"

Then silence again. Leticia's feet hurt, and so did her hand from carrying her travel bag, so she put the bag down next to her and began rubbing her fingers.

A man's voice could then be heard asking, "What is it?"

The young woman answered by saying, "There is a girl here who says she is your daughter."

"What?" the man said.

The door now opened wider, and a man peered out. He had on a pair of pants but no shirt, sox, or shoes. He wiped the sleepiness from his eyes and weakly uttered, "Leticia?"

Leticia could see the man was her father, Felix Pampo, and shouted, "Daddy!" She threw her arms around his waist and gave him a big hug that seemed to be only halfheartedly returned.

"What are you doing here?" he asked the little girl.

"Didn't aunt Ernesta tell you that I was coming?' Leticia asked incredulously.

Her father then looked questioningly at the young woman who had a blank look on her face as she shook her head and shrugged her shoulders.

"No, Leticia. No one told us anything."

Leticia could not believe it. How could aunt Ernesta go through the trouble of writing down the directions, explaining how to travel to Pampanga, which was a long journey, and never tell her father that his daughter was coming?

Leticia was invited into the house and limped into a small living room. "What's wrong? Why are you limping?" her father asked.

"I think I have a lot of blisters," Leticia replied.

"Take off your shoes and let's have a look," her father said.

But as the little girl sat on a chair and removed her shoes, her bloody sox were seen to be crusted and stuck to her underlying skin.

"Please don't pull them off. They hurt too much," Leticia said.

Her father looked at the young woman and said, "Fill the bathtub with warm water. We'll soak them off while she gets cleaned up."

As the woman was leaving the room, Leticia's eyes began searching the house. She then asked her father, "Where's Mama?"

Letty's Story

The woman stopped, looked around at Felix but did not say a word.

The two of them exchanged only a glance, and then Leticia's father replied, "She's not here, Leticia." No further words were spoken, and Leticia remained puzzled.

Temporarily, however, her confusion and questions took second place to trying to get some relief from her pain. She sat quietly in the chair, silently waiting for the bath to be ready. When called, she hobbled into the bathroom, took off all her dirty clothes except for the bloody socks, and got into the water.

She was a small girl and easily stretched out in the tub. The heavenly feeling of the warm water caressing her body was indescribable. She just rested in the water, absorbing all the relief it brought to her aching muscles and painful feet. Later, she tried to remove her sox, but they were stuck fast to her skin. She thought it best to generally wash up first and just continue soaking her feet. She lathered up and soaped her sox as if they were her real skin, hoping to soften the crusting scabs that held them fast.

Finally, she was able to remove her sox, but they peeled off her blistered skin along with them. The soapy water began to sting and burn the delicate pink underlying skin, but Leticia was happy to have herself separated free. Besides, she was now home with her daddy, and if painful feet was the price she had to pay to be there, it was okay with her.

As she lay in the tub relaxing, no one came into the bathroom, but she could hear the voices of a man and a woman loudly discussing something in the next room. She could not make out exactly what was being said, but the tone of their voices made her feel uncomfortable.

When the water became cool and the skin on her fingers began to shrivel like prunes, she got out of the tub, dried off, and opened the door calling for her father. He came and helped Leticia put ointment and dressings on her feet. He then helped Leticia into the kitchen for something to eat. She was starved. She had many questions running around in her mind, but the dinner table was not the place to ask about family problems, so she quietly gobbled down every bit of food given to her until she was full.

It was now late in the evening, and Leticia was weary from her long journey.

However, as she was sitting quietly with her father, listening to the radio after eating, curiosity got the better of her and she asked, "Daddy, where's Mama?"

Her father responded, "It's late and you're tired now. We'll talk about it tomorrow, Leticia."

At that point, Leticia was shown to a bed where she "settled in," and almost instantly, the calm repose of a totally relaxing sleep overtook her mind and body completely. The soothing balm of sleep healed all issues for a little girl, at least temporarily. During the ensuing days, Leticia was consumed by questions and doubt.

All her father would tell her was that her mother was in Manila working at a hospital, but it seemed more complicated than that. Leticia's mother never came to visit and never wrote letters.

Her father did say that Flora, who was a former maid for Ernesta, lived with him to "help out." This was particularly troubling to Leticia because Flora did not act like a maid but rather like the dona of the house. The woman was "cold" and seemed to just tolerate Leticia, being very nitpicky over small inconsequential events that were turned into "big deals." Leticia wondered when her mother would come. She waited and waited.

As she was becoming more uncomfortable with her home situation day by day, her father finally told her that he was going to send her to school and had enrolled her in Holy Family Academy, which was a Catholic school. She had been placed into the fifth grade and was to start immediately.

Leticia had always loved school and looked forward to going as a new adventure; besides, it would be a chance to get out of the house and away from troubling thoughts. She was not disappointed. She enjoyed Holy Family Academy so much that she did not mind the long walk to school which was several miles away. Sometimes, her father would give her enough money to ride the jeepney in bad weather.

Because of her prodigious reading skill, Leticia did very well and achieved excellent grades. She made friends quickly and adored the nuns who were nice to her. Life seemed to be improving for her until the start of the sixth grade.

Leticia's father always paid her tuition each month and would do so by placing the money in the pocket of her school uniform which routinely hung overnight in her room ready for the following day. Leticia would then normally give the money to the nuns.

However, one month, she could not find the money in her uniform. She was very upset, at first thinking that she had lost the money. She was afraid to tell her father. Nothing was said to her at school. When the same thing happened the following month, Leticia didn't know what to do. She knew this time she had been extra careful and had definitely not lost the money. The only thing she could think of was that her father was not able to give her the money, and she did not want to make him feel badly, so she said nothing.

Several months went by. The situation had not changed. Leticia still had no money to give the school for her tuition. In a kind and casual way, the nuns at school asked the little girl about her tuition. Leticia replied by saying that she would ask her father. She now had to say something.

With great trepidation, Leticia finally got up the courage to ask her father why he had stopped giving her tuition money for school. Leticia's father told her that he had not stopped giving her school money and that each month up to the present, he had placed the money into her uniform pocket like he always had done. He did not seem to believe what Leticia told him about the money disappearing.

Crying, with sobs deep enough to prevent her from catching her breath, Leticia swore that she was telling the truth. "Why would I lie?' Leticia sobbed. "I love going to school, and I know that I won't be able to go if I don't pay the tuition. Please believe me."

That evening, the atmosphere at the dinner table was very quiet and tense. Afterward as Leticia lay in bed trying to find the mental peace which would allow her to fall asleep, she heard the loud voices of a man and a woman arguing in the next room.

From that night forward, Flora treated Leticia in similar fashion to how she was treated by her unkind aunt on the farm. Regardless of how well Leticia behaved and did her house chores, she could not please Flora, and it seemed that her father either couldn't or wouldn't do anything about the woman. The worst thing of all was that no tuition was ever given to the little girl again.

At school, the nuns approached Leticia once again about the problem. Their attitude was kind, but deeply concerned. They spoke to her at great length and finally, it became obvious what the real problem was. However, Leticia was facing dismissal from school.

For her entire young life and for many years into the future, all her problems were "always about the money" especially when it came to her family and relatives.

But this time, luck was with her. Through the sobs of her conversation with them, the nuns saw a little girl who was in school because she loved it and wanted to be, not because her parents were forcing her to attend. These compassionate and wise nuns truly liked this intelligent and cooperative little girl who was always willing to work hard. And so, a very grown-up bargain was struck between Leticia and these teachers—one that brought out the character of this little girl that would lead her to a future that she could not yet imagine.

The nuns told Leticia that if she were willing to clean the school after classes, that she would be allowed to continue and finish her final year of the sixth grade in elementary school without any tuition payment. Tears of happiness now welled up in the little girl's eyes as she hugged the nuns. Leticia did not view the cleaning of the school as work but as a kindness extended to her which would allow her to continue doing something that she loved very much—going to school.

Increasingly with the passing of her final year of elementary school, the happiness and love that she felt in school was becoming nonexistent at home. Flora became more intolerant and irritable with Leticia, and her father seemed to drift off into a world of ambivalence until the little girl could no longer stand feeling like an unwanted stranger. The father that she remembered and revered from the war no longer existed, somehow having died in that horrible conflict but still walked around as a person she no longer knew or loved. The mother she once knew seemed not to want anything to do with her anymore.

For Leticia, life became an unfathomable mixture of feeling more comfortable with unrelated friends than with her own relatives. After graduation from elementary school, Leticia's father sent her back to her aunt Ernesta. The little girl felt like a truly displaced person with no one to cling to. Her father seemed to prefer having a strange female with him rather than his own daughter, and her own mother never voluntarily wrote or visited her.

With a sadness deep inside that could not be measured, Leticia left for her aunt Ernesta's house.

A Flower Blooms

Upon arrival at Ernesta's house, Leticia was completely dejected.

She realized that she was being shuttled from one relative to another. It seemed that no one wanted her around, least of all her mother and father. She had stayed with Ernesta before and did not feel particularly enthusiastic about returning. She knew that this time her experience would be no different than her last visit. She plunged even deeper into depression.

Leticia moped around for days without any particular sense of direction, doing in a halfhearted way, whatever Ernesta told her to do. She really did not care about anything and was like someone walking around in a perpetual dreamlike state. At night, she would crawl into bed with her own private thoughts, seemingly locked in an isolated world devoid of affection. The loneliness would bring on the tears that flowed until exhaustion gave way to the blessing of sleep.

Ernesta was a public health nurse. Streams of people were always coming to her house, and on many occasions, she had to travel to the homes of poor people to render care. Leticia saw these people come and go but because of her personal sorrow and loss of will, she paid little attention to them. She was all wrapped up in a self-pity that stifled her ability to relate and left her in a distant numb world of "I just don't care."

One day, when Ernesta had to travel to the homes of some patients, she decided to take Leticia with her. Whether Ernesta took Leticia simply because she needed someone to take away some of her workload or to try to shake Leticia out of her lethargy was not known.

The little girl would help carry necessary medical supplies and, at first, only did little things that Ernesta asked of her while patients' needs were met, but there were so many people and so many needs. Although Leticia always did what was asked of her, deep inside, her actions were still only half-hearted. Ernesta kept taking Leticia to the villages and kept showing her new things to do to help the patients, but although she absorbed all the lessons like a sponge, neither what she learned, nor the grateful responses of these poor people to Leticia seemed to fill the bottomless void of hurt in her broken heart.

Ernesta's workload became overwhelming. She began to see only the patients who were able to come to her house and no longer made the long trips to outlying villages. However, as time passed, Ernesta had added greatly to the knowledge of practical nursing care that Leticia's aunt Marta had taught the little girl, showing her how to properly do basic wound care, simple physical therapy exercises, and as she became more proficient, even instructed Leticia how to safely administer medicines by injection. Ernesta continued to teach; Leticia continued to learn. Then one day, completely by surprise, Ernesta told Leticia to go to one of the villages all by herself! Understandably, Leticia was frightened. She was frightened not only because she was being asked to give medical care unsupervised but because travelling was not always safe, especially to unfamiliar areas so far away.

In spite of her fears, she went.

Her motivation for going was no motivation. She did what she was told not because of dedication, desire to help others, or even the results of the consequences for saying no, but because going to the villages was just something to do and a way of getting out of the house. She preferred doing things for the patients rather than house chores. The real reason Leticia went to the villages all by herself was that she just didn't care anymore. The saddest of all sadness for a little girl—she had lost her reason for being.

Ernesta gave Leticia one of her own white coats that had been cut in the sleeves and length to fit. Ernesta believed that the medical coat and canvas supply bag would be protective for Leticia on her long trips alone because there was a great deal of respect for medical personnel who were almost nonexistent in the outer provinces. This, in fact, was true.

Leticia's first trip was the hardest, but all the subsequent trips became easier. She became a familiar site to many people on her numerous trips. No one had ever seen a child nurse before because all medical personnel were adults, but because *any* medical help at all was so scarce, Leticia found very quick acceptance and protection in the areas that she visited.

It rapidly became evident that Leticia had learned her nursing care very well from both Marta and Ernesta. She did her best to help and the people appreciated any little thing that she did often giving her vegetables or an occasional chicken from their meager possessions to say thank you. They gave what little they had with great pride, and Leticia knew to always accept what they gave graciously in the same spirit with which their offering was given. This endeared the little girl to these poor people. In some villages, she was called "our little angel nurse." She became treated as a very special person.

And yet there was something still missing deep within her.

On the surface, she was warm and friendly, returning in kind the affection the patients and other villagers heaped upon her; but as soon as she left the villages to travel back to Ernesta's house, the emptiness would return. Time after time, she continued to visit the patients in the villages at Ernesta's request, with each visit seeming to blend imperceptibly into the next.

Then one day, Ernesta told her that in one village she would be taking medicine to a family with a baby that had been sick for a very long time and that this baby should be the first patient seen before all others.

As she was told, Leticia went directly to this patient upon arrival and found the family completely distraught. Leticia could see the mother holding the baby and patting its back because the baby was having trouble breathing. The mother said that the baby had not eaten or swallowed anything, but that its breathing had just suddenly become progressively more difficult.

Leticia administered the medications that Ernesta said to give and removed the baby's clothing, but nothing helped. The baby's fight for air became greater.

Each heave of its tiny chest seemed to suck in the skin between the ribs as the chest pulled in. Each strained breath made a high-pitched wheezing sound that was becoming louder as the lips were turning blue. The baby's eyes were open very wide in terror looking directly at Leticia, begging her just for one gulp of life giving air. As the baby thrashed in Leticia's arms, her tiny hands frantically grabbing at Leticia's clothes, Leticia didn't know what else to do.

The helpless looks of the baby's parents made Leticia feel a cold panic. She gave the baby a second injection of the medication and initially it appeared to help, but after a minute or two, the baby resumed its deeply labored breathing in its last losing fight for life. Leticia's eyes were transfixed to the pleading eyes of the baby, eyes that were begging for the last time to breathe.

Suddenly, the baby's whole body stiffened, and the labored breathing began to subside, having given way to the terrible exhaustion of a losing battle for life. Seeing this, the mother knew her baby was dying. She realized that the "little angel nurse" could not save her little baby girl. While there was still an occasional breath sound heard, the mother begged Leticia to "please baptize my baby." The father brought a cup of water and held it near his baby girl who was now becoming more still.

At that moment, Leticia's whole life seemed to flash before her eyes in an instant.

She had never baptized anyone and didn't know how to do it. She had seen only one baptism, and that was at Holy Family Academy when the visiting bishop had come to give confirmation to her and her classmates. Leticia thought, *I'm not a priest*, but she could not refuse this mother the last act of human kindness that would ever be done for her dying baby. She strained to remember what the bishop had said and done.

Leticia looked upward and raising her eyes to heaven said, "*Please, God, forgive me for everything that I have ever done to displease you, and please allow me to help this little baby come to you without sin.*" Leticia then put her thumb in the water and with it, made the sign of the cross on the baby's forehead, saying at the same time, "*I baptize you in the name of the Father, and of the Son, and of the Holy Spirit. May God have mercy on you and receive you into His loving arms free of sin, amen.*"

Almost at the moment Leticia finished, a last breath was heard from the baby, its body went limp in her arms, and the tiny hands and arms that had so desperately clung to Leticia's white coat slowly fell away to dangle lifelessly toward the floor.

The little baby was dead. For a moment, all was silent in the room, as the lives of all the people there also seemed to stop. The mother then gently took her baby from Leticia and, cradling the dead infant in her arms for the last time, sat in a chair slowly rocking back and forth quietly humming an unrecognizable song.

As Leticia slowly gathered up all the medicines and was putting them into her canvas medical bag, one of the other family members started to hand her some vegetables. Leticia stopped, placed her hand on the man's outstretched arm, and with tears filling her eyes, slowly shook her head and said, "Not this time."

After she left the little cottage, Leticia began to walk faster and faster, and then she started to run, dropping her medical bag to run still faster. Eventually, she could run no more and just flopped down to sit on the roadside. With tears still streaming down her young face, she just sat there looking down in the dirt.

Then, she looked up into the sky, her eyes searching the clouds for the face of her God. Her own face slowly became contorted in anguish, her mouth hung wide open for many seconds without uttering a sound, and then letting out a long, pitiful cry of pain that came from the very depths of her soul, she screamed, "Why-y-y" that seemed to hang onto the wind, echoing in the countryside forever.

She then continued sobbing, at times with stuttered breath. Leticia mourned this way until dusk. A tiny life had passed away, never having had a chance to live. From this day forward, Leticia's life and the way she felt about her own misfortunes would never be the same.

It was as if she had been healed by a dying baby.

Purgatory Reclaimed

Time passed ever so slowly, and little changed during Leticia's first two high school years.

Her family relationship with her parents was now essentially, no relationship. Any money for Leticia's school support was now disappearing, and Ernesta wanted her out. Being caught in the middle, and nobody wanting to keep her, Leticia ran away to her grandmother.

"Can I stay with you, Grandmother?" a sobbing Leticia asked.

Basilia was always the kind woman she had been since memory. "Of course you can stay, but we have to get you in school," Basilia said reassuringly.

And so it was that Leticia was placed in Alcala High School for the following two years, from ages fourteen to sixteen.

Everything changed for the better! For the first time in long memory, Leticia could finally relax. The firm but kind hand of Basilia made chores almost enjoyable. She encouraged Leticia to study fostering a desire to learn more. To this day, it was the remarkable influence of Basilia that helped save Leticia from prior despair, and until the end of Basilia's life, there wasn't anything that Letty would not do for her grandmother who she loved and respected above all others. In addition to a "new life" that began to flow around her, a new joy of life was becoming very evident.

As she was approaching "sweet sixteen," Leticia was blossoming *everywhere*.

Her short black ponytail gently cascaded down along with her pulled-back hair framed a truly beautiful unblemished, golden face, which needed no makeup to enhance. A brilliant white smile shone like pearls becoming wider and wider as she became more emphatic as her dark brown eyes flashed in mesmerizing appeal as she spoke.

Watching her walk across the room was a thing of beauty with her graceful twist of the hips and her head elegantly perched on square shoulders that sustained perfect posture. Her bouncing breasts protruded directly forth with defined nipple outline not overly big, but with proportional sculpture in exquisite profile, supporting an aristocratic gait that outlined the form of athletically muscled legs of perfect contour.

It was this vision that greeted the new boys of Alcala High School, rendering many speechless and, at the same time, producing many unsmiling girls who had the misfortune to stand next to Leticia lining up for class. But what won the day for Leticia in all things was her likeability. It was very hard for others to dislike her. Both boys and girls—but especially boys—simply just wanted to do things for her without her asking for anything.

She was a true gift and delight to be around. After finishing dinner one evening and helping Basilia with the dishes, they began to hear music coming from outside their home. Pretty music of love ballads, and then a little later, the singing of male voices began to accompany the music. Some were a "little screechy," but the boys were trying in such earnest that it didn't seem to matter to those listening. Basilia looked outside the window and called Leticia. It was the first site of kind that she had ever seen! Leticia was being serenaded by several boys who had brought musical instruments, and the music was beautiful, and the women thoroughly enjoyed what they heard.

But while she felt very flattered, Leticia did not know exactly what to do.

However, her ever present beautiful smile and flashing eyes seemed to say to Basilia, "What am I to do?" She thought, *There are so many boys here.*

In a very aristocratic manner, Basilia told Leticia, "You must respond because it would be a big insult not to acknowledge the serenading." Leticia now realized that being serenaded was a very rare event. So, after the singing ended, Leticia vigorously applauded with great enthusiasm and loudly proclaimed that she wanted all the boys to come into her house for cake and ice cream.

This was the beginning of a great adulation of the boys for Leticia that lasted for her entire time at Alcala High School.

Leticia had arrived!

Then it was boys, boys, and more boys! They fell all over themselves trying to be nice to Leticia and to make themselves as noticeable as possible. Letty found herself being called the most beautiful girl in Alcala, and in fact, *she was!*

Unfortunately, all the attention being paid to Letty did not sit well with the other girls. Soon after, a beauty pageant had been started in Alcala High School, and it was unanimous for all the boys that Leticia be encouraged to enter as Miss Alcala. However, just before the time to finalize entry, Leticia's entry money disappeared mysteriously, which would cause Leticia to be shut out of the pageant. Since Leticia had no money, it appeared she would never have a chance to compete.

But boys are boys, and at times like these, they would not allow them to be denied.

The boys themselves put up all the money for Leticia, causing great consternation and anxiety among the other girls. In the end, Leticia did not win, but the decision of the judges was greeted with such an outpouring of catcalls and booing that order could not be restored for a full ten minutes. The judges tried again to restore order, but the raucous noise only got louder.

The judges still would not relent, the boys would not relent, so there took place a Filipino standoff. To resolve the issue which was becoming somewhat heated and to "save face" for the judges, the judges created a completely new title for Leticia as Miss Alcala Health for the high school. This was completely appropriate as it was obvious to all that Leticia was *very* healthy!

After that, since Letty was a student nursing assistant to the high school, it was routine to see lines of boys constantly seen in the nursing office for all sorts of odd and sundry ailments. At the same time, very few of the females in the Alcala High School Nursing Office ever appeared.

The coming of spring heralded the last year at high school for Leticia. It came with the bursting forth of glorious petals of all kinds, picturesque and fragrant flowers that unfolded into splashes of color totally consumed in Alcala's lush land. Everywhere Letty was seen, she appeared as a picture framed by nature's art.

Along with the burgeoning landscape, a new and strange status for girls who were associated with her came into being: *girls*—some followed because they genuinely liked her, some imitated her out of envy, some followed because the girls wanted the boys and Letty was where the boys were to be found.

But there was more to it than that.

Teachers had noticed and recognized the elegance and class that Leticia exuded, and all the teachers treated her with mutual respect now calling her Ms. Pampo in such a way that all the other girls desperately coveted the title.

Then came "the Letty look"—and it came in spades!

Leticia loved to read anything and everything she could get her hands on, especially magazines and books about the USA.

The beautiful clothes that she saw in pictures were things she wanted to have. Basilia thought the clothes were too avant-garde, but Letty had a way of persuasion that brought Basilia to Letty's way of thinking.

So started homemade clothes designed and crafted by the two that produced very elegant and classy but casual blouses made of lace and ribbons topped off with black pedal-pusher/ toreador slacks not yet worn by other Filipino girls. Shoes were completed by black pumps or loafers. The ensembles created a type of sexy-elegance plus class that immediately caught the eyes of all the boys starting a kind of Pied Piper effect.

Both the boys *and* girls would go to class every day in great anticipation of seeing what Leticia would wear. The focal attention on Leticia reached a point one day when one of the boys (a star soccer player and son of a local mayor) actually tried but failed to kidnap Leticia. Such was the intensity of feelings. After that time, Basilia and Grandfather Candido made sure that Letty was always chaperoned—a very wise decision.

The girls—well, they just wanted what Letty had so imitation followed Leticia everywhere. Business was good for seamstresses as many girls could not sew. The girls just wanted the boys to like them too.

As always happens, imitation is just that, so many girls could not get what they wanted which led to inevitable disagreements and outright fighting. These outbursts of hurt feelings were usually settled by the high school principal who talked things over with the girls over ice cream.

One would think that with all this going on Letty would be a real "heartbreaker" just toying with all the boys, but there was a great deal more about her, something very deep within her that would never go away—ever.

Leticia's life had been deeply scarred in many ways, but in all the tragedy and pain was the one thing in her mind forever burned into her consciousness that would guide her always and that was the little baby who had died in her arms.

The reality of death and finality consumed in her the desire to try to do something about it. To Letty, her act of *baptism* was her defining moment, a one on one with God, something she felt good and right about, and she wanted to do more, and so, Catechism was the way.

During high school, because of her deep religious feelings and the good fortune of being so popular and admired, Letty spent a lot of time talking to her classmates about church, religion, and in particular, *baptism*, and her charisma was instrumental in having many young students baptized.

So because of all the things that had happened in her life, Leticia still believes that because of those that she helped bring to baptism, God has showered special blessings on her and always will. Even still to this day, when someone asks her, "How are you doing?"

Letty responds with a cheerful, "I am very richly blessed!"

At the end of high school graduation, Basilia was crying. She knew of all the events that had taken place in Leticia's young life and remembered carrying her around in her arms as a baby.

She was crying because she knew that "her" Leticia would be going away from Alcala, crying because she was so proud that Leticia was graduating, crying because of Letty's mother and father not having gone to the graduation, but most of all, she greatly loved Leticia and realized that she would probably never see her again.

Graduation was now over, and high school now finished. Leticia felt elation and excitement give way to a kind of deflation as if a wind behind her was no longer pushing her forward. A different kind of wind was replaced by one of hot, humid air, which held speckles of dust that forced her eyes shut and caused her to cough.

She was riding in a jeepney on her way to Manila, a long, tiring, thirsty trip. Leticia had not seen her mother for some time and wanted to talk to her. Her mother, Alicia, did not live in a house, but lived at the hospital in a dormitory. Letty needed some shelter. She was quite fortunate to be allowed, by the hospital, to live in her mother's dormitory together, but the one room was small and cramped.

Although Letty was uncertain about her future, she had actual hands-on experience in medicine which was extremely valuable having been taught by her aunts Marta and Ernesta. Her mother was a nurse, and she was living in Alicia's dormitory at the hospital, so it was only natural that medicine was on her mind.

And so it was, Leticia thought she might want to go to nursing school. But wanting to go and being able to go were two different problems. Before being able to get into nursing school, one year of prenursing was mandatory. Money was *always* a problem, but her mother did manage to "scrape up" a little, and Letty was very amenable to do *any* menial chore to help.

She was able to get enrolled into Far Eastern University and vigorously applied herself scholastically becoming very successful passing the SAT examination.

Once again, as so many times recur, the intense strain of study needed an outlet after her year of prenursing completion. This time, Leticia just spent time "moping around," and it actually felt good not to do anything for a while. However, the "a while" became a very short time. After feeling great becoming the "ultimate mope-a-dope," *dope* was exactly the word. Leticia almost forgot the nursing school entrance examination that had come up almost like a flash, in rapid succession, seemingly in the blink of an eye!

Still unbelievably oblivious of things taking place, events were swirling around and destiny was about to take a hand. While walking about casually on the hospital grounds, a jeepney stopped with a screech and shouted to Leticia, "Are you going to the exam?"

"What exam are you talking about?" Letty asked.

The girl repeated, "You need to take the nursing school exam right *now!*"

"But I can't go," Letty said. "I'm not prepared, I didn't bone-up, and besides, I don't have any money."

With the greatest of luck, Letty's girlfriend was wealthy and said not to worry.

In a genuine magnanimous gesture, she said she would pay the exam fee for Letty, but that there was no time left and the exam had to be taken *that* day or a whole total semester would be lost before it could be taken again.

"Take a chance and fly by the seat of your pants," advised her friend. "The only thing we can lose is a terrible loss of your semester time, Leticia, and the loss of my money," said her girlfriend with even more anxiety.

Then, away all these students went, off to a much anticipated but dreaded examination!

Several weeks passed—a time interminable. Then on a very bleak and rainy day, a letter came stamped Chinese General Hospital, addressed to Ms. Leticia Pampo. Letty's emotions all welled up inside her, complete with tight knots and stomach pains. She thought she was about to throw up but did not. Not knowing was bad for so many weeks, and what she now felt was much worse. She was afraid to open the letter.

For minutes that seemed to be an eternity, she sat down, just staring at the white correspondence. Then with a deep sigh, she opened the letter: PASSED!

She screamed out loud that might have heard supine patients in the hospital sit instantly right up.

Passed. Passed. Passed!

Leticia was accepted and was now on her way to the next starting nursing school class.

MY NEW LIFE IN MY NEW WORLD.

Leticia

RON GRADUATES MECHANICAL ENGINEERING.

FINALLY SOME TIME TO RELAX.

Letty's Story

LETICIA MEETS THE ENGINEERS.

FROM DISASTER TO VICTORY

WINNING WITH MY INVENTION INSERTS

HOW VERY PRECIOUS THE BEAT OF A BEAUTIFUL
HEART—LETICIA'S BIRTHDAY: AUG. 5, 2012

Coming Down to Earth

Letty entered nursing school with a sense of awe.

At the same time, she was required to submit to all the reorientation procedures that were created to instill one of the most important tenets of the school, *discipline*. It went beyond saying that all the nursing students were required to live on the school campus dormitory in Chinese General Hospital in Manila. Letty had to pay for her own food and lodging and did not receive any monetary subsistence during training.

Hazing was *not* allowed and was forbidden by the school. Although the nursing director was very strict and rigid about it, hazing happened anyway. Actually, it happened the first night Letty arrived at school and began with the purposeful slamming of a door behind her.

The juniors and seniors were called the higher-ups. The higher-ups had summoned Letty in their quarters, which was an imposing site for a probey like Letty.

Leticia was not allowed to talk.

For many long minutes, the lowly probey just stood in the center of the room full of the seated higher-ups, just "eyeballing" Letty very critically in every possible angle and vantage point, visually critical of her hair, clothes, shoes, everything.

The higher-ups did not like Leticia's beautiful posture as they felt not bowing her head low enough insulted them. None spoke. The silence was deafening. The tense silence made Letty very uncomfortable.

Then suddenly, *all hell broke loose*!

All the higher-ups began shouting questions at Letty all at once rendering no possible way that any single sentence could be understandable. Letty's ears hurt, and in this cacophony, it was not possible to respond, so she did not respond, making the girls even angrier.

However, Letty knew that no matter how bad things would get, the higher-ups could not physically abuse her as such would be an expulsion event for the perpetrator. Finally, all the shouting and noise calmed down to nothing and individual seniors began to speak. But again, Letty was not allowed to speak except to answer a question.

The probey's interrogation unbelievably lasted for several hours distilling down to just one question, "Why was Letty recommended by the president of the Philippines Magsaysay to this nursing school?"

"So you're a big shot, are you?" they shouted.

Several chimed in.

"How did you know him?"

"Why were you recommended?"

"Did you have an *in* because the president knows you and the president's daughter?"

"So, Ms. Muck-a-Muck, give us an answer!"

Leticia infuriated the girls even more in two ways by not answering this specific information (which she really didn't know) but also because Letty spoke English, not Tagalog, so they really had a speech chasm that had gotten even wider.

They couldn't get anywhere with the English-speaking probey, so they ended the interrogation and let Leticia go back to her room with a sweating uniform and a restless night that was to last for months, as she knew very well that it wasn't over.

In reality, Letty did not know either President Magsaysay or his daughter. Apparently, there was some sort of mixup during Letty's transcript papers. Leticia had gone to Castillejos Zambales, which was the town and province of President Magsaysay. Somehow, Letty became associated (wrongly) with President Magsaysay's daughter. But this didn't help Letty's situation.

The hazing continued relentlessly every night. The higher-ups kept waking Letty up after their shifts were over. Letty was sent to buy food for them, always shine their shoes, and tidy up their rooms. This was done in addition to all the other things she had to do for herself.

However, although hazing was illegal and frowned upon by the director of nursing, Letty never reported the hazing. Leticia was no wimp or snitch. Still, it fell to the task of the probeys to clean and scrub the bedpans, and somehow, Leticia got *all* of them. Every stinking job connected with vomit, urine, and feces became Leticia's prize as it became known, yet still, she never ratted out the hazing that she endured or any of the other girls.

Whenever she got an order, Letty responded cheerfully saying, "Okay, ma'am, I'll do it."

When patients called for any reason, Letty always said, "It's okay, ma'am, I'll answer the calls for you."

Leticia endured the hazing for six months from the day that it all started. After that, the higher-ups began to talk among themselves, little by little saying, "You know, Leticia might be okay. She has really taken all our crap that we dished out and never bitched or complained at all."

Since that time, when all the other nurses routinely snuck out for snacks, Leticia was included, not to be another hazing "gopher" but as part of the accepted few, no longer a pariah.

The probey year ended, and Leticia received the first thin black stripe to her cap. The capping ceremony was a very important and solemn ceremony attended by a procession carrying an actual lamp by all the nurses and representing the Lamp of

Knowledge, Hope, and Mercy. This was something Leticia would remember forever.

Autopsies—the most dreaded participation of the second year of school, and the most difficult thing in nursing to get through for Letty.

It wasn't the usual unsavory smells of hospital wards with the very occasional purulent wounds and dressings requiring hands-on care, it wasn't deformities or lost body parts that required the physical therapy necessary to stretch to move, but it was having to touch the dead bodies.

These dead bodies had been real people who had lost the battle of life and death; people who, some of which, Leticia knew, had talked with and shared some of their innermost thoughts, and feelings and who wanted to so badly live. These people were now still, silent, and cold, with some of their eyes open, holding the final nonseeing and vacant look transfixed into eternity. Still others had their faces contorted in horrible pain that only death could end.

Leticia had trouble touching those to be autopsied as she was required to do, not because she couldn't handle things necessary for nurses to routinely do, but because all too vividly, memories flooded in, and brought back to her mind, the experience of that little baby that had died in her arms, the "little angel nurse" who couldn't save the precious little baby.

Leticia was a very compassionate girl, and sometimes, that compassion just overwhelmed her. During the unfolding of the second year, Leticia began to have sudden abdominal pain that became increasingly more severe. She was found to have appendicitis and needed an emergency appendectomy. Immediately, a problem arose for both Letty and the doctors: Letty had a very low blood pressure prohibiting the use of a general anesthetic.

The doctor, in a reassuring manner, said, "I'm sorry, sweetheart, but we can't put you to sleep. We have to operate you under local. We'll do the best we can for you. You'll be all right."

Letty trusted what the doctor said. After all, she was a nurse, she was one of them. Leticia was given the local anesthetic, prepped, draped, and the operation started.

Letty began to move about and squirm.

"I can feel it! It hurts! It hurts!" screamed Letty. "Wait, Wait!"

The anesthesia did not take effect, but surgery kept proceeding. Leticia was being operated on *without* anesthesia.

Afterward, Leticia was not certain whether she just passed out because of the pain or something else happened, but it was not until early next morning until she finally awoke. "You're all okay now," said the doctor.

Letty, however, felt quite the opposite. Pain ensued with every cough and also the dreaded small bit of vomit that occasionally came up. She pulled tight against her abdomen with a pillow to blunt the effect of the coughing-produced pain.

Pain, up close and very unforgiving and personal.

Because of this experience, compassion remained for her, fixated within her very bowels, something she would always try to remove or alleviate. Leticia had matured and grown into one of the most caring nurses of her profession. After her ordeal, Letty got a short vacation to recuperate.

During that time, her cap proudly sported a second black stripe. As she went about doing her nursing care, she did "little things" like removing all adhesive tape against the skin slowly, using her finger against the adjacent skin as soft traction that caused a minimal amount of pain, a technique that a very fine plastic surgeon had taught her, as opposed to other care givers who always appeared to be in some kind of hurry and pulled off dressings fast, causing more pain than necessary and occasional unwanted bleeding.

She was also very sensitive about needles. People who were already sick and in a lot of pain did not appreciate "getting stuck" to have blood drawn, even the soldiers. Letty was particularly gentle drawing blood and doing anything involving cutting procedures, always making patients feel like she had all the time in the world to spend with them in spite of the fact that "someone else" was always pressing her because of other problems.

She had a soft, sexy voice, and spoke slowly which was very pleasing and reassuring so that many of the VA soldiers in growing numbers would always ask to be her caregiver. When she was off duty, the patients would be disappointed, remembering that, "Uh-oh, now we'll get the vampire."

One particular soldier who was blind began to always ask for Letty. His only contact with Letty was her voice, but he became infatuated with her especially after all the other soldiers had remarked about what a "babe" she was. Letty's voice seemed to fit very well the image he had conjured up in his mind. The soldier introduced Letty to his family, and afterward, all kinds of baskets of fruit and gifts were sent to her.

However to Letty, this soldier was someone that she took good care of as a patient, but he had fallen in love with her. Leticia began to feel very uncomfortable, so much so that she started to become afraid of him as he wanted to be around her everywhere. She was beginning to feel "smothered."

As her third and final year began, Leticia received her third black stripe on her cap. She now felt somewhat like a top sergeant. Weeks afterward, the blind soldier was told that he was being transferred to a second VA. Together with his family to say good-bye, he came to the Nursing Dormitory and brought a huge basket of fruit and a magnificent sweater as gifts.

He stood very tall and proud and wore his military army uniform that was covered with medals of valor on his chest attesting to the fact that he was a true hero. He was a striking figure indeed. He then told Leticia that he wanted to marry her.

Letty stood speechless. For a minute, there was complete silence between them. For some unexplained reason, Letty was afraid of this man—a man who had always been courteous and, true, a little smothering, but was offering to spend all the money necessary for her to continue further higher schooling and was willing to buy her a new house.

Now for some reason, she felt trapped. Letty's heart raced and pounded in her chest, her mind flashed with thoughts of confusion.

She thought, *What am I to do?*

Letty excused herself and went to the housemother's office to speak privately. Letty was asking for help, but surprisingly, the housemother just said, "Look how proud he is in his uniform. Don't you feel sorry for him?"

"Yes, Housemother, I do," responded Letty, still shaken with what was said, "but I'm only nineteen years old, and I couldn't get married until 21 anyway, even if I had plans to do so."

"But don't you have any pity for him?" Housemother asked.

It was in that exact instant that Leticia realized what to do and why. She now knew that if she were to marry this soldier, she would be doing it for pity and not for love. She could not accept his proposal, but what to do and say? The man was a good man, a hero who loved her. She just could not hurt or insult him.

Leticia came back into the room, took the blind soldier by the hand, and led him to the housemother's office where the housemother left for privacy, trying to soothe the dashed feelings that were to come.

Leticia then genuinely thanked him for everything and said, "I am only nineteen years old and cannot get married until twenty-one. My mother would not allow me to get married at this age. So I am not able to marry you now. Both of us would need more time to get to know each other better."

The soldier and his family left.

Leticia never heard from him again.

Afterward, Letty still felt deeply troubled, her heart pulled strongly one way, her head pulled the other. She had hurt this good man, and Letty did not like hurting people. She thought that if she were older and more mature, maybe she might have considered this soldier's proposal. In the end, Leticia came to the great realization that deep in her heart, she could not marry for pity. It would be wrong. She had to marry for love.

Choices

The third year of nursing school, it was just great!

Many things changed for the better. Many new friends had been made during this latter year, and a lot of pressure seemed lessened as top year had many advantages, but one of the best was that it was now possible to have some fun. Being gregarious and a "people person" helped a lot. Everyone in the class asked each other where it was likely that they would be working and, believe it or not, *for a paycheck.*

A paycheck—a way to be self-sufficient, a time the future might be charted.

That was a great feeling!

Although working for money would be very important, Leticia wanted to do something with her life, and therefore, she looked closer and closer into the various fields of nursing medicine that she could go into.

Many doctors tried to persuade her into specialties of their own showing how interesting things were as *good* nurses were as rare as diamonds, and *Leticia was definitely a diamond in the rough.*

As she surveyed the possibilities of the medical field, the doctors fell into her own special little "other" broad categories:

- *surgeons* did everything and knew nothing
- *internists* knew everything and did nothing
- *pathologists* knew everything and did everything but did it all too late
- *pediatricians* were just big kids that never grew up

- *orthopedists* were big bruisers but usually very nice guys
    Being small like Leticia was a handicap
    One big patient with a spica body cast could make a pizza out of her
- *anesthesiologists* lived in a world of sleep and of doing a lot of passing gas

Leticia thought, *Oh my, what am I to do?*

There was a *big* universe out there, and God gave Leticia the only thing he truly does give: *choices* and Letty wanted a lot of them.

As the world opened up, Leticia was working with the patients when a man in the physical therapy department named Marco began to be especially nice to her and very polite. He was small in stature, appealing in features, and sociable. However, he was about twenty years older than Leticia, so initially, Letty was not interested in a romance as she thought it would be like dating her father.

He was nice enough, but Leticia was very attractive, so young men were always smiling at her. As time passed however, Marco was extremely persistent, and Letty, being young and naive, began to get worn down against Marco's overtures, so Letty mistook flattery for deep affection and caring.

And so the older man who was twice Letty's age persuaded Leticia to marry him.

Almost immediately, Marco told Leticia that he did not want her to work anymore and that she should just take care of their family. She thought that was great as very shortly, Marco got her pregnant. Leticia was an obedient and faithful wife and always said that she "wanted to be a perfect wife." So Letty accepted Marco's rather dominating attitude, which always started with money first keeping Letty on a very "short leash" for buying anything.

He told her that it was very important to strictly adhere to their budget which Letty accepted as Marco, at times, could be "touchy" and irritable.

Their lives seemed to go smoothly at first as long as Letty never disagreed with Marco or criticized him for anything as he would sometimes get quite agitated. After her first child, Leticia was immersed in the care of the baby, and as a lover, Letty was warm and affectionate, totally focused on her family.

She enjoyed being intimate with Marco who was, at first, gentle with her. Marco wanted a second child immediately, and so Letty very quickly had two boys to care for. Almost immediately, Marco wanted another child, but the third pregnancy did not go easily, as Leticia had a lot of pain and bleeding, eventually requiring complete bed rest for three months in order to save the pregnancy. A little girl, Carlita, was born healthy and well.

Leticia had suffered a great ordeal and needed time to recuperate. But as she began to get out and about, with other people smiling and greeting her, especially men innocently saying hello, Marco became sullen and suspicious with no cause.

Leticia was still not well. Again almost immediately, Marco wanted to get Letty pregnant again. Leticia refused. For the first time, Marco began to smack her around. This came as a shock to her! From this time on, lovemaking changed from enjoyable to rough, dominating, violent forceful entry, which was progressively more painful for Letty and almost a punishment, not love.

Marco had been refused by Leticia, and this changed everything, *or* had Marco always been this way and Letty had never realized that this man was not who she thought she had married, and that Marco's keeping Letty constantly pregnant was a form of domination.

For better or worse became progressively much worse.

Leticia did conceive a fourth pregnancy and had an extremely difficult time. About halfway through the fourth pregnancy, Marco began to disappear for long periods. Coincidentally, so did

Leticia's sister, Adelina. As Letty struggled, her mother, Alicia, seemed more attentive to Marco than Leticia's plight. Then, one night, when she was unable to sleep because of pain, she heard grunting and groaning in the next room.

Thinking someone was hurt, Letty opened the door and found Marco with Adelina together in adulterous intercourse. Marco became furious and began beating Leticia, making her bleeding flow profusely. *Unbelievably, Alicia became angry with Leticia* for catching Marco with Letty's sister Adelina in the adulterous affair. After that time, Marco put Adelina up into her own apartment and used the money that *Letty* had to budget for *her* children.

As Letty came to term, she conceived a very tiny blue baby and called him Bernardo. Bernardo barely survived!

Adelina was not seen again after the night she had been caught, but a few months later, Adelina produced a baby girl named Lynn by Marco. From that point on, Marco had fathered another child by some Chinese girl.

Between Marco and Leticia, they're relationship became violent!

It appeared that Marco was all about domination and forcing his will on Leticia, *not* love. The more she resisted, the more he beat her. *Marco's kicking of Leticia's abdomen produced many bleeding events.*

Leticia's beauty seemed to make everything worse. No trust in their relationship existed as Marco's jealousy, and envy were unbounded. What Marco was doing with Adelina and other girls, *he* projected on Leticia calling her a whore just for saying "good morning" to another man. A little old man with a beautiful wife like Leticia brought out an ugly, Napoleonic, inferiority complex culminating in Marco *placing a gun to Leticia's head* and saying, "If you don't do what I always tell you to do, I'm going to use this!"

Leticia knew that it was only a matter of time before Marco would vent his rage on her, for the very last time!

Leticia Runs For Her Life

"I can't stand it! I can't stand it! Flesh and blood can stand no more," cried out Leticia in anguish as she tried to stand up but could only "huddle up" forward, wrapping her arms around her abdomen because of the pain. Repeatedly kicked like a dog, she could barely walk.

Marco was usually careful always to punch Letty in the abdomen, the back, arms, and legs, *never* the face in order not to show any signs of bruising. She always had to wear long sleeve blouses and slacks, regardless of the heat on summer days, so bruises and swelling would not show.

In her bathroom, curled up in the fetal position, she cried and stayed there, terrified of what might come next. After a while, Marco left the house. All was quiet, *but this time*, it was different. Leticia looked in the mirror and saw her face which was badly swollen, the left eye purple and almost completely shut and blood trickling from her nose.

The beatings Marco had inflicted on Leticia had become progressively more severe and intense, *but this first time, he had beaten Leticia's face, and the cruelty was now very visible.* Leticia was a mess. She tried to cover her facial bruises with makeup, a bandana, and her largest sunglasses, but to no avail. Letty had to go to work, and for the first time, other people got to see the results of the ferocity that had been inflicted on her!

She had suffered in silence for a long time, never having spoken a word to anyone, always suffering in silence. When Leticia had slowly walked into the high school infirmary, leaning forward and protectively favoring her abdomen, others saw Leticia's face and bruises for the first time!

Shock, disbelief, and then disgust greeted all others around the beautiful girl who was no longer beautiful on this day. Two doctors and two dentists in the public health service sent Leticia to the emergency room, took many pictures, and reported the pummeling of this diminutive little girl by Marco.

One female doctor who was married to a lawyer was so angry that she said to Leticia, "There are others who can help."

But Leticia realized that she had no money and no resources. "What can I do?" she cried with tears flowing down her battered face.

Both doctor and lawyer said to Letty, "If you do nothing, you are certainly going to be killed. Stay hidden. We have to make a few calls," they advised.

The next day, Leticia was told to go to a bus stop at a travel agency.

The agent said to Letty, "Ah yes, you're the one we're waiting for. We're preparing paper work for the consulate and passport. It seems there are some very nice people who want to help you, but first, you must have a physical exam by the doctor to be sure that you're not pregnant or have any infectious diseases."

Leticia wound up in Chinese General Hospital, and to her amazement, she found that the director of the hospital that she had to see was her godfather who had been her sponsor at the wedding of Leticia and Marco. After Letty told her story, the director placed a guard to protect Leticia from Marco and assembled all the medicals necessary for a passport and visa.

"You must run away and go to a place far away," the director said.

What Marco had been doing to Leticia *for a long time* had now been exposed. Surprisingly, one of the guards, a Mr. Aginaldo, who actually was an assistant in physical therapy to Marco, helped Leticia hide.

"I don't like Marco either," Aginaldo confided to Letty.

Many people stepped up to help as Leticia was a school nurse employed by the government and well respected. Hospital personnel hid Leticia as did teachers and the school principal. Many of Marco's relatives turned against him. His brother and a cousin, who was a policeman, gave Letty a few US dollars, some clothes, and luggage. All these things were kept in the school, waiting for Letty to use.

Then, the time came to run for her life!

But while the travel agent gave Letty all the necessary papers and airport schedule, he made the mistake by reaffirming the flight by calling Leticia's mother, Alicia. For some reason that Letty never really knew, *Alicia took the side of Marco* against Letty and told Marco that Letty was running away.

She was caught!

That night, it all began again! Leticia thought all hope was gone. As she lay behind the bed, cowering in fear, Marco dragged Letty up and threw her on the bed, repeatedly beating her and raping her over and over again! It didn't stop until *he* was exhausted! He then threw Leticia into the bathroom and locked her in.

There was now no hope.

Am I to die now, in this way, she thought, *without even my mother to pity me?*

Leticia rolled up in a ball and just kept sobbing.

A little later, all was quiet, and then, she heard a voice that she recognized, Marco's cousin, the policeman. He unlocked the bathroom door, and they both ran to his car.

Letty looked terrible! He took Letty to a beautician he knew who cut her hair very short, put a lot of makeup on her face to disguise her, and tried to fix her up a little. He then told her to hide. The policeman then gathered Letty's luggage from the school nurse and took Letty to the airport. But Leticia was late for the flight, and it had taken off.

Her mind kept thinking, *I'm not going to make it. I can't make it. I'm going to die tonight!*

Marco and Alicia, together with some other of their cohorts, now arrived at the airport and furiously began looking for Letty. They couldn't find her! Since her flight had gone, and nobody could find her after hours later, they all gave up looking, reluctantly thinking Leticia had escaped and gone away.

Actually, all this time, Leticia remained hidden under a small nook under the stairs. She remained there totally quiet, never uttering a sound. However, Leticia's mind was anything but silent. Over and over again, she thought, *I'm running away, running from those I love. What right have I to do this?*

It was like a dagger piercing her heart! Then other thoughts flashed before her. *I'm being forced to leave those I love. I'm not leaving of my own free will. I'm forced by the probability of death from the beatings by Marco. I have no choice.* Her mind cried out, *I want to live! I want my children to live! I know others will say I abandoned them, but being forced to leave, not leaving by free choice, is not abandonment. I know my children will say someday to their children that, "Our mother abandoned us," but they will be so wrong! They will even probably resent me, deep down. But the bottom line is, would these children be better off with me dead, without a mother forever, replaced by God-knows-who, or would these children be better off with both me and them left alive to be temporarily without me and someday bring them to me to a better place where we all could be happy and safe? If my children then—and now—believe they were abandoned by me and freely tell everyone this, then this is the price I must pay in order to do what's right and best for them.*

Letty's Story

Leticia knew it was so incredibly hard to do what had to be done. She had come to her own peace with her own conscience and her mind with God.

Letty waited until the very last flight possible after 6:00 p.m. when it was dark, and her appearance looked different, making it harder for her to spot. With her legs bent under her for so long in her hiding place, she could hardly stand up. Then with all the energy she could muster, she made a last dash for freedom, a last dash for her life!

She ran, stumbled, and finally fell into the open door of the plane stairway! Breathless, she flopped into the plane seat, completely exhausted. But she wasn't free yet.

A few people were still boarding.

She tensely waited and waited and waited, waiting for the others to sit, giving Marco all the more time to find her, to catch her for the final time and to pull her off the plane. Then, *she heard a loud clunk*; the door was closed and locked.

A pleasant girl's voice said, "Welcome to Flight 309 to Hong Kong..."

Leticia did not even hear the rest of the stewardess's speech as she felt in her own world of limbo, blankly looking and staring out the window as if in a trance, but looking for something out there.

The plane then began to taxi on the runway. Faster and faster it went, then smoothly rising higher and higher. The golden sunset shown brilliantly against the puffy white, billowing clouds with the plane now rising higher still, beginning to enfold the plane, seemingly into the arms of God.

Leticia was safe, and she was free!
She would never be beaten and abused again!
God had protected her!
Her destiny directed her—to her new life in her new world!

Years later, Leticia did bring some of her children to her "better place" to live in the USA. These children became members of the United States Marine Corps, Postal Service, and a fine registered nurse and had themselves married and had produced children and grandchildren.

The truth is that *not any* of Leticia's children, and the wives of their relatives and others who begat these children would *ever* be in America today, if it had not been for what Leticia did—*everything* came directly and indirectly from her!

Leticia's decision to save her own life and make better the lives of others became the best thing that ever happened to everyone.

Abandonment—hardly!

Two Worlds Collide

All throughout the years of her very young life, Leticia had admired intelligent people, particularly engineers. She herself was very intelligent and possessed all the characteristics and traits of the fine professional nurse that she would eventually become, but she had always had a problem understanding mathematics.

Far from being deterred by the subject and others who were quite skilled at it, Leticia tended to gravitate to those who were mathematically inclined and, therefore, made friends who were usually a little older than she, finding that she was very comfortable in this venue. *She could not possibly know how circumstances, thousands of miles away in "another world," would be determining her destiny forever, for the rest of her life.*

As the Vietnam War was "heating up," a young high school Polish boy was just graduating. He was confused about which path to take, but he was extremely fortunate in having two great assets: loving parents who set his feet on the correct path of life and a natural aptitude that gave him the gift of being good at everything he attempted to do.

The boy's father was a pipefitter, a manual laborer at the ESSO Petroleum Refinery, and had struggled mightily during the Great Depression and World War II.

Because of this, he had instilled in the boy the importance of learning how to make his way in life using his brains, rather than breaking his back for a living. Therefore, since his father possessed great hands-on skill and the Polish boy had mechanical ability, his parents wanted this boy to go to college. His father would always say, "I want you to be better than I am."

And so the boy entered Stevens Institute of Technology to study engineering. Things were far from easy. There was great financial hardship necessitating his father to place two mortgages on his house, hold two jobs simultaneously, and his mother had to get a job in addition as a garment inspector for the Maiden Form Brassiere Company.

Everyone dug in for the long haul, and four years later, in 1963, the Polish boy graduated from Stevens Institute of Technology with a degree in mechanical engineering. Everyone was proud of the boy including himself, but he was not fulfilled; he wanted something else.

No sooner than he had just graduated, the boy sat down at the dinner table with his parents and said, "Mom and Dad, I want to go into medicine." His mother and father were upset because they all knew that the family could not afford medical school.

"We cannot afford what is owed now from the cost of engineering let alone medical school," they said.

The boy said to his parents, "I have never failed to keep all my promises to everyone, so I'm going to make a promise to both of you: I have taken a position with National Lead Company as a chemical engineer. With my salary, I will pay off both mortgages and all else that I owe. I will pay for all my own premed expenses at Seton Hall University *at nights*. I will pay my future medical school tuition by myself. I think that I can do all this in three years' time.

The boy's reception to his promise for his parents was *negative*.

"Nobody can take on such a load as you're going to attempt, and besides, what if you're called into the military service?" asked his father.

"If I must go into the military, I will give you all the money that I have saved, and I'll send you all my military pay every month until I come back," he promised his parents.

"Three years is a long time, son," his father said.

"I know, Dad, but I've got to try," said the boy.

"Son, nobody can handle the load you're describing and for three years? Don't try. You're going to kill yourself," his dad emphasized.

But the boy would not be deterred or discouraged. For a year, his father saw the boy board the Jersey Central Train at 5:00 a.m. each day, then return home from South Orange to Bayonne, New Jersey, by bus, having done his full-time day job *plus* his evening premed studies and repeat the schedule every day but never failing to pay the monetary support to his parents, and *he was receiving all As in his premed classes.*

As the second year began, the boy and his parents once again sat down at the dinner table, and his father said, "I didn't believe anybody could do what you've done. Your mother and father are so very proud of you!"

Tears filled his mother's eyes, but the tears were of joy and pride.

"From now on, son, I'm behind you 100 percent," said his parents.

"No matter what happens from here on, we know we have a truly great son. How else can we help?" they asked.

"You're already doing it by just letting me sleep in a bed each night," said the boy.

"Son," said his father, "what are you going to do next?"

In the past year, the young Polish boy had grown in many ways—stature, maturity, and the respect that others now freely gave him. He was no longer just "son" anymore. To his parents, with great pride, they would always call him our Ronnie, announcing to all others.

As the end of the third year was now close, and all promises were fulfilled, his dad asked, "What now, Ron?"

Ron's reply was, "We're going to medical school! We are going to have a doctor in the family!" he proclaimed with great glee and well-deserved pride.

In the summer of 1966, Ron resigned from the National Lead Company and accepted a seat in the Class of 1970 of the University of New Jersey Medical and Dental School.

Destiny had taken a hand.

Leticia had always wanted an engineer.

She never dreamed that she would come to love a man who was *both* an engineer and a medical doctor all wrapped up in one!

And Now, the Rest of the Story

Medical school was hard, challenging, and intensely demanding.

The first two years had been primarily scholastic and having to memorize and remember a myriad of confusing facts.

For example, the students had to be absolutely sure that people were dead before proclaiming to the instructors that these people had gone to visit "the great bye and bye." No kidding, there had been rare occasions when suddenly and unexpectedly, a "corpse" would sit up under a sheet with a quizzical look on its face as if to say, "Where the hell am I?"

In 1968, the eighty stalwart few entered the clinical years as third and fourth year medical students.

The University of New Jersey Medical and Dentistry School was in a period of great turmoil and transition. The medical school was being transferred *from* Jersey City Medical Center, a rather huge, awesome, complex of multiple comingled buildings, *to* Newark City Martland Medical Center, another huge, awesome, complex of multiple comingled buildings.

As the third and fourth clinical years began, there was a whole lot of comingling going on there! To add to the confusion and uncertainty, there were the riots and police cars occasionally riddled with bullets looking like Swiss cheese in New York City. Things were out of control, and in an attempt to get the people on the side of law and order, the police department would place the actual massacred police cars in which policemen had died, *on display* for everyone to see in many places all around town in Manhattan.

It was doubtful whether this type of stark visual attempt at "wake upmanship" was effective because it was not known whether any of the perpetrators of the mayhem and killings actually refrained from doing these things as nobody came forth, willingly or unwillingly, to acknowledge anything. Really, come on now, did anybody seriously think to "own up" and say, "Yeah, man, it was me. I did it. I did it!"

The times were very restless, complete with the overlap of the Vietnam War.

Needless to say, medical school at this time was "a little different," yet maybe, not so different. It was difficult to study and learn when their student class was riding "The Silver Bullet" (the students' euphemism for the Coronary Care Ambulance), having to go into buildings, stores, and homes, anywhere a suspected immediate heart attack was taking place, while having to be on guard and careful not to be hit with bricks, garbage, and debris hurled down, as there were many areas where some people didn't want anyone coming there, not even on an errand of mercy.

But study and learn they did, together with a good dose of public relations. Then there were "other things."

As 1969 rolled around, a contractural dispute with the interns and residents occurred at the Martland Medical Center Hospital creating a stoppage of work. The senior medical students were "moved up" as acting interns. This created *a lot more work.* All of the senior class was always very tired and needing rest, but as Charles Dickens wrote, "It was the worst of times; It was the best of times."

We didn't realize it then, but the Class of 1970 was becoming the toughest and most resilient fourth year medical students/ acting interns to suddenly burgeon forth, a group that then and in the future, was capable of doing almost anything, and become some of the best doctors to be.

Our student Class of 1970, eighty souls in all, was broken up into groups of five, and each group remained with this unit of five routinely throughout each of the service specialties. Individual students got to know each other pretty well, some more than others.

One of the good sidekick buddy-ups was Fred Meier. It was easy to learn from Fred because he was a little higher in class rank than I and was always generous in imparting useful information necessary to know and grow in ability.

In addition to all this, he was an all around "good guy" that was completely reliable. Reliability was a priceless commodity in medicine and, in many instances, was the only thing that prevented complete catastrophe.

One day, when they were in the wards making their rounds, *it happened!* There was a flash of white as they both happened to look up from their charts.

Then simultaneously, they looked at each other and again, almost in perfect unison, said, *"Did you see that?"* and both dashed over to the wardroom door.

Both of us then tried to look casual, peeking around the open door of the ward.

"Oh my god, did you see that?" Ron exclaimed to Fred in a surprisingly low voice like a whisper.

A girl was walking down the long corridor of the ward toward the end of the unit. She was in a dress all in white and had a white cap on her head with a black stripe crowning her uniform, obviously an RN, a registered nurse.

The day was heavily raining, drenching most of all the caregivers who had just come into the hospital as the change of shift was occurring. This nurse had been caught in the deluge and her dress was quite wet, but *holy smokes*, how she looked!

The wet dress tightly clung to her in *all* the right places below the waist, revealing magnificent sculptured calves that ascended up to the knees, then higher up snugly wrapped around very svelte athletic thighs and buttocks. Although she had nurses flat shoes on, it was obvious that if she were to wear high heels, her statuesque legs would be even more impressive.

Ron and Fred just stood there ogling this nurse from behind, a very appealing behind, as she kept walking down the very *long* corridor, and they thought, *Thank God for long hallways!*

As they finally got a sense of presence, they saw the letters on the unit that said, Coronary Care Unit—*that* was supposed to be their beginning rotation.

Both of us thought, *Oh, God, please say it is so!*

The nurse passed through the swinging doors and disappeared.

Ron said to Fred, "Hurry up, or we'll lose her in the maze of beds and medical equipment and machines." Now all doctors know that they are never to run. They only walk swiftly with purpose, but the swift walking turned into a short gallop.

During the instance of "burning up the shoe leather," Ron suddenly got the thought, *Hey, wait a minute, we haven't even seen her face. What if she has a face like a moon pie?*

Ron and Fred tried to look casual and professional, panting after their brief gallop. They diligently kept checking out the nursing forms as there would be no question that when they found "the right nurse," they would know it. There would be no mistaking her back (side).

Then in a corner, near the sixth patient bed, was this unmistakable form, now being even more enhanced as she was standing on her tiptoes, raising up high an IV setup to hang the IV pole for the patient.

Trying to look very dashing and doctorial, Ron and Fred tried a pincer maneuver moving to each side of the bed for maximum vantage. As the two medical students inched closer, being careful not to disturb their "quarry," her sides revealed an equally statuesque profile that matched her rear view.

As it would happen, having completed regulation of the correct IV drip rate, she turned full face toward Ron. She wasn't just beautiful; she was *stunning!*

Ron tried to come up with something clever to say, but neither Ron nor Fred could come up with anything except, "Duh, can we help you?"

Slick, really—slick.

Both oglers felt like two genuine *dolts*.

"No," she softly said.

As Ron was mesmerized by her face, Fred was staring at her uplifted breasts where her nursing name tag was tilted up and oh so *prominently* displayed. Success. Fred memorized her name.

She then said, "Excuse me, please," and walked back deeper into the Coronary Unit.

Ron and Fred then checked the medical student roster for the groupings assigned to the Coronary Care Unit.

As they were perusing the list posting, a soft, sexy voice said to them, "I'm Leticia Pampo, the coronary care charge nurse. Your two-month rotation begins tomorrow. For the next two months, you're my responsibility."

What great luck *and* we're *assigned* to *her*!

Brains, looks, and a veteran.

We've died and gone to heaven!

GETTING TO KNOW YOU

Two months. Only two months to get to know her.

With all the work to do and things to learn, this was going to be a prodigious task, indeed. As precious time passed and days slipped by all too quickly, Ron thought about her. Ron thought about her a lot. Ron thought about her *all* the time, actually.

She was always courteous and professional, but she did not "mix" a lot even with the other nurses. There were, however, two other nurses that she seemed closer to named Fe and Sylvia, but they usually had different nursing shifts. The fact that when Fe and Sylvia got together with Leticia, all three would somehow disappear, and nobody seemed to know where they had gone. This gave an aura of a mystery, which was intriguing.

For the times that they conversed in the Coronary Unit, although she was always pleasant, all things said were of an impersonal nature and always medical, never personal. Ron's difficult problem remained so and was getting more difficult. Ron never saw any male companions that she appeared to like, although there were always lots of interns and residents hanging around her like flies on honey. For sure, the only thing collecting flies was Ron, an impossible and exasperating situation!

It was a fascinating mixture of absorbing the medical book knowledge, learning a lot of "practical" hands on medicine that was priceless that broadened Ron's medical abilities, but learning absolutely zip, zero, nada, about this beautiful girl that kept to herself and was as tight-lipped as a clam. In addition, Ron was a sensitive guy and seemed to feel that there was "something" about her that was not only her aloofness, but a kind of Pathos, a sadness that did not seem to fit her persona. She didn't seem to want to get close to anyone, male or female, except for Fe and Sylvia.

Ron thought, *How can this beautiful girl be sad when there are so many opportunities for her?* What was so bad for Ron was that he really liked Leticia, but other than in a professional manner, he didn't exist. It didn't look like there was much hope. He could not get her attention; she just didn't care.

The workload was now taking its toll as all the medical students were always very tired. Cat-napping was rampant as everyone was trying, as best as they could, to "recharge their batteries" so as to keep going because each medical student knew that there would always be the next inevitable call to take care of another emergency.

One evening, when Ron was making his rounds very quietly, Leticia and the "skeleton crew" were on duty as the hour was quite late, and all the patients were sleeping.

There was a soft, eerie, yellow-green glow that bathed a large portion of the nurses' station command room that clustered all the EKG monitors, continually monitoring the cardiac status of twelve patient bed stations.

It was almost the appearance and feeling of a Star Trek space ship command center, although Ron definitely was *not* Captain Kirk. As Ron looked at all the nurses at the desk, quietly working and seated, the color of the night magnificently enhanced their beauty, all of them, but particularly Leticia.

All looked younger, accentuating their "bedroom-eyes" as the soft light seemed to erase any and all blemishes, but what stood out most of all were these gorgeous eyes, purposeful, elegant, and focused. *Any* patient would feel completely safe with these "angels of mercy" guarding their lives. All the patient beds were darkened and quiet for sleep with only dim night lights faintly glowing, each close to the floor.

Only the EKG monitors were visible with each patient's rhythm, keeping constant record of the silent "blips and green tracings" throughout the night. There was no movement; none of the usual hustle of nurses purposefully tending to the care of their patients.

As Ron slowly moved to check one of the patient's charts, he accidentally dropped his small pocket pen light, creating an unwelcome noise, with all the nurses becoming startled and looking towards him, casting angry eyes at him and the irritable and disturbing sound.

All the nurses then settled down, and Ron thought, *Oh crap!*

But he was very tired, and dropping his pen light was just another sign that his coordination was diminished by lack of sleep. There were several patients who were of particular interest to him, and therefore, he decided to position himself between two beds on a tall, circular, waist-high stool. Being as quiet as possible, Ron moved toward one of the Mayo stands, sat down, and then spread out the EKG tracings attached to the charts. He proceeded to compare the charts to the active "instant time" running monitors.

Each patient had his individual EKG monitor mounted on the wall above his head. Since the beds were about five feet apart, Ron had a perfect vantage point to scan about four monitors at one time. He relaxed in the evening glow, deliberating on the meaning of the paper chart EKG's and following all the adjacent four active monitors.

Time passed, and no extraneous sounds were heard except for some whispers of the nurses. Ron's back was getting stiff and sore as the stool had no back support, so he put his chin in his hands and propped up his elbows on the Mayo stand, thus relieving at least some of the stiffness that was becoming more pronounced in his neck as well.

No sound, just the constant "dancing" of the EKG monitors giving off their soft, green, flickering light. The electrical "dance" continued on and on and on. Ron began to relax even further and further, his eyelids getting heavier and heavier. He caught himself in one instant closing, then snapping his eyes open simultaneously with his neck but to no avail in a losing effort.

His eyes closed again longer, and then a sharp opening again, but this time without any movement of his neck, except for a slow movement forward of his body onto the Mayo stand, for a last final trip to "slumber land."

Then—

Bang! Crash!

Ron didn't know where he was, but he felt a severe pain on the right side of his face on the orbital rim. He was lying on the floor, crumpled under the railing of the adjacent bed, and instinctively, he didn't move.

There was now total chaos and pandemonium almost instantly!

The Coronary Care Unit jumped to active life—bright white lights went on, sound alarms began to blare, and all the patients became instantly fearful. All the nurses ran to their respective patient responsibilities, with one nurse running over to the still motionless medical student.

"Are you all right?" she asked.

There was no response from Ron.

Lita, another nurse, said, "He really hit his head very hard. I heard a loud crack when he hit on the floor. He may have fractured his skull."

Ron began to regain consciousness. The nurses kept him lying on the floor and carefully checking him for broken bones, especially his cervical spine and skull. His vital signs were okay. Still keeping Ron on the floor, Leticia called for the portable x-ray machine. Leticia had put a cervical collar on his neck as the technicians took all the x-rays, and she was the only one who allowed Ron to be moved in any way. Ron did not want to open his eyes. The bright light focused into his pupils for examination bothered him. Ron's face was beginning to significantly swell especially on his right side, so Leticia applied ice packs.

In what seemed like an endless length of time, the radiologist diagnosed, "No fractured skull, face, or cervical spine."

Ron was still quite dizzy, and for the first time in his life, he had other people put him in bed—girls no less, but he didn't care. He was just not in a position to enjoy it!

Ron heard Leticia say, "Our census is, low and we have an open bed here in the CCU, and besides, he's one of our own, so I'm going to keep him in the CCU for observation."

Just before she left the bedside, Ron heard Leticia softly say only one word, "Gago."

What could that mean? He had never heard that word before, and in addition, it was in a foreign language. *Well*, Ron thought, *at least she, finally has said one personal word to him.* He felt better already! About one hour later, Lita came to the bedside to check on Ron's status.

He was very curious, excited, and anxious to find out what "gago" meant. In somewhat of a whisper as if not to divulge a secret, Ron asked Lita, "Please tell me what *gago* means."

Lita stopped, looked at him with a quizzical facial expression, and began to smile.

Oh boy, this must be good, he thought.

The medical student then again repeated the question. Lita leaned over, closer to Ron's face, and also in a similar soft whisper, said, "*Gago* means idiot."

Oh no!

From the height of exhilaration to the depths of despair... flying in the clouds to crashing and burning in flames! Ron was absolutely destroyed! The one girl he really liked regarded him as an *idiot*! Suddenly, *all* his injuries hurt a lot more. And sleep, it was not possible, not only because of the pain, but because pain medications could not be given as he was on cerebral injury precautions. What a bummer! The night could not end soon enough.

Ron's ego was so demolished all he wanted to do was to get out of that bed and go home all by himself.

The inevitable morning came. Ron just lay there, with his right eye very swollen and almost completely shut. He didn't feel like opening the other eye either. Then, just lying in his bed feeling totally miserable, he could sense and hear someone close to his bedside.

"Good morning. How do you feel?" said the voice he knew only too well.

The subtle fragrant scent of Sampaguita wafting the bedside as Leticia moved about.

"I feel better, but like I was in a bar fight and came out the loser," Ron said.

"You sure look like it," Letty said. "You have a magnificent black eye. I have your x-rays, would you like to see them?"

Trying to regain some semblance of professionalism, Ron said, "Absolutely." He then perused the films, handed them to Leticia, and said, "Thanks. I understand that you were the one that picked me up off the floor last night. Thank you for that."

Leticia nodded in acceptance. Then, in her usual detached professionalism, she said, "Did you take a good look at your skull x-rays a little closer?" Letty asked.

Ron looked at the skull films again and said, "Yes, but I don't see any fracture line."

"Look at the skull films again," persisted Leticia.

Ron repeated, "I still don't see anything. No fracture line. No nothing. I don't see anything at all in that skull."

Leticia then said, "I don't see anything in that head either. It's empty!"

Ron just looked at Letty, with his one eye open, and saw her, just staring sternly at him. Then her features softened, and a smile creased her lips, wider and *wider*.

Like a bolt in the blue, Ron got the joke. The two both sat on the bed and laughed for a long time together. When the laughter was over, Leticia became serious and said, "I'm really very sorry for thinking that you were stupid and clumsy. I didn't realize what had happened to you and how hard you were working to the point of complete exhaustion when you fell. The other nurses saw you working exceptionally hard and said the same thing on your behalf. I really feel that we did you a great injustice." Leaving the bedside, Leticia said, "I'll be checking on you after you're discharged tomorrow."

Ron got dressed and went out of the CCU the next day.

The sun was shining in spite of the weather being overcast, the sky was blue in spite of a slight drizzle of rain, and the air even smelled good on a smoggy Newark, New Jersey day.

Somehow, even his face that looked swollen and battered just didn't hurt at all anymore!

The Ice Is Broken

The next time that Ron walked into the CCU, he noticed a completely different attitude of all the nurses towards him. What had transpired had now become known as the episode. All the nurses now smiled at him a lot, but he wasn't quite sure whether they were smiling and laughing with him or at him. At any rate, there was no doubt that he was now a very recognized medical student. But the most important thing to him was that Leticia was much nicer to him and more sociable.

Each day, he tried to find the courage to ask her for a date, but always, he would chicken out, thinking, *What if she says no?*

That would have devastated him.

What got his courage up was the fact that it had become known through Fe that the reason Leticia was always disappearing was because she was moonlighting at St. Clair's Hospital in NYC. There was no romance anywhere "in the wings."

Oh my god! he surmised. Is it possible that there is a clear field? But if there is, he knew nothing of her personally and didn't have a clue what she might want to do. Asking for a night out to go dancing might seem too forward as her customs might be different coming from a distant culture.

Hmmm, what would be fun, sociable, non-threatening, and not too forward, he thought.

Ron got a good-sized headache, thinking about it and then came to the conclusion, "I'll ask her to go bowling!"

During a break, he asked if Leticia would like to go for a cup of coffee. *Say yes*, he thought. *Say yes.*

Her response was, "Okay."

Ron then thought, *Great, I'm on first base, riding high!*

Ron diligently surveyed the cafeteria tables, looking for the most out of the way and inconspicuous table possible. As they sat down, drinking their coffee and making small talk, Ron gulped hard and popped the question, "Would you like to go bowling with me this week when we're both free?"

His mouth suddenly got quite dry and a sinking feeling took hold in the pit of his stomach. Leticia didn't respond right away and was silent. Ron thought, *Oh no, I'm going down in flames.*

Actually, Leticia was silent because she didn't know what bowling was and wasn't sure what she would be agreeing to. Letty said, "What would we be doing, and how do I do this bowling?"

Whew! Maybe I'm okay after all, Ron thought.

So he simply explained bowling was a sport, lots of fun and exercise, didn't need special equipment, didn't cost a lot, and that he liked it a lot.

"Okay," Letty said. "Where do I have to go?"

"I'll pick you up at the nursing residence," said Ron.

"All right," Letty agreed. "But I have to get back to the CCU now, so I'll see you then."

"Scored! I did it!" he enthusiastically proclaimed. He felt feet tall and smiled from ear to ear all day long!

The day of the first date arrived, and Ron came to the nursing residence to collect Letty. At almost the exact same time, each of their emergency call beepers simultaneously sounded off with the ominous *beep beep beep*!

We were both called to come to the CCU—*STAT!*

On arrival, the CCU was a beehive of activity. Several new acute patients had been admitted, and *all* needed attention immediately. All the nurses were doing exemplary work but because of the intern/resident strike, the regular staff was undermanned with only one cardiology fellow for the entire Coronary Care Unit.

Leticia and Ron were immediately rounded, briefed, and directed to help the sickest patients. Ron said to Letty, "Well, I guess bowling is out," but the humor fell flat. Letty said nothing and kept working.

After about two hours, the patients in the CCU began to stabilize, and everyone had a chance to catch their collective breath.

The cardiology fellow who was supervising the unit said a well deserved, "Good job. We haven't lost anyone, but we're far from out of the woods."

Still being a medical student, Ron was the least experienced of the entire CCU group and he was quite uneasy. Since that was the case, the fellow assigned Ron and Leticia (who had more experience than Ron) to the least acute, although very critical, patient who was suffering from a cardiac tamponade.

The fellow explained the condition being created when blood gets *between* the pericardial sack and the heart muscle itself, then the volume of blood increasing progressively putting increasing pressure on the muscle reducing the heart muscle's ability to pump, eventually leading to death, unless the blood volume can be drained away and stabilized because the pericardium has little elasticity. The effect is analogous to a water bottle that can expand no further, creating great internal pressure inside.

Ron said to himself, "And *this is the least sick* of the group!" Trying to show his best professionalism, Ron said, "Okay, so how do we handle this problem?"

The rejoinder to the fellow was, "Hopefully, the blood in the sack will stabilize on its own with the medications given, and we won't have to do anything else, but if the chest x-ray, EKG, and vital signs begin to deteriorate, then we will have to do a decompression. This would mean that you will have to take a long intracardiac needle and syringe, advance the needle tip into the pericardial sack under EKG control, and drain out the blood until the heart is able to acceptably pump."

Ron said, "But I've never done this before, and it's major serious. I don't know whether I can do this."

Getting a little annoyed, the fellow said, "Do you want to be a doctor or not?"

In a subdued voice, Ron said, "Yes, sir."

The fellow then said, "Never forget that you're *always* going to be dealing in life-or-death situations as long as you're a doctor. Some of your patients are going to die. Just *you* be damn sure that if a patient does die, that *you* weren't the *cause* of your patient's death. Also remember that the unwritten creed of our profession is this: see one, do one, teach one." He then said to Ron, "You're going to do *both* steps all at once, and you're going to have someone showing you how, so man up. I know all doctors are scared the first time. If you weren't, it would mean a lack of caring, and that would mean that you could never be a good doctor. You're really very lucky because Leticia is very good at reading the nuances of the EKG, and she has a hard ass attitude regarding losing a patient of *'not on my watch,'* so the two of you will make a good team.

"Also remember, that if circumstances arise that force me away from the bedside of the two of you and the tamponade becomes rapidly worse, listen to Leticia as she watches the EKG. She will be your eyes as you advance the needle properly. Blood will start to drain from the needle's syringe. If the EKG becomes erratic or irritable in its tracing, pull back a little as you are going too far in. Pull the needle completely out of the heart and chest when you're not getting any blood draining." The fellow again strongly emphasized, "Remember, Leticia is very good, so *trust her eyes.*"

As Leticia and Ron continued to observe their special responsible patient and generally perused all the other activity in the CCU, everything seemed to stabilize and calm down. There were two on-call rooms directly adjacent to the CCU. Nurses' aides had brought some food as none of the group of care professionals had a chance to eat anything. All were very hungry.

After eating, since Leticia was a charge nurse, she commandeered one of the nursing call rooms. Both Ron and Letty were tired from the extremely stressful night, and both felt very drained. Their charge was far from over as the morning shift was still many hours away. They sat down for a moment of solace.

Finally, Ron spoke, "Well, I guess bowling is out for our date."

Both smiled and began to laugh with a certain giddy affect.

Then Leticia said, "Our date may still be salvaged if the patient doesn't get worse."

"What do you mean?" Ron asked.

Leticia responded, "Do you play chess?"

Ron nodded, "Yes."

Letty then said, "I don't know how to play, but there's a small chess set in the drawer. Maybe you could teach me."

This was certainly a "different" kind of date, and it was kind of nice.

Ron and Letty continued to play chess until the first early golden rays of the morning sun began to shine through the curtains of the tiny room. All the patients slept peacefully, and it hadn't become necessary to needle decompress the cardiac tamponade.

This was the first date ever for Leticia and Ron and started a long journey of complete trust and caring, knowing that they could totally rely on each other regardless of what was to come. The dates and their reliance on each other have never stopped even to this day.

Leticia continued to save many lives into the future but never so precious and personal as the one she saved for the life of her Ron, *twice*.

LETICIA MEETS STANLEY AND THE BLUE BEETLE

It wasn't a "normal" date; actually, there really never was anything ordinary about Letty and Ron together, but then again, they did go bowling and had a great time.

However, Ron could not seem to find the right place to take Letty, although she seemed really happy for us just to be out of the hospital. Then while talking to Fred in the hospital cafeteria, Fred said, "Oh heck, Ron, why don't you just take her to a good movie. It works for me."

Maybe this would be a good idea, and I think I know just the right place too, Ron thought.

Journal Square—that's the place to go! Journal Square was literally the hub of all activity in Jersey City, New Jersey. Everything passed through there—subways beneath the square, all the bus terminals top side of the square, stores for shopping, and best of all, the absolute *jewels* of entertainment for three movie houses: The State, The Loew's, and The Stanley. All three were opulent and very appealing but far and away. The best of the best was The Stanley.

The Stanley had to be experienced to be believed. In many ways, the newest movie theaters today could not come close to the Stanley as they all appeared to be just boxy rooms that showed pictures on walls, but the Stanley was totally unique.

Leticia was intrigued after listening to the buildup after all that Ron had told her.

"Is this movie theater as good as you say?" Leticia asked.

"No, it's better," insisted Ron.

He then said, "I'll tell you more, but I have to tell you some things about my car."

"Oh, I don't care if your car is old—not really being interested in the car. Tell me more about your fascinating movie house. I can't wait. It seems almost incidental to the movie," Letty said.

She was super excited to go, and Stanley *did not* disappoint! The journey from Newark to Jersey City usually took about one hour by car. They approached an old, but shiny, clean, dark blue Volkswagen beetle.

Ron pointed to the car and said, "Well, there it is."

Leticia smiled and said, "Have you ever been in a jeepney with a lot of people inside on a hot day?" She further admonished, "You think *your* car has something wrong!"

The only thing unusual about this little blue car was the backseat that was neatly piled up with several big, fluffy quilts. *No big deal about that*, Letty thought. *Maybe he's just bringing them home.*

But Letty was still far more interested in the "unique" movie house and wanted Ron to tell her more. The history of the Stanley began during the 1920s as a vaudeville palladium and, because of this, had a huge stage and platform. which was also used as a concert stage for really big orchestra presentations.

The silent movies melded well with the music, but as vaudeville began to fade and lose its vogue, the Talkies were introduced in the 1930s and became the rage and a whole new era of the movie industry. Suddenly, in order to keep their audience and fill seats with people, and to keep things profitable, the old vaudeville palladium had to be redone.

Everything had to be bigger in size for the new coming movie theaters, more elaborate, sumptuous, elegant, and classy. These theaters had to be a place where everyone would always look with great anticipation to see the most current great movie. The combo of this kind of theater plus constantly appearing new Hollywood movies became huge spectacles. The Stanley then emerged with the theater as the best of the best through the 1930s and reached its zenith during World War II when The Stanley was always packed.

As Ron parked his car and the couple walked to the end of the block on Journal Square, Leticia saw an unbelievably huge and ornate movie theater. She had never seen *anything* this big! There were innumerable flashing lights projecting forward on the marquee. As they moved in line to buy their tickets, they moved through large, shiny, smoke-tinted colored double doors with wide golden brass framing the doors and centered on elegant, semi-circular, figurine carved door handles.

The doorman opened the doors for the couple. Leticia's eyes opened to twice their pretty size. The Foyer was absolutely immense and *easily* capable of housing hundreds of people inside. This foyer was totally covered with plush dark maroon carpet that contained golden figures emblazoned on the ancient Greek heroes like Hercules. All the walls had the most current movie marquees, about four feet by five feet in size, with pictures of the biggest movie stars, scenes of their movies, all enclosed in glass cases that opened for replacement.

The foyer, as well as the whole theater, was fully air-conditioned. At its back end, the foyer had multiple dark-brown mahogany framed stained glass windows that all opened completely, extending for the back end so that a large volume of people could all move easily into and exit the theater.

Multiple popcorn, soda, and candy cases were filled to capacity. Ron and Leticia avidly collected the irresistible hot, buttered, great-smelling bags of their popcorn and were shown to a pleasant usherette, whose flashlight directed the way to walk. Leticia found that their seats were all plush velour with the back of the seats automatically reclining simultaneously together with the lower portion of the seats rising and lowering vertically, as one would either sit down or stand up so that they would move out of the way when other people would leave, thus taking away any obstructions to movement.

As they looked around, the movie had not started yet, and the theater lights were very low and subdued. Soft, soothing music seemed to be coming from everywhere. The movie curtain extended the full length of the theater top to bottom and was color-coordinated maroon identical to the color of the foyer, except the curtain was total maroon in color without any design, but had a golden border strip at the floor about two feet high extending the full expanse of the curtain.

Then came the most amazing thing of all! As Leticia looked around the theater, trying to get her bearings, she was astounded to realize that she was sitting in an "outside" amphitheater! The Stanley was actually capable of giving the illusion of being outside!

The lights gradually became a little less dim and Leticia could see real, white, statues of the ancient Greek heroes and gods, all standing at strategic places positioned at the *entire* periphery of the theater. Then slowly, the lights dimmed *very low* again, but this time, something else was happening.

Letty's mouth hung open and gasped in awe! As she looked up, the entire ceiling of the theater completed the appearance of the sky opening up with stars twinkling, an occasional comet flashing by, and most incredibly, there were clouds moving across the night sky in what appeared to be 3-dimension!

All this and the movie had not started yet.

To complete the entire experience, as the movie did begin to unfold, at several times during its length, there were instances when the theater-created smells consistent with the action playing out on the screen. As something exploded on screen, the people in the audience could actually smell the scent of gun powder burning. At The Stanley, this was the first time that smell-o-vision had been tried to enhance the best movie experience for its audience.

To Letty and Ron, the absolute best smell arrived when the theater blew hot, freshly popped, buttered popcorn into the air. It was totally irresistible!

When the movie/date was over, Ron asked Letty what she thought of it all. She was completely silent for a few seconds. Then as they were exiting the theater, as if collecting her thoughts, she began gushing forth things that she had just seen, constantly in total random order, that did not stop until they got to Ron's car. Her movie/date had been totally overwhelming!

Then it came! The next big surprise which he had not yet been able to show her.

It was late evening now as they left The Stanley, and it had gotten quite cold and surprisingly very windy, making the temperature seem even colder.

Leticia began to walk much faster in an attempt to get into the car as fast as possible. Ron's fingers were numb from the cold so as he fumbled with his car keys, their desire to get into the car heightened further. Their breath turned into expressions of visible vapor reaching about twelve inches beyond their lips and noses.

"Oh quickly," Leticia exhorted, "put on the car heater."

"I will," said Ron, "but I've got a bit of a problem that we're going to have to deal with. I've tried to tell you but never got to it as we were so preoccupied," Ron revealed.

As their teeth were now chattering, Ron pointed to the back seat of the blue beetle.

"Okay, so?" Letty said in a stuttering voice.

"We don't have one," Ron blurted out.

"We don't have *what?*" Leticia asked.

"A floor in the back seat of the blue beetle," responded Ron.

"You're kidding!" she said.

"No, I'm not," Ron insisted.

"Do you see that pile of quilts in the back seat and cardboard below the seat? *There's nothing under it!*" To show Letty, Ron removed all the cardboard on the bottom of the rear seat and revealed a huge hole in the car where the rear tray of the feet of passengers normally sat.

"Oh my god!" she said, startled. "I am looking directly at the pavement of the street. We're *both* outside and inside the car at the same time!"

Trying to lighten the mood, Ron said, "Well, if the brakes fail, we can just put our feet down and stop that way."

"That's *not* funny," Letty said. "How did this happen? You certainly weren't that dumb to buy a car that didn't have a floor, did you?"

Ron replied, "Actually, when I bought the car, I didn't realize that Volkswagen places their car batteries under their rear seats. The blue beetle had a defective battery that seeped acid and corroded my back seat floor to nothing."

Leticia then said in her usual professional way, "Okay, so this is our problem. How do we keep from freezing to death as we get home *and* prevent burning off the soles of our feet on our nifty impromptu brakes?"

"I've got it covered." he said, "and I mean literally." Ron hastily opened the car and got a huge quilt from the rear seat as fast as he could, completely wrapped the quilt around Leticia, then grabbed a second quilt, bundling up her legs and feet. Then Ron put the heavy cardboard into the bottom back of the hole in the car, creating a makeshift bridge over the chasm. He then put a rainproof poncho over that and further draped over a third quilt anchoring to all the door handles and straps from the side door frames. While the car was running with heater full blast, Ron put a fourth quilt on himself and then just waited until both of them warmed up and stopped shivering and rattling their teeth.

After a short time later, Letty said, "Boy, I sure feel a lot better now."

Ron answered with a big, "Me too!"

"Is it safe to ride in this car?" Leticia asked.

"Sure, I've been doing this for some time now," responded Ron.

Then he put the blue beetle in first gear, and away they went. As they were travelling, they looked rather like a moving tent with only two heads poking out. This must have been quite comical as several people were pointing to them and laughing. When they had stopped at a red light, one of the other cars signaled them, indicating that they wanted to roll Ron's window down.

Still laughing, the other driver asked, "Hey, buddy, what kind of a silly rig is that?"

"Not to be outdone," Ron replied. "It's a special love tent." And flashing a great big grin in addition, Ron said, "We *always* have a great time."

The other driver then said to his female companion, "Hey, Jennie, where can *we* get one of these things?"

Ron and Letty continued in this manner toward Newark and were really beginning to have fun again. Letty was very impressed with The Stanley, but surprisingly, both of them had to pause a few seconds to remember what the name of the movie was. The complete presentation of The Stanley itself and the actual real life drama in the blue beetle had overpowered and blotted out all else.

Leticia thought, *Wow, real life couldn't be more fun than the movie that we just saw.*

With still a little ways to go to get to the hospital, Leticia said, "You know, I'm getting a little hungry after all this action."

Ron didn't say anything at first, thinking, *Uh-oh, how much money have I got left?* He searched his mind and figured, *I think I've got about $5 left, I think.*

Ron had to pull in his ace in the hole when Letty again asked, "Are you getting hungry too?" Boy, was that a clue or what?

He answered, "Sure am, but I'm thinking of the best place that we can go." *Best* meant *cheapest*, but Ron was a slick dude. He pointed the Blue Beetle straight into the parking lot of one of the drive-up stands at a place called Gino Giants.

"Hospital cafeteria food isn't the best, but you're going to love a Gino Giants with fries and a coke. They're great, the best burgers in the whole city, *and* they serve it to you in the car in addition!" Ron proudly said.

One of the hostesses then walked up to the blue beetle, and after Ron rolled down his window, he placed his order for Letty. The hostess just couldn't resist asking with a coy little smile, "What kind of a rig is this?" The hostess could still see only Ron and Letty's heads.

Trying to be funny and a little James Bondish, Ron suavely said, "This is our moveable love machine."

The hostess replied, "Really? Does it work?"

With a somewhat sly and debonair flare, Ron enthusiastically said, "You can't believe how much!"

"My god," the hostess exclaimed. "I have to get my boyfriend into this thing."

As the hostess left to get their Gino Giants, Letty ducked under the quilt and was laughing hysterically. Later she said, "You know, I haven't had so much fun in a long time."

No question, their date was a resounding success!

Letty absolutely loved the Gino Giants that Ron had introduced her to, stating, "I've never tasted better. The other nurses who have not tasted this don't know what they're missing."

Leticia would continue to enjoy them for a long time into the future. Both of them just ate under their quilts, snuggled, and talked about many things. Ron felt that he could just not talk to her enough. She was smart, witty, and fun, and really had something to say way beyond just small talk. He had known many girls, but he was beginning to feel more and more that she was truly special he wanted to know her more, a lot more. Many more dates ensued. Surprisingly, these dates became times when they would get together and just talk. They really enjoyed being together and began to realize how much they were the same in so many ways.

Sometimes Ron would think, *Oh my god, I'm going way beyond just conversing with her. I'm actually grilling her.* He began feeling really bad about this, but she never complained, either being oblivious to the friendly "interrogation," or not caring, he didn't know. He asked himself why he was doing this, and his mental answer became aware to him: he was *not* looking for what he wanted in a girlfriend—*but what he did not want.*

It was easy to meet lots of girls and have fun; both he and they would always be at their best, and so negative things would not be seen.

If he were to get "serious" with a girl, he wanted to know whether they would accept the things that would drive apart other couples. After all, all the fun things in life are easy—it's the hard, undesirable things that make life impossible or not, endurable or not. What Ron had come to realize, was that he was becoming far more than just fond of Leticia; he was seriously thinking of her as the possibility of being someone that he would consider marrying.

In every way, he was beginning to think that the answer was *yes*.

The Ride of a Lifetime

Time. Time was now a big factor.

The rotation through coronary care was almost half over, and this meant leaving Leticia and Newark to go to St. Elizabeth Hospital for OB-GYN and then the VA in South Orange for internal medicine, *each* another two months long. The two of them were getting to know and like each other a lot, but juggling the hectic schedules they kept was almost impossible, but the operative word was *almost*.

One day, Leticia asked Ron if he would like to go to Connecticut. Leticia had belonged to the International Student Association and had been invited by an American family sponsor. This seemed to be a great idea! It was a time to relax and get away for a while, meet new interesting people, do all this as a fully paid for trip courtesy of the sponsor, and most of all, gave both Ron and Letty more time to be together in a very appealing setting.

It was wintertime, and the snow was falling. Wood on the fire producing its characteristic entrancing aroma, toasting marshmallows—how much more romantic could it be? And Letty had asked Ron to go! Jumping to go on this terrific date, Ron gassed up the blue beetle, outfitted up some new cardboard flooring and heavy quilts, and away they went to Connecticut!

The meeting in this new state (which neither of us had visited before) was fantastic. It was just the right mix of fun and interesting people from many different countries. Also, the American sponsors had left several gaps in the weekend program so that all the students could enjoy any of the events available. The season afforded the possibilities of skating, skiing, hiking, and sledding, along with prodigious amounts of picture taking as many friends were made.

During one of the events, Letty asked about a bobsled which she thought was quite curious. The sample sled was very old, ancient actually, with wooden runners and rope that was used to control the steering front runners, the back runners being fixed. The rest of the bobsled was all wood.

Letty was all about wanting to try new things, so a bobsled was what they were going to ride. Before leaving the lodge, everyone had breakfast croissants and hot chocolate, and then away they went! They were told that they had to go up a hill by ski lift to get to the bobsled before they could launch.

Launch? Are you kidding me? Ron thought.

He looked up the hill and thought for sure he could see clouds up at the top, which was *not* visible.

Uh-oh, this may not be such a good idea, he thought as Ron was getting a queasy feeling in the pit of his stomach. But Letty was all excited and jumped right onto the ski lift calling, "Come on, let's go!" Ron had to fish or cut bait. He couldn't chicken out now, so onto the ski lift he went also.

The ride was a *long* way up, and as the people down below the "hill" became smaller and smaller, Ron thought, *My god, I'm going to lose my breakfast!* Leticia, however, kept talking excitedly about what they were about to do.

Finally, after a time that seemed to last forever, they reached the top. Boy did they ever reach the top! Ron could swear that the air up there had gotten thinner and rarefied.

Oh, man, do we really have to do this? he thought.

But Leticia excitedly said, "Come on, let's go. What do we do now?"

Die probably was the thought firmly in his mind.

One of the ushers pointed to a bright yellow sled that was to be ours.

The color of the sled sure matches the color of my courage right now, pure yellow, Ron mused.

It was a two-man sled. "Sure looks narrow," Ron said as the usher indicated Ron should sit down at the back of his seat and spread his legs.

It was now Letty's turn. Brimming with enthusiasm, she literally jumped into the bobsled and plopped down between Ron's legs landing onto his "private parts."

"Aaahh!" he moaned.

The usher who was now laughing said to Ron, "Are you okay?"

Trying to regain some semblance of composure, Ron exclaimed to the usher in a very forced, uncomfortable whisper, "It's not exactly the ride that I was looking for."

The usher then laughed even harder. Leticia, however, who was always facing forward in the bobsled, was totally oblivious to all the hilarious happenings that had occurred. When they were completely seated in the bobsled, the usher then casually told the Dynamic Duo that last night a slightly wet mist had blanketed the hill, which had rendered the snow to ice conditions.

This was important because many of the skiers didn't want to ski because their footing was treacherous. "Don't worry though," the usher said. "You guys should be okay."

Oh no, we're going to die, Ron kept saying in his mind.

"Maybe we should—"

Uh-oh, the usher got his hands on the back of the sled and is now pushing us and running behind the sled. After one *big* push, my god, they're off! As they came to the point where the top of the "hill" was flat, the sudden steep slope down almost instantly appeared, their faces directly down like the very top of a huge roller coaster just beginning its major plunge down.

There was a rumbling roar which began to get louder as the wind blew in their faces.

"Wee! Wee!" Letty was screaming in great exhilaration. "This is great!"

The only wee-wee that Ron was concerned about was the wet stuff now in his pants.

Leticia was totally oblivious to the danger. Faster and faster they careened down, down. Then, oh no! The sled was beginning to turn and rotate ever so slowly, like a slow-motion movie.

They were now out of control! The runners of the bobsled no longer bit into the snow and the whole sled was running on a sheet of ice. Ron frantically pulled on the ropes, trying to gain any kind of control, but all was impossible.

"Aaah! Letty was now shouting even louder, but not in fear, just pure exhilaration.

The bobsled was now starting to slowly spin. They were now going sideways! Ron couldn't utter a sound. He just kept thinking in his mind over and over again, "Oh s——, we're going to die! We're going to die!"

Letty was having a ball! She thought all that was happening was supposed to be that way as she never was on any kind of a sled before. Down and further down they went. Now the sled began to turn and rotate even more. My god!

They were rumbling and screaming (Letty in excitement, Ron in abject fear and panic) down this "hill" backwards! Even worse, They were beginning to veer off course, off the path of the "hill" roaring now to the side of the "hill" that did *not* have snowside mound curbs.

The edge of the hill was the woods!

That meant trees—*big* trees—the kind that could really hurt you if you smashed into them, crashing into these pine trees could be lethal going this fast! Going backwards, Letty screamed, "Look how far up the mountain we've come already! This is great!"

As the bobsled careened further ever more down and backwards, snow began to be dumped into the sled as they were hitting branches of Frazier Fir trees above. Tree after tree was hit, but only by the blessing of God did they avoid the tree trunks that were populated in the woods.

Now they were totally off the "hill" and the sled began to slow down a bit. The roaring rumble began to muffle, and they were on regular snow again. Something hard bashed the bobsled, and a very strong bump and bang turned the sled, finding us moving forward again.

Then another softer bump in the front of the sled buried itself into the biggest and most welcome Frazier Fir Ron ever saw in his whole life. The rumbling and wind had stopped. There was now silence.

Letty and Ron were covered with snow and pine branches with pine cones to boot.

For a moment, both Ron and Leticia said not a word, being in a kind of stupor, just glad to be alive—Letty having experienced the thrill of it all, Ron trying to unwind the terror he had felt. He began checking his arms and legs and found that he was okay, but also, he felt his backside finding it was softer than usual and just a tad "mushy."

Matters were worse in that he had split his usual store pants, not having had a regular ski pants outfit. Leticia just leaned back on Ron's chest and said in a low, slow, sexy voice, "I'm going to keep these pine cones forever. This has been the greatest ride that I have ever been on. Can we go again?"

She was totally oblivious of the fact that they had almost been killed by a runaway bobsled. Trying to find *any* possible way out, Ron coolly said, "We can't. I split my pants almost in half and I have no other."

By this time, other people who saw their ride and the dramatic events that unfolded were running over to us and kept saying, "Are you guys all right? My god, we thought that you were both killed."

In reply, Leticia kept telling everyone what a fantastic ride she had had and what a great and skillful bobsledder Ron was. She actually thought he was a hero! Ron just smiled and hoped that nobody would say anything about the funny smell coming from Ron and his pants.

The Speakeasy

Before I knew her, I liked her. Before I liked her, I loved her. This simple thought kept running through Ron's mind.

All the things they had done and the really neat places that they had been were always casual, except the rigid program that both Ron and Letty were going through. It seemed that something next was going to happen if Ron was going to get the show on the road. He wanted to go somewhere special where Leticia could feel feminine rather than always being in the surroundings of the hospital. And so Ron decided to change the venue and do something more romantic. The idea popped into his mind almost instantly. He would take Letty to The Speakeasy.

At an earlier time, Fred had introduced Ron to this place and it seemed perfect.

The Speakeasy was a nightclub that was frequented by the college crowd and was a great meeting place for young people to get-together. It was a perfect place for people to relax and, at least for a while, step away from the routines of daily life, especially for medical people, who had to deal with tension almost constantly.

The Speakeasy had a fabulous band called The James Boys that was so popular that it was actually beginning to rise in the music charts for their song "Where Is Love?" that seemed destined for bigger things. When going home afterward, people would always be singing and humming this song.

As you would expect, The Speakeasy was very low key and the intimate atmosphere was conducive to dancing. Girls would sometimes ask guys to dance when they hadn't brought partners. Surprisingly, the attire was quite elegant as the girls always wanted to look their best, but casual clothes were also welcomed.

The dance floor's soft multicolored lighting had scatter lights that were constantly in motion except for the very low white lighting on the floor to show pathways to the bar and restrooms and also the ever present bar, which was framed by many people clustered around it.

Tables, especially near the cozy sides of the room, were at a premium. So it was that The Speakeasy was what Ron decided to take Leticia to, and to make the evening even more enjoyable, he invited Fred and his girlfriend, Linda, as both couples already new each other. The entire day was filled with excitement and anticipation! Then, 7:00 p.m. rolled around, and it was time to collect Leticia at the nurses residence.

Upon entering, Ron noticed that there were six people in the living room, three young men and three female nurses who Ron had met before, and one of whom was Lita. They were chatting in Tagalog. The residence had two stories.

Ron politely asked the nursing head mother to call Leticia to notify him that he had arrived. He then sat down in a couch and relaxed in an open adjacent room and waited. About ten minutes later, he heard a door close on the upper second floor landing and footsteps coming with the unmistakable sound of clicking high heels.

As he looked up, there was Leticia beginning to descend the staircase.

She was absolutely radiant! Her dress was silk with golden color that shimmered as it appeared almost alive. Its oriental style with Mandarin collar and thin black contour lines maximally accentuated the athletic body so gracefully moving towards him revealing the subtle, but definite proportions of a statuesque beauty. Her long black ponytail flowed downward, framing her face, from the top of her head to the left side of her cheek and down further to her left shoulder ending at her left breast. She wore no jewelry except for two very thin candlestick earrings.

Highlighting her hair was a small gold ribbon of silk that matched the color of her dress. Her makeup was elegantly placed with very little eye shadow and only the faint blush of soft pink lipstick. She wore her black coat draped over her right arm. As she continued to descend the staircase, Leticia's eyes met Ron's, and she burst out in a beautiful flashing white smile.

Then as Ron got up to meet her, suddenly, the three nurses ran past Ron stopping Leticia's descent. All the nurses were nervously talking in Tagalog to Leticia as she just stood on the stairway listening. They seemed to be imploring Leticia to leave by the side hallway.

Ron was confused, but Leticia finally just said to Ron, "Come with me to the back door. It's closer to the car."

With a quizzical look on his face, Ron agreed. When they got in the car, Ron said to Letty, "What was all *that* about?"

Letty was reluctant to answer but started to laugh, saying, "My girlfriends did not want their boyfriends to see me."

"Excuse me?" Ron replied.

"No, it's true," Letty said. "They say that as soon as other boys see me, they lose their boyfriends. These nurses were trying to get me out of the house before any other boys saw me." "Are you serious?" Ron asked.

"Yes," she replied.

"So you're a real mantrap are you?" Ron asked as he laughed.

"But it's worse than that, Ron," Letty said.

"Uh-oh, what do you mean?" Ron asked.

Leticia then tried to explain, "You are quite a muscular guy. Haven't you noticed how all the other Filipino nurses now are always grabbing and touching your biceps and arms whenever they are close to you, and haven't you noticed how I always try to bump them away to get between you and them?"

"No kidding, really? I hadn't noticed," Ron said.

Leticia then admitted, "Remember Lita?" Ron nodded. "Well, the last time I talked to her, Lita said to me, 'Give him to me. I saw him first!' I told her that I can't just give people away like a dog or a cat. It doesn't work that way. You wouldn't believe how desperate some of the girls are."

"And what did she say?" Ron asked.

"Well, she wasn't happy, but she got the message to butt out," Letty said.

Ron then said to Letty, "You mean you really didn't want to give me away?"

Leticia's eyes then softened and just simply answered, "What do *you* think?"

It was then off to The Speakeasy, and the anticipated great time to come! Ron and Letty arrived after Fred and Linda, which actually turned out well because Fred had already commandeered a choice spot, out of the way, but still close to the dance floor.

They just chatted and settled in for a little while enjoying the music, especially while fast songs were playing as those were not quite Ron's cup of tea; he liked the slower more romantic tunes. The nightclub was crowded, but there were few waiters that could be seen, and the bar was on the other side of the dance floor, even farther than their table. Both couples wanted drinks, but Ron and Fred couldn't get an order. Then an interesting thing happened.

Leticia said, "Let me try." Then she just stood up with her magnificent posture but didn't move. For a couple of minutes, she remained motionless. Several other men spotted her and began to give her room to walk. She continued to walk toward the bar, but when she got there, she couldn't get a space.

Suddenly, a big bouncer-type of bartender called out in a loud voice, saying, "Give the little lady some room!"

"I'd like some drinks, but I can't get through to get served," Letty said.

"Pretty girl, you should be able to get anything you want. What is your pleasure?" the burly bartender said.

After ordering drinks for all four of the friends, and then placing the glasses on a circular tray, the bartender called for a waiter, saying, "Hey, Sam, grab these drinks and part the waters for this little lady to get back to her table, will ya?"

"Sure thing, boss," was the waiter's response.

As others looked about at what was happening with looks of "Gee, I wish someone would do this for us," Leticia said to the bartender, "Thank you for helping and saving me."

"It was all my pleasure, pretty girl," was his rejoinder.

The waiter then took all the drinks for her and said to Letty, "Follow me." He then created a pathway making it easy for Letty to get back to her table.

Fred said, "Are you kidding me? Did you see that?" Leticia just said nothing and demurely smiled. What Leticia had accomplished by a classy demeanor and "lost little girl look," Ron and Fred were not able to accomplish by fighting their way through all the other people. Linda sort of got lost in the shuffle. After enjoying and finishing their drinks, the slow songs began to play.

Ron asked Letty, "Would you like to dance now?"

Leticia just nodded and then said, "I'd love to."

The crowded dance floor was just perfect as it was almost impossible to move, pressing their bodies together tightly.

As they danced, their eyes slowly found each other and seemed immersed only in each other, looking nowhere else. Neither said a word. Their faces came slowly closer as their cheeks caressed, becoming ever so much more relaxed. Letty's head then gently rested on Ron's neck and shoulder with their encircling embrace becoming stronger.

It feels so good to hold her, Ron thought.

As she slowly moved her hand onto the back of his neck, Ron gently pressed his lips to her forehead and kissed her, her perfume becoming ever more intoxicating. She didn't move. Then as they separated, their eyes met once again with neither one hearing the music playing, or knowing where their feet shuffled. Their eyes saying all that needed to be said with just a glance, implying a communion of fathomless intense desire. Then quivering, their lips pressed slowly together, then, more firmly, locked in now total embrace, in a time unknowing. As the music ended, the crowd began to thin, their embrace continued, but without anyone else seeming to notice. Slowly holding hands, they made their way to the table and sat down. They were in a place all their own, reserved only for those whose deepest and most cherished feelings are given one for the other, only once. Ron and Leticia did not seem to hear anything Fred and Linda were saying. They were totally consumed in each other, as if they were the only two people alive on earth.

Fred and Linda later left to go home. Ron and Letty did not care and hardly knew their friends already had gone. She had touched his very soul, and he did not want it to end—ever. As they just sat there transfixed in time, a waiter came up to them and said, "We're sorry, but everyone has left, and we have to close up now."

Slowly, they got up and left. Snow was now lightly falling and it was very cold. Moving toward their car, the snow crunched under their shoes. Letty was very unsteady walking on the ice and snow, so Ron lovingly put his arm around her shoulder and ushered her to the door of the Blue Beetle. The door and handle of the car were frozen, and Ron needed some mighty tugs on the door handle to free it to get them both inside. They were shaking badly from the cold as they turned on the heater high and just snuggled tight under their quilts. Their eyes said everything; there was no sound, except the humming of the engine. Once again, they were totally lost in each other completely.

As the car started to move and made it to the streets again, at every red light, Ron would place a *very* long kiss on Letty's lips. Suddenly, other motorists would start honking their horns, until the next red stop light.

When they finally got to the nursing residence, it was quite late, well beyond curfew, but the house mother was always lenient. Neither wanted to move and leave the car. They remained, again just lost deep within each other in that special place where only people in love can reach. The windows steamed up the car. Boy did they ever!

Still they remained, a night that neither wanted to end, but end it had to. Ron gave Letty a steady arm to lean on as there was ice everywhere, and the snow had continued to fall.

As Ron gave Letty a final long kiss, the door closed slowly behind her with their eyes still fixed on each other. Ron slipped and slid all the way to the car, got inside, and let out a loud shout in exhilaration, "Yahoo!"

What a Christmas date this had been!

On his long ride home from Newark to Bayonne, every second was wrapped up in his thoughts of Leticia. His mind was in a whirl! He tried to recall all the things that she had done at other times. They were beautiful and she was genuine.

At The Speakeasy, when another man would stop at their table and ask her to dance, Leticia always answered, "Thank you, but I'm already with someone I like a lot," as she would be looking directly into Ron's eyes.

She even turned Fred down as she looked at Linda and said, in a very polite way, "I think Linda wants to dance with you." This showed a lot of class.

Leticia was the ideal blend of very sexy woman and sweet little girl that men just couldn't resist, but with all her considerable charms, she *never* flirted. She always made Ron feel ten feet tall, like she was interested *only* in him even if they were in a busy, crowded room.

He thought, *How unbelievably lucky he was when he once fell off a stool and found Leticia dusting him off and getting him up off the floor*. It seemed like ages ago, but was only yesterday.

As his ride went on, along with the rhythmic swish of the wind shield wipers, further thoughts kept popping into his mind about Leticia. She had a very unusual quality about her, like that of a little lost girl, so that men always wanted to help her. They would always open doors for her (like the bartender had done). They would pump gas for her even at self-service stations and carry packages for her. But Leticia never asked for anything; people just spontaneously did things for her. And her voice, even if she were on the phone and the other party could not see her, had a slow, soft, sexy voice that was not phony or forced, so that men immediately would warm up to her.

Ultimately, she was a "kiddie magnet." Ron and Letty would be sitting in a church pew when a small child would be standing facing backward in the pew; the child would make eye contact with Letty, and both would smile and wave to each other. It was that kind of warmth as a person that Leticia exuded, and Ron could both sense and see it.

As he finally got home very late that night, after all these things ruminated in his mind, he sat down in the low light of the night as all were asleep. He just sat there, then sat there longer as he could not go to sleep. Ron just wanted to sit in his chair continuing to think about the wonderful girl, who, for some reason, had chosen him to become close to, and how fortunate he was. It was at that quiet, dark hour of the night which sounded only the soft ticking of the wall clock for accompaniment that Ron came to realize that he *never* wanted to be anywhere else.

Being away from Leticia made Ron feel like a part of him was missing, and he never wanted to feel like that again. It had become true when it was said,

> Before I knew her, I liked her;
> Before I liked her, I loved her.

Ron had become deeply and forever in love with Leticia.

The Surprise

The 1970 New Year's Day passed into history.

During the ensuing days and weeks, Leticia and Ron were inseparable; it was as if they almost melded together into one. Wherever they went, they were always holding hands. Some nurses thought the hand holding was romantic, others thought it was corny, but as time passed, it was obvious to all that Ron and Leticia were deeply in love. They even tended to finish each other's words and sentences, seemingly knowing what each other was going to say before things were said.

And it became infectious as it was not surprising to see more couples beginning to hold hands everywhere. They seemed like two swans on a pond, always coming together if someone tried to separate them. The two lovers worked hard, played hard, and always seemed to drain every day of life that had been given to them.

As some would say, opposites attract, but this was most certainly untrue of Letty and Ron. They were as completely the same as a man and woman could be—*true soul mates*. But time is relentless, and both knew that the last year of being a senior medical student would now be over in the first week of June. Ron kept doing all the things he had to do on a daily basis, with seemingly little effect on the upcoming matching program that he was beginning to enter.

Although he wanted to be chosen by a very good hospital for internship, if he was nervous, he didn't show it. He had sent out multiple résumés of his curriculum vitae, his grades were good with honors, and all his medical school instructors held him in high esteem as supported by glowing references; therefore, he felt that he would get a good internship position, that it was only a question of which hospital and what part of the country and state he would wind up in. He had a list ranking the hospitals as choices 1, 2, 3.

The bottom line was that by the first week of June 1970, Ron's career was going to spring forward in every way, and he knew it. That was why he had such a confident "air" about him. By June 1, he would be a true MD, and the world would be before him with limitless possibilities.

But for Leticia, things were different. They loved each other deeply, but their careers were marching on a different treadmill of the medical scene. Leticia's career was also moving forward, but she was a salaried RN working for the Martland Medical Center of the University of New Jersey Medical and Dental School, so she already knew where she would be living.

Although very close in all things, little by little, day by day, Leticia was becoming uneasy. She began to worry and think, "What if his matching position puts him in a state far away from Newark, New Jersey?"

She knew very well that it might be very difficult to be together. Might the two of them slowly drift apart simply because of circumstances? More worried, she thought, *What if one of the other many new nurses in Ron's new hospital prettier than me, with long blond hair, be more appealing?*

It hurt her just to think about these things, even if only imagined. So Leticia decided to say nothing of her deeply anguished thoughts and bury her fears, hope for the best, and pray that all things would work out fine. After all, Ron had never changed one bit since the time they first noticed each other, which seemed so long ago as so many thoughts flashed through her mind, tormented.

Then it came! May 1, 1970. The matching results of hospitals, interns, and residents.

Published announcement revealed that Fred had gotten Jackson Memorial Hospital in Florida. Ron's published notice was the Hospital for Joint Diseases and Medical Center in Manhattan, New York City, a magnificent "plumb" that Ron had hoped for as his number 1 choice, exactly what he wanted!

Fred and Ron both wanted to celebrate immediately, but Fred noted that the Match that had been made was contingent upon writing an acceptance agreement to the hospital confirming the acceptance. Ron said to Fred, "Accept the Joint Diseases Hospital, are you kidding? Give me a pen and the confirmation response letter before the pen runs out of ink!"

Ron was on cloud nine! He immediately called Leticia to tell her the good news! Both were excited, but most importantly, Leticia now knew that her position was in Newark, New Jersey. Ron's was in Manhattan. This was close enough so that they could see each other and not be forced apart by distance.

What was even better, Leticia had been moonlighting in New York City at St. Clair's Hospital, so she knew her way around geographically quite well. The matching party was a fantastic blowout! *All* the interns, residents, and nurses were there including Fred, Linda, and of course, Letty and Ron. However, the party was saddened in only one small way. All these people realized that as they were now being scattered all around the USA, they might never see each other again. But for this particular night, *they were in nirvana!*

All knew that they now had earned the right to make a mark in their lives. Although matching was just another "rung on the ladder" to be climbed toward success, all these doctors knew and realized that the ceiling was limitless. It was this feeling that Ron and Letty were swept up in, a feeling that would never come again, but a feeling that neither wanted to ever let go of. The party lasted to the early bright sunlight of morning requiring many to be brought home by taxicabs. Some of the celebrants never got to their homes at all, winding up in other places.

With matching now over, it seemed that a large balloon had decompressed. All the prior hubbub vanished as did most of the familiar, friendly faces that Leticia had known and, *Ron was one of them!* No phone call—nothing. This was totally unlike him. Leticia called the local hospitals emergency rooms, but none had reported an accident that might have involved Ron. It was as if he had just vanished off the face of the earth. An unusual uneasiness, then sadness, filled Leticia's heart. The days passed, her phone remained silent—no calls, nothing. Almost a week went by—still silence.

Leticia began to move about in the Coronary Care Unit very mechanically, as if in a trance, performing her daily tasks as a robot. The other nurses were quick to realize that something was wrong with Leticia. Ron was nowhere to be seen, and Leticia was very quiet, now sitting by herself in corners of the cafeteria, just wanting to be alone. Leticia was very genuine and could never make a pretense that all was well.

Some of the nurses like Lita, who had been jealous and who were never successful with men, actually would say to Letty in a snarky way, "So where's your boyfriend now?" That really hurt.

Letty always wore her heart on her sleeve. There was no denying it. Her face answered for her heart, and she was heartbroken. Despondent in her mind, broken in spirit, but worst of all, alone in the devastating thought that she had been cast aside by someone that she loved and trusted, she was confined in a private hell that was all in her mind.

After work in the silent hours of the night, she would not eat. She would just quietly weep, making hardly a sound, her tears wetting her pillow, until blessed sleep would intervene, bringing relief to a tormented girl so hopelessly in love.

Over and over, she thought, *How could you just leave me? I love you. I love you with all that I have to give.*

Then she cried out for the first time aloud in anguish, "Don't leave me! Please don't leave me! I can't stand being without you. Without you, all is emptiness. I will follow you anywhere you want to go."

But the silence continued, crushing all her hope, being all alone. Then, about two weeks later, a soft knock on the door, but no answer. Again, multiple times, the door was knocked, still no answer.

As the knocking was beginning to abate, the door slowly opened only a crack, revealing a young girl whose face was wet with crying and whose eyes were very reddened. The door was now widened. Leticia then saw Ron's face as he was casually standing before her with a soft, quizzical smile.

Neither spoke for a few seconds. Then Ron said, "Hi, can I come in?"

When Ron walked into the room, he saw Letty's room disheveled, her uniform undone, and mascara staining her face. As he looked at her, she still said not a word.

Jokingly, he said, "What's the matter, don't you know me? Did you forget me already?"

She still did not yet speak.

He then said, "If it's a bad time for you, I can come back another time."

Finally, Letty said in a soft whisper, "Where have you been?"

"It's a long story," Ron replied, "but I have a little surprise for you."

She didn't know whether it was a good surprise or a bad surprise, so she looked at him with a somewhat cautious expectation. Seeing that and noting the disheveled shape that she was in, Ron said, "Why don't you wash your face, clean up, put on some comfortable clothes, and we'll talk, okay?"

Letty agreed, and Ron began to clean up her dishes and straighten up the room for her. It had been a mess for quite a few days. Then later, they sat on the couch and just looked at each other, without saying a word. Gently, Ron's fingers slowly brushed away the hair from Leticia's face and eyes saying, "Now that's better."

Lovingly, he kissed her forehead and cheeks and then her lips saying, "It's been a long time, I've missed that."

Then, there was a gush of words from Letty. "What happened? Where have you been? I've been worried sick. I thought that you left me!"

"Never," responded Ron.

"Then what happened to you?" asked Leticia.

"Well, do you remember the four years I just graduated from?" Ron asked.

Letty nodded positively.

"Well, it's all gone. I've got no money at all," said Ron.

"But I can give you money from my moonlighting work," Letty said.

Having a lot of pride, Ron responded, "No, it doesn't work that way, not for me."

"Then what?" Letty asked.

Ron explained, "The only thing that I have of value is my Steindorf microscope, so I decided to sell it. The problem was that the Steindorf is a very special and expensive microscope. I found out that my scope had appreciated greatly since I bought it four years ago because Steindorf was the best, and they don't make this particular microscope anymore. Turns out, it's a collector's item. But to sell my microscope and get a fair price, I had to visit many places in New York City and New Jersey to talk with them, and they all wanted to examine my microscope. Finally, I sold it for the highest price that I could get, but it took me a long time to complete the deal and get my money."

He explained further, "Then there was more time lost, but *I had to find exactly the right item to get, not just anything, but a very special thing.* Matters were made worse in that I have no knowledge or expertise in buying things like this."

"So what did you finally buy that couldn't wait?" Leticia asked.
"*This!*"

Ron left the room temporarily, later holding a very large box with beautiful multicolored wrapping paper and a very large red bow and ribbon. He handed the box to Leticia and said, "This is for you with all my love."

Although the box was big and cumbersome, it was light and weighed hardly anything at all. A present for her! Excitedly, Leticia carefully removed the bow and ribbons, being careful not to tear up the paper as was her custom. She always was prone to save everything. As she opened the box and looked inside, Letty saw another slightly smaller box inside. This second box was wrapped in a similar fashion. Letty smiled and said, "This really is a surprise, isn't it?"

Ron said nothing, letting Leticia continually search for something inside. The second box now revealed a third box, again slightly smaller, decorated in a similar fashion. There was a quizzical expression now on Letty's face, but again, Ron remained silent.

"Oh boy, this is really turning out to be a treasure hunt, isn't it," she said.

Ron just nodded affirmatively. The multiple box opening occurred several more times until the final, last seventh box which was *very* small and as light as a feather. She removed a little red bow and paper and found a tiny black velvet box inside. Leticia's hands were trembling as she now knew what this kind of a box meant and what would likely be inside.

She hesitated and then said to Ron, "Please open this for me."

Ron opened the small, black, velvet box, revealing a diamond engagement ring. It had two parts, the first the diamond ring itself with a bivalved second ring that cradled the first, both coming together into one ring, *very unique.*

As he placed the ring on her finger, he said that he chose this special ring design because it showed perfectly the two parts that became one just like the two of them coming as one from two worlds.

A more appropriate and fitting ring could not be made.

Ron then said to Letty, "My microscope has become your ring, and your ring will always have my heart until the day it beats its last, forever stilled, until I die." Leticia jumped up and let out a scream of pure ecstasy! She then began to cry uncontrollably. Truly, he had once again touched her very soul. They kissed and held each other so tightly that Ron thought Letty would push out all of his breath. Nothing else was said between the two lovers. No further words were necessary. No further words of "Will you marry me?" were said. They knew in their hearts that the answer was yes. They knew their two souls were now one. The two lovers just continued gently caressing, kissing, and holding closely, enfolded in each other's arms on the couch, with tears, now of joy, coming from Letty's eyes.

This continued as both fell into a deep, wonderful sleep unrealized by the world around them. They just slept, both wanting to never wake up or disturb the moment. They belonged only to it and to each other completely.

Leticia would never lose trust in her Ron again.

As daylight began to gradually filter into their room, Ron still slept, curled up on the couch as the prior night had left him. Leticia began to slowly open her eyes and awaken. She did not want to move lest her wonderful thoughts suddenly vanish, things that yesterday she could only dream about. Was it true, or was it still just a beautiful dream? She slowly looked down to her left hand. On her fourth finger was her ring that Ron had given to her.

It was *not* a dream—it was true!

She was living her dream, for real! It did not matter where she was, she was home, and home became wherever she and Ron were together. Both began to stir and slowly awaken to the new day, a bright inviting day that seemed to call the lovers toward more wonderful things yet to come. As the beauty of the prior wondrous night faded, they began to speak about only intimate thoughts that only lovers share.

Leticia then said, "Although I love you so very much, you didn't *have* to give me a ring. I would have followed you anywhere. The formality really doesn't matter."

Ron replied, "It does to me. It's a matter of pride and honor. You're coming with me."

"Where?" Leticia asked.

"All the way!" was the response as Ron elaborated. "I will marry you no matter what, with a drunken judge and rent-a-witness, big wedding or no wedding, a dowry or nothing, just the clothes on your back and not a penny in your pocket. I want you to completely understand that I am marrying *only* you with only your heart and soul as my wedding gift to *both* of us. God is marrying us, and I know that he loves us and we love him. We don't need a big, formal wedding. A big wedding doesn't mean that we love each other any less. I am giving you *all* that I have to give you, and I always will."

Leticia then lovingly said, "Oh, Ron, you stubborn, splendid, adorable fool." She then wrapped her arms around his neck, kissing her constantly for a long, long time.

And so, on May 15, 1970, they were married, in the Municipal Court of New York City, for a $5 court fee, a microscope to pay for her ring, and a heart freely given only to each other.

The first of June, 1970, now came full circle, and with this came *graduation* with all the pomp and circumstance expected for a medical school graduation. Ron's parents were bursting with pride and seemed if "walking on a cloud," almost oblivious to the events of the graduation itself and even all the people surrounding them. For them, it was the greatest event that they had ever experienced in their lives, even greater than Ron's graduation from Stevens Institute of Technology from engineering seven years ago.

Ron had kept all his promises to his parents, and for them, Ron could do no wrong ever. However, he also felt the awesome responsibility that came with the love and pride his parents freely and completely gave. Leticia looked radiant in her conservative golden-tan suit and pill box hat standing close, side by side, and constantly holding hands as they always did during all the photographs being taken of everyone. Leticia held her hand more tightly this day and was trembling, somehow feeling that she was an "outsider" with Ron's parents present. This was the first time that she had met them personally and felt quite nervous.

Ron was always the same, his parents were formally polite, but there was so much going on with all the graduates and parents talking with everyone that no real personal conversations were made. There were many graduation parties after the formal ceremonies, and all the graduates were eager to remove their caps and gowns, moving from other houses to meet friends. The day was one of festivities ongoing and then finally settling down with special, familiar people and friends in small groups, and *Leticia was most certainly one of them.*

Destiny was once again guiding their fate.

Time, Success, and Trouble

The internship flew by!

As hard as the work was, it was very interesting and enjoyable.

The chief of surgery, Dr. Wilder, was very well-known and respected, and because of this, many of his patients were famous people. As an intern on staff for the chief, it was not uncommon to bump into Zero Mostel, Connie Stevens, and Elizabeth Taylor as they were rapidly whisked away by the chief's office through security.

"You'll never guess who I saw in person today," Ron would say to Letty, and then he would regale her with how beautiful these people were.

One of his prized possessions was a book in his library titled *Atlas of General Surgery* by Dr. J. R. Wilder who autographed his book for Ron writing, "Now you have joined the team." Because of the famous people coming and going all the time, Dr. Wilder always treated "his boys" (as they were called) very well.

Their food, when they were on call was always catered first class, and boy was it good!

During that year, a group of Jamaican nurses had been contracted for help and turned out to be superbly skilled. They had been trained in England and Ron always found it interesting that these nurses (who were all black) had British accents and were very pleasant to listen to. Not only did they speak so well, but they were *all* very classy. Since they worked so hard, and Leticia knew well their rigors, she would sometimes ask Ron, "Can you help them out sometimes?"

Ron answered by saying, "We always have good catered food courtesy of Dr. Wilder and lots of extras, so the interns always save some of these great dinners to give to these Jamaican nurses who greatly appreciate them.

In Ron's eyes, he saved the best food for the best nurses and felt that this was only fair. Leticia told Ron, "You're darn right! And when push comes to shove, and life is on the line, you only want the best of the best in the trenches helping you!"

As the year was beginning to end, confidence ballooned, and Ron told Leticia that he thought he was ready for anything. That was good because residency matching again threw Ron into the mix. He wanted orthopedic surgery and got his first choice getting the Henry Ford Foundation Hospital in Detroit, Michigan. It was once again time for Ron to learn how much he really didn't know, and learning was painful under of the instruction of the higher-up residents who themselves had gone through the mill the same way. Only this time, residency was from July 1971 to December 1974.

Ron's bosses were Drs. Edwin Guise and Hal Frost, and *that* made residency very exciting as Dr. Guise was team physician for the Detroit Lions football team and Hal Frost was the only true genius that Ron had ever known. It was a great privilege learning from them! The conversations that Ron had with Leticia about football and medicine were incredible. The senior residents always had to go to the games as Dr. Guise was responsible to care for the injuries to players like Mel Farr, Charley Sanders, and a whole litany of others.

We thought the world was our oyster, but the pearl was about to go empty. An old problem was about to almost destroy them—bleeding and pain! It had allowed Leticia a brief respite, but now it was back with a vengeance! She tried everything—bed rest, medications, but nothing seemed to help.

All the old beatings, being kicked in the abdomen many times before by Marco, and prior difficult pregnancies had created significant problems.

Massive, multiple uterine myomata had formed.

The doctors talked at great length with Ron and Letty, but all possibilities left them with only one best cure. Leticia was extremely upset and was crying uncontrollably! Ron asked the doctors to excuse them for a while so he could be alone with Leticia. Finally, Ron was able to calm Leticia down. He then said, "You know what has to be done is inevitable, don't you?"

Still sobbing, Leticia said, "Yes."

"We both know that if we don't take all these bleeding tumors out, the result will be continued pain, bleeding, then hemorrhage, and possibly infection and death," Ron emphasized.

Leticia answered, "Yes, I do."

Then neither spoke. They just held each other ever so tightly. Leticia then said, "You know that I will never then be able to have a child with you—ever. I will be barren, and you are so young, strong, and healthy."

"I know," answered Ron.

Leticia then stopped sobbing and went totally silent. She slowly lifted her head and, looking deeply into his eyes, said, "You deserve much better than this. You should find another good woman and divorce me. I want you to. I can't be together with you anymore in the way we should."

Ron's eyes began to flow with tears making no sound. After composing himself, he said, "Before I ever leave you, the sun will set and never rise again in the heavens."

Letty responded, "But Ron, if you keep me, you—"

He put his fingers on her lips stopping her from speaking and said, "I once before told you that I would *never* leave you, that we were going all the way together no matter what, to the very last beat of my heart."

Leticia's sobbing began to stop as both said nothing for a long, long pause. And then Leticia softly said, "That long?"

"Until my heart ceases to beat forever, you will always be mine," he responded.

They embraced for a long time, with Ron continually kissing Leticia's tears away.

As he held Leticia's hand as was always their custom, the doctors were called into the room and Ron said, "I think *my wife*, and I are ready now."

Leticia then stated with her head held up high. "I'm ready now for you to do the hysterectomy and take these tumors out."

The Inheritance

Leticia's surgery was successful and the years passed.

All the orthopedic training completed, Ron and Leticia settled in Florida and began a successful private practice, working together in the office. Disney World, saltwater fishing and crabbing, and trips to the Keys were wonderful. Ron did not forget the hard work his parents had put in to give him his engineering education. He brought them from the cold of New Jersey to live in Florida, where his father's emphysema would be less troublesome and his mother's arthritis caused less pain. Ron then gave his mom and dad a beautiful condo and sent them to Spain, Miami, and the Keys to enjoy.

After all the travelling Letty and Ron had done for educational reasons in New York, New Jersey, Michigan, and Kentucky, they felt it was wonderful to settle down and just get to know each other again. But all things don't always go smoothly.

Ron had a brother, Robert, who took a road travelled differently than Ron. Robert was a "good guy" but was not interested in the scholastic venue as was Ron. This created friction as his parents tried in vain to instill scholastic efforts in Robert. It was made worse by the why-can't-you-be-more-like-Ron approach by his parents who meant well but couldn't seem to get on the same ground with Robert.

During the period when the Vietnam War was raging, Robert decided to join the marines. Although fearful, Robert's parents and Robert were justifiably proud. Initially, Robert's attitude in the Corps was that of a John Wayne Marine, but after he got shipped out to Nam, his attitude began to slowly change in his letters.

He became less enthusiastic, progressively to the point of saying things like, "Agent Orange is killing Marines as many as the Cong and try to stay out of the military if you can because what's going on here in Nam is not what you think it is." He had lost his John Wayne swagger.

Leticia and Ron had talked about Robert's plight, but neither knew exactly what was happening. Eventually, Robert got through his hitch safely but came back home disturbed similar to other soldiers like PTSD. It took a long time for him to heal as a first marriage failed ending in divorce. A beginning second marriage seemed to fare better.

On a trip to Florida by car with Ron, Robert was very jumpy. Both brothers were warm and cordial, but Robert voiced to Ron once, saying," You're doing great, but I want to get mine too!"

Robert was struggling with something, but he never let anyone in to explain what was wrong. Ron told Leticia about all the distress Robert had experienced, and she asked, "How can we help him?"

"I don't know," Ron replied, "and I'm sure it's a lot more complicated, but I'm beginning to think the bottom line is that Robert believes that I caught the Brass Ring in life, but he got the short end of the stick and got screwed."

They talked more, and Letty said, "You know, maybe he's right, and he did get screwed for whatever reason." Again, she asked, "How can we help him?"

Ron responded, "I don't know. Let me think about it some more." He did and told Leticia what he thought best to do. Leticia agreed completely, and their decision was made together.

Then one day, Robert had come to Florida from New Jersey to help Ron install a new telephone system in Ron's office. In the evening, the family sat in the cool night of the screened in veranda all playing cards. Ron was holding Leticia's hand and said to his father, "Dad, I have something important to say to you and all of you here at the table."

"Okay, shoot," his father said.

Ron then began saying, "Dad, you and your mother have always been very good to me, and I have become successful and don't need help anymore, but Robert does. I want you to give to Robert *all my inheritance* that you may have put away for me. I don't need it now, but *he is struggling, and he does need it.* Please agree and do this for me.

Leticia heard and saw Ron saying this as his father's face became at first mellow and then very proud. "I always knew I had a great son," his dad said with his eyes sparkling.

"Can we shake on it?" Ron asked.

"You bet," his dad agreed.

This was all happening out of the blue, and at first, Robert looked stunned at the unexpected magnanimous request. Getting his composure back, he threw his arms around Ron saying, "Thank you so much, I can't tell you how much this means to me."

Shortly afterward, their father died. The promise was kept. Leticia saw Ron personally take Robert's wife to the bank and place the money from his dad's safety deposit box into her hands for Robert. Although his father was dead, honor and loyalty was still very much alive!

As Leticia and Ron were going home, she heard Ron softly say, "Rest well, Dad. All is well."

A Price Too High to Pay

Leticia saw Ron becoming distracted for about the last year as this was not like him.

She asked, "What's wrong, my love? What's bothering you?"

Ron replied, "I've practiced eight years now and have been quite successful, included having treated and helped many of Disney World's toughest compensation cases."

Leticia, waiting for an explanation said. "And?"

"It's not enough. I want to do more. I want to go higher," Ron stated as the astonishment in Leticia's face continued to grow.

"But you're the best now," Letty said emphatically.

"Am I?" asked Ron.

"Then what is it you want to do?" asked Leticia.

"I want to be a plastic surgeon," he said.

Totally aghast, Leticia said, "You mean that you want to be one of the few surgeons in the world who is an orthopedic surgeon and a microsurgical hand surgeon and a plastic surgeon all rolled up in one?"

"Yep, that's it," Ron casually replied.

"But my love, do you realize what will happen to you when you revert from full prominent attending surgeon status to just lowest resident in training again in another state of the country when even the nurses will give orders to you and sometimes crap all over you because nobody will know how distinguished you really are?" she asked. "No doctor in practice for years like you can go back again to so low a position. It's too hard and too far a come down," Letty declared.

"Ya think?" Ron answered.

Neither spoke for awhile. Leticia knew of the tremendous focus he was capable of. She asked, "Have you thoroughly thought everything through?"

"Yup," he said.

Leticia knew very well Ron's mind and knew he had already made his decision, so she said, "Okay, so where and when are we leaving Florida?"

Ron smiled, looked into Leticia's eyes, and said, "I'm married to the greatest and most generous wife in the world." He then embraced Letty and kissed her for a long, long time. He then answered her, saying, "I've applied and have already been accepted to the Southeastern Michigan Plastic Surgery Program under chief of surgery Burns Newby. The first rotation starts in nine months."

Leticia asked again, "Are you sure? Do you realize your orthopedic patients will then vanish and the loss of savings will be horrific as money will be hemorrhaging out, but almost nothing coming in and that it will take another five years *after* you start practicing as a plastic surgeon to establish yourself again?"

"Yes, I do," Ron declared.

"Okay," Leticia said. "I know that you're only one of a few men in the entire world that can pull off something like this, and that's why you're special, and I'm so very proud that you're mine!" Without further hesitation, Leticia emphatically said, *"Do it!"*

The next few months brought confusion and some unhappiness as Ron's practice began to gear down and patients were referred to other doctors.

And then suddenly, it happened!

Leticia received a call from the hospital. "Go to the hospital, STAT!"

Leticia phoned Ron, "Your mother is very sick!" Stopping everything, Ron sped down I-4 to get to his mother's side. She was in radiology.

As Leticia caught up to Ron at the hospital with a look of grave concern, the doctor showed the x-rays to Ron and Letty. They revealed *massive pulmonary embolisms of both right and left lungs*, with only about 25 percent of her left lung functioning.

Both Ron and Leticia knew his mother was dying in front of their eyes, and Ron could not be able to save her! Both Leticia and Ron stayed with his mother, Antoinette, to the last gasps of breath. She was conscious and trying to talk but couldn't, straining for breath to the very last moment of her life, with her eyes saying good-bye to Ron for the very last time. Then, it was over.

Leticia saw Ron, this big, strong, determined man, totally breakdown. In anguish he cried, "Oh, Mom," with tears streaming down his face, burying his face into her chest and clutching her head as he stroked her red hair.

She was gone.

Leticia and Ron stayed at bedside for a long, long time afterward.

The next day, Leticia stayed close to Ron, still trying to console the inconsolable.

"I could have spent so much more time with her when she was alive, but I didn't. I was always off doing something for someone else. Selfish, selfish, selfish!" he blurted out. "I can't do this anymore. I have no heart for it. It's too big a price to pay."

But in a soft, loving voice, Leticia answered Ron, saying, "There was no greater pleasure for your mother than knowing her son made people better every day and saved lives. She knew that *her* life made people better through her son and that *she* had made a difference in this world because of that. *How proud she always was!* Are you going to throw it all away? All your mother stood for? Are you going to say that all she did for you was for nothing? That you're going to quit now? Something that she knew you were always destined to do and be?"

Nothing else was said.

Later that evening, after Letty and Ron stayed with his dad, his father spoke similarly as Leticia had expressed.

His father said, "Your mother would have wanted you to do what you're attempting. You were the light in her eyes. *Go for it! Finish it for her!* And don't worry about me either."

And he did!

THE FLAME GOES OUT

In 1984, Ron graduated his second residency and became a plastic surgeon, a true multispecialist.

During his two-year absence, both Leticia and Ron had flown from Michigan to Florida several times because of his father's deteriorating health, so Ron was happy that his training was finished. The "pressure cooker" was released, and all began to relax and live life again.

Then about a year later, there was *another fateful call!*

In a voice sounding short of breath, his dad, Michael, was on the phone and said, "Ronnie, I can't make it anymore!"

Ron and Letty rushed home and found his dad gasping for air. He had developed *congestive heart failure!* Immediately, they took Michael to the emergency room. For a few days, his dad slightly improved, and all felt a sigh of relief.

Then, about 4:00 a.m., the hospital called asking Ron to come to the hospital STAT. He immediately rushed to the hospital and upon arriving at the nurse's station, the charge nurse told Ron, "I'm very sorry Dr. L, but your father has just passed away."

Ron slowly walked into his dad's room and saw him looking as if in restful, sleeping repose. He had just gone to sleep and never woke up. He had gone home. Michael and Antoinette were now reunited with God.

Although Michael's passing was not as unexpected as Antoinette's was, it was no less devastating. Leticia realized the depth of Ron's grief. He lost his beloved mother, *leaving* for residency, and now, he lost his beloved father *coming* from residency. This was truly a price too high that he had paid. But Leticia knew the workings of Ron's mind better than even he did sometimes.

He had lost both his parents and for what? Letty saw Ron become even *more* determined and drew deep down from within himself, an even greater resolve.

"I'm going to be better than I was. I'm going to do things that few or no others can do," Leticia would hear him say, and she thought, *How magnificent!* He continued his prodigious drive until a casual call from his brother Robert about two years later. Leticia said to Ron, "Robert is having a little problem with his stomach and wants to talk with you. Other doctors are treating him with medications, but he's not getting better."

After listening to Robert's complaints, Ron felt uneasy and said to Leticia, "Let's ask him to come to Florida and we can see what's what."

On arriving, Robert looked well enough but couldn't keep his food down.

Letty said to Ron, "A GI series, you think?"

"Good idea," he responded.

A large tumor in his abdomen the radiologist reported. "I would recommend an exploration of the abdomen."

Ron chose two of the finest general surgeons to operate on Robert, and in addition, he chose to assist at the surgery himself as a third surgeon. The exploratory revealed a massive tumor of the pancreas obstructing the duodenal portion of the intestine. Microscopic exam revealed *cancer!*

"Can we get it all out?" the other surgeons asked each other.

They kept exploring further, and then the worst was found—*metastases!* The cancer had spread to Robert's liver.

"Looks like that's it," one of the surgeons said.

"But he's my brother," Ron said. "I can see only *one* liver lesion. Can't we at least try to give him *any* chance at all?"

All surgeons paused in silence. Then they said, "We don't think this will help, but we know some of the rabbits that you have pulled out of the hat for others, so we're going to remove all the tumor from the intestine and cut out the only metastasis in the liver we can find, okay?"

"*Do it!*" Ron agreed. Robert was looking at certain death otherwise.

Leticia helped care for Robert after the grueling six-hour surgery, and Ron kept his brother in his home. Leticia did *everything*—wound care, IVs, bathing, cleaned bedpans, *everything* as Ron completely closed down his office, pouring over every bit of the medical literature he could find that might help save his brother.

About a month later, it was time to let Robert go home to his family in New Jersey and start chemotherapy.

Robert looked well enough as his wife was ready to collect him at the airport, but she was so ecstatic to see Robert better and was so happy that she was almost too exuberant. Leticia said to Ron, "I don't think that Gloria understands how sick he really is. You better talk to her privately."

Ron had a huge dilemma. Should he tell Gloria and Robert that it was likely he was going to die, or should he trust in God in situations like this with the advice prior great surgeons before had said, "When you can offer nothing but dire prognosis, love and *hope is something that you can always give them.*"

So as Ron watched Gloria's exuberance, he spoke to her and said, "Robert is very sick. We've taken all the cancer out that we could find, but there are no guarantees. Cancer is cancer. It's going to do what it's going to do, so be very sure to get Robert to the chemotherapy sessions when home, okay?"

Leticia looked at Ron, saying, "I don't think Gloria understands. She seems homed-in on the cancer is out part and doesn't seem to hear the rest."

"Let's hope for the best," Ron said, "and pray for them."

About five months later, Gloria called Ron, saying, "Robert has lost a lot of weight and can't keep his food down again. I'm very worried."

Immediately, Ron told Gloria to come to Florida right away to the doctors he trusted! Leticia and Ron looked aghast when they saw Robert who was now emaciated and looked like a skeleton. He managed only a faint smile as they greeted him at the airport.

An immediate exploratory was done. The cancer was *everywhere*. There was now nothing else that could be done except for pain relief. Robert never left the hospital and died several days later. Ron closed his office and did not work in Florida again.

Leticia watched her beloved just want to sit each day, doing nothing. She knew that the flame that had burned so brightly in all he did was gone. Maybe never to be rekindled again. Ron had lost all that was dear to him except Leticia, but the worst dagger in his heart was the fact that he was never able to save those he loved most, which, in the first place, was his reason for being.

If he couldn't save them, was he really ever good enough?

Dying

October 1996 was a very nice month, generally sunny and not too cold yet as typical for days of Indian Summer in Missouri.

After church, it was Leticia's custom to practice in the bowling center, and Ron would always accompany Letty, hoping to improve her game. For some reason, Ron did not feel his usual energetic self that Sunday, but he thought that the heavy load of caring for the patients had just worn him out. Surprisingly however, both Letty and Ron had posted very good scores that afternoon, reaching the two hundreds for their three games each.

On the way home, Letty said to Ron, "I forgot some things for supper. Can you pick them up at Kroger's for me?"

"I'll get them for you," he said and drove off to the store.

After picking up a few small items, Ron began to feel weak all over and began sweating profusely in a store temperature that was cool. He managed to get his packages into his car, got in, and drove home. As the garage door closed behind his car, Ron just sat behind the steering wheel and did not seem to want to move.

Not hearing Ron enter the house, Letty finally opened the door and called out, "Aren't you coming in?"

Ron didn't answer.

She walked to the car door and asked, "What's wrong? Why aren't you coming in? I have things cooking on the stove and need some help now."

Ron still didn't answer.

Letty then saw that Ron's face was white as a ghost with beads of sweat pouring down his forehead. Finally, Ron reluctantly spoke in a very soft whisper and said, "I can't lift my legs out of the car."

Letty asked, "Why not?"

"I just can't. I don't have the strength," was Ron's reply.

Now very concerned, Letty asked, "Did you hurt your back again?"

Ron said, "No, I have no pain anywhere, but I feel very weak and can't move my legs even to lift my legs out the door off the seat."

Being a nurse, Letty realized right away that Ron was probably suffering a "silent" heart attack. She immediately administered two aspirins to help prevent blood clots from further forming, placed him supine beside the car with a soft car pillow behind his head, and called 911 for help. She remained at his side tensely waiting for the possibility that she would have to perform CPR before the ambulance could get there.

She kept talking to Ron constantly, reassuring him that the ambulance was coming.

Ron, on the other hand, did not talk but kept looking into Letty's eyes, eyes that seemed to plead "Please help" and with eyes possibly realizing that he was looking at them, maybe for the last time on earth as he was still conscious.

As the EMT people arrived, they placed electrodes to see what the EKG looked like. Leticia saw a tracing that was wildly erratic as an intravenous line was started STAT and a bolus of Lidocaine pushed in.

Ron was already in shock. Quickly, the EMT personnel put Ron on a stretcher, into the ambulance, and off to the hospital with Letty in hot pursuit! As she drove her car, tears flowed down her face as she realized that she was losing her beloved! She was now frantic to get to bedside, but she was not allowed to because a whole cadre of medical personnel surrounded Ron.

She anxiously waited and waited longer as each agonizing second seemed to be a century long. Her mind was in chaos, but with everything only about Ron, his warm smile, how he would always bring her a special cup of coffee in bed each morning before leaving for work, his loving, protective concern when he would be away, the strong bond that had only gotten stronger through the years. All thoughts of Ron came flooding in all at once, but what she also felt was the stark realization of the horror that she was losing him maybe forever. The feeling was almost intolerable! Waiting, waiting, waiting.

Then, the doctor emerged from the treatment room. He told Letty that indeed Ron had suffered an insidious silent myocardial infarction, and it was "touch and go" for a while, but so far, Ron was for now stable.

"It's very lucky for him to have had you there at the exact time that you realized what was happening, you undoubtedly saved his life, Leticia," the doctor said.

Letty was then allowed to go to Ron's bedside. All the frantic activity of the prior hour now subsided. Letty and Ron were now alone in the room. All was silent as Ron helplessly lay there motionless, with his eyes closed, with the EKG monitor constantly dancing and the IV fluids constantly dripping, sustaining his life.

Again, Leticia's mind flashed back twenty-six years, a time when she herself was caring for other patients, but now the problem was up front and very personal, it was her Ron who was very ill and might not recover. She kept speaking to him, but he did not respond. Several hours passed. Letty remained at bedside, but Ron still did not awaken. She kept speaking to Ron hoping that he might still hear what she was saying, praying to him and for him, but still, the room was silent except for her prayers, forced back by tears.

I don't want him to hear me sobbing, Leticia thought if Ron might be able to hear. More time passed. Leticia too began to fall asleep, the strain having totally drained her. Then suddenly, she awoke. She thought of the time long ago when Ron too had fallen asleep and then fell off a stool, striking his head on her CCU floor in the Martland Medical Center when he was still a medical student. She remembered that time so very clearly, so long ago. How pathetic he appeared, and from that time, how much she had come to love him so deeply.

"Oh, he can't die. He just can't," Letty softly sobbed.

Then, with just the two in the room, Leticia heard a faint noise, a small movement on the bed. Ron's hand began to move! Still, he said nothing, but he began to open his eyes. She was so happy to see this, that she could not contain her tears, and at the same time constantly saying over and over again, "Thank you, Jesus. Thank you, Jesus."

A little later, Ron was able to speak very softly. As they spoke to each other, sharing how deeply they cared one for the other, Ron said something amazing. "I think I know what it feels like to die!"

He continued, "The problem is that it feels too damned good!"

Leticia immediately stopped talking and said, "What, come on now. You're freaking me out!"

"No, I really mean it," he said.

Trying to explain further, his amazing disclosure continued, "From the time things began, there was never any pain, just a generalized feeling of progressive and profound weakness. Then I couldn't lift my legs out of the car. Apparently, I was beginning to go into shock.

When that happened, I felt like my total body was melting like wax very slowly down into my shoes. There was total calmness like the most restful sleep that I have ever known. I did not seem to want to fight the sleep but rather began to embrace it. It felt too good to wake up. I did not feel anything going on around me or hear anything people were saying to me. I think that if I had stayed into that feeling, that the shock would have been complete.

It just felt too good to remain there, and at that point, I think that I would have been permanently gone and died.

Leticia then said, "What you've just told me is fantastic! You mean that there were no voices, no light in the distance, or images of familiar people or loved ones?"

"No," Ron replied.

However, what neither Ron or Letty knew, round 1 was over, but round 2 was about to begin! As Ron was speaking to Leticia, he began to keep his eyes now completely closed, and his speech was becoming softer and garbled. The EKG monitor at his bedside was becoming erratic and began to fade as alarms were starting to sound off.

Leticia jumped up onto Ron's bed and, with all her might, punched Ron's chest, trying to do a thump-version as she had been taught in CCU.

As she did this, she screamed out at Ron, "You promised me to never leave me," and started CPR! In just a few minutes, medical personnel took over.

Ron did not feel the pounding on his chest, the CPR, or the electric shocks coursing through his body from the paddles that were used to restart the rhythm of his heart. Mercifully, both the quick action of the medical personnel and Leticia had saved Ron's life. As he began to mentally awaken, Ron only had a sensation of being very cold.

It was very hard to open his eyes and actually felt better if his eyes were kept closed. He had the sensation of being moved from something soft to something hard and having only something thin covered over him. Then, that something hard began to move as he felt vibration with just a little bit of a breeze caressing his face.

Ron could hear voices, saying, "Out of the way, please," with the vibration getting stronger and faster. Then suddenly, a loud rumbling noise followed almost immediately by a gush of cold air that flowed from his feet to his head. Another noise drowned out a louder sound that seemed to swallow up all others with a monotone woop woop woop that was coming closer to him. Someone elevated his something hard onto another and put straps onto him.

Still, someone else kindly put a blanket on Ron because he was constantly saying, "I'm so cold."

"Everybody in?" said a voice.

Then, a loud sudden slam was followed by a very loud, rapidly increasing crescendo of woop woop woop. Ron then heard someone say, "How's our patient doing?"

A young woman began shaking Ron's arm while saying, "How are you doing, Doctor?"

Ron's response was, "I've been a damn sight better. I'll tell you that."

The young woman then communicated by speaker phone to the hospital base that the patient was stable, alert, doing well, and already starting to complain about the service.

On that thirteenth day of October 1996, *doctor* Ron had his first medical helicopter ride to Barnes-Jewish Hospital, St. Louis, as *patient* Ron. The first ten days were filled with fear and exasperation. Whether to operate or not, do it quickly or not, which procedure to use, or no operation at all, in the end, the result was to use conservative medical treatment and *not* to operate, at least for now.

Although Ron was not feeling his best (to say the least), he was fully alert and aware of all the medical problems and possible complications attendant upon all the surgeries that the doctors were considering.

In spite of the fact that he knew these doctors were excellent, Ron did not want to have his chest possibly "cracked." Letty spoke to Ron at great length, and they both agreed that Ron was going to choose conservative treatment by

- anticoagulating his blood to thin it down,
- increase the blood flow with Imdur which helped to open the coronary arteries.
- use Toprol and Vasotec to help allow Ron's heart to beat with less strain, even though Ron did not ever have high blood pressure.

Complicating Ron's myocardial infarction was that his heart had been damaged in such a way that he had persistent multifocal ventricular premature contractures (PVCs). This meant that the muscle of his heart was irritable and damaged in *many* smaller focal areas, not just one big one, making his heart muscle potentially unreliable at any time.

In addition, Ron's first cardiologist said that considering the specific anti-arrhythmic drugs necessary to treat irregularities that Ron had could just as easily kill him with the drugs themselves. A second cardiologist who was a laser specialist said that because so many focal areas of irritability were present, ablating all of them were probably not realistic, and she did not feel success would be high, and death was a distinct possibility.

After all the conferences were completed, Ron and Letty asked to be alone together at bedside. Leticia began to cry. Ron tried to console her, gently stroking her long black hair and kissing her forehead and tearful cheeks. Ron then said, "You know, I'm not dead just yet, and there is still conservative treatment left for me."

"I know," said Letty with a very low, soft voice.

They continued to talk for a long time, then called Ron's cardiologist into the room at bedside. In the same manner as they had always done, Leticia stood up alongside Ron, holding his hand, and said, "My husband has elected to do *no* surgery or dangerous anti-arrhythmic drugs, or laser ablation. He wants only conservative non-invasive treatment, and I want what he wants, and I agree with him completely. Ron too is a doctor, and I am a registered nurse so we are both fully aware of, and agree with, this decision."

The cardiologist nodded his head in agreement and left. The room was now totally silent.

Letty continued to hold Ron's hand; both did not speak. Then Ron softly said in the manner of a man fully resigned to his fate, "I guess it's all in God's hands now, and I'm at peace and content with *our* decision. No matter what, I know that *this* one decision is correct. He hasn't ever given me a bum steer yet."

Both gave each other a faint smile and spent the rest of the evening caressing each other and saying little else. Leticia then left Ron's side only until the other medical personnel declared that visiting hours were over. She was so reluctant to leave. And so, another momentous decision had been made and both knew that their destiny was now totally in the benevolent hands of a much higher power.

Depression

Leticia entered Ron's hospital room and happily said, "You're going home!"

"What?" asked Ron.

"It's true! The doctor has discharged you," Letty gushed.

As the medical attendant pushed Ron's wheelchair down the hall with Leticia alongside, the sliding doors of the hospital exit opened, and Ron looked around. The wheelchair stopped for a long pause as Letty went to get her car to collect Ron. Ron just sat there very quietly.

As he looked about, everything seemed different, even the air smelled fresh and clean. He looked up to a sky he thought was bluer, blue without clouds, that seemed so much bigger. The colors of all things were richer and more vibrant, especially the trees, flowers, and bushes which seemed so much more alive. The sounds about him seemed to be musical, but no radio was playing. All his senses seemed so much more vivid and awake as they exploded at him all at once. He was going *home*!

As Letty drove her car to curbside, the medical attendant helped Ron to get inside, smiled, and said, "Good luck," and disappeared through the hospital sliding door. The car started rolling out of the driveway, and they were on their way, excitedly going home. Letty kept talking to Ron, but he didn't say much, and just kept looking around, drinking in all the sights and sounds around him.

Their journey by car from St. Louis to Poplar Bluff was a little over three hours, and since Ron had just gotten out of the hospital, he tired very quickly. Despite Letty constantly talking, the ever present drone of the car, and the elevated temperature of the car purposely kept raised to keep him warm as the doctor had recommended, Ron could not keep his eyes open and fell asleep.

He awoke to the closing of his garage door with his car now inside. For a few minutes, all was quiet, and neither said anything. Letty spoke first and said, "Seems like we've done all this before," recalling the fateful and dramatic days of the past few weeks.

"Yep, I hope it's not going to be déjà vu all over again," he said with a wry little smile on his face.

Leticia helped Ron get into bed, and almost immediately, he fell fast asleep. Initially in the days ahead, Ron was getting better physically and appeared to be getting stronger, thanks to Letty's good cooking and the strict diet he had been placed on. However, there was something different about him. Mentally, there seemed to be something missing, and Leticia began to notice this change almost immediately. She was correct in the realization of the severe trauma to his body that Ron had endured, but she did not quite understand fully what was going on in Ron's mind.

She thought, *I'll just give him more time. He'll come around.* But as the time passed, he didn't. Leticia loved Ron deeply and was extremely protective and vigilant as he had always been toward her. She observed Ron constantly and saw him becoming ever more quiet and withdrawn, sleeping all the time. Ron was always introverted, but this was something different.

The nighttime was the biggest problem, something real, not imagined. Ron would lay in bed, many times wide awake, just staring at the ceiling, not saying a word.

"Are you okay?" Leticia asked.

The hesitant, slow, thoughtful response was, "Yes, I'm okay," but in fact, he wasn't. Ron was going through a living mental hell that Leticia did not realize. Several weeks passed. The same situation recurred.

Leticia again asked so many times before, "Are you okay?"

This time, Ron opened up, "No, I'm not."

Leticia immediately sat up and looked at Ron's face. "What's wrong, my love?"

Ron responded, "I can never sleep at night because my heart always has PVCs that get their strongest at night, erratically always pounding in my chest, and I feel that every one is going to be my last one forever. The feeling and this thought is frightening—*I'm scared!* Every night at bedtime becomes a night of living hell, *not* rest. I sweat because of fear, and it doesn't stop until the pounding and fear literally exhaust me until I do fall asleep. In the morning, the pounding never goes away although it's much less intense, so that I don't even realize the PVCs are occurring although they are as I take my pulse randomly to check, and they are always there."

"Oh my god, I didn't know what you're going through," Leticia said with deep concern. "Can I do *anything* to help you?"

"No, I wish we could," he sadly replied, "I think I'm stuck with the situation, and that's it."

"Oh, Ron," she said and then began hugging him tightly, constantly kissing him as though it were to be the last night of his life.

Days and weeks went by, then months. Still, with the same awful scenario every night. Ron always dreaded the night, knowing what was coming, not being able to stop it, expecting to breathe his last that coming night of dark, and maybe, eternity. He prayed every night, but the pounding continued, no pain, no headaches, just the constant basketball bouncing around in his chest.

Ron asked himself, "Is this really going to be forever in my life? Is this really living?"

He was obviously depressed. He knew the depression made things infinitely worse, but he had to fight it! Leticia knew that too. She tried in every way imaginable to cheer him up, but each little step of success was followed by two steps backward. She knew that he was losing *their* battle.

Leticia asked Ron, "I know that you don't want to, but what about trying—"

Ron immediately stopped her in mid sentence. He knew what she was going to say. "No," Ron sharply said, "No! No! No! I never have agreed with the complications and side effects involved that went along with antidepressant drugs in the first place. The drug companies are always touting the latest and greatest new drug that comes along, have very flashy ads, especially with pretty young women always smiling, sometimes suggesting if one drug didn't work, consider a new second drug simultaneously, but then, naming all the bad side effects and complications including possible suicide, cancer, and death, that could happen by taking these drugs, but *always, always,* bailing out by making the statement in their infomercials to be sure to ask if the new drug is right for you, essentially the implied message being, 'You buy it, you try it. You call a doctor if a complication happens, then let him or her deal with it if he can. We're out of the problem and covered legally.' Excuse me? I don't think so," Ron emphatically said.

He added, "We both know that considering my erratic PVCs, who knows what another medication like anti-depressants might do to my heart, when all the pills I'm taking now rattle around in my legs when I walk around?"

Leticia agreed and said, "I know that you're right. I'm sorry that I've upset you, but what are we to do?"

"I don't know," Ron replied. "I think that I'm just going to have to deal with my problem all by myself."

"Deal with *our* problem," Leticia added. "Whatever happens, we will deal with it *together.* I will never give up on you. I love you until whatever comes."

Hugs are good, and Leticia wore out her arms around Ron's chest.

It was now about 6 months after Ron's heart attack. It seemed nothing had changed. Leticia enforced Ron's strict diet and sometimes had to force him to constantly walk around the neighborhood as initially, he lacked desire because of his depression. Letty bought a gravitational traction table to relax Ron's back and kept him in physical therapy but curtailed bicycle riding because for the same reason, the PVCs got worse using the bicycle.

Although Ron's internist and cardiologist both said that repeated scans and echocardiograms showed Ron's heart muscle repairing itself and heart circulation improving, Ron physically did not feel much better as the PVCs persisted in every way.

Ron began to realize that after all this time, and for many reasons including his personal worry, that if he were to try to resume his surgical profession, and if he were to injure a patient because of his heart not functioning properly at exactly the wrong time, there would be no moral or legal forgiveness, especially to himself. And so Ron resigned himself to never perform surgery again, a crushing personal decision, as he loved his profession, but accepted his fate.

Letty then asked, "But, Ron, what will we do? How can you waste such a brilliant mind?

But Ron had now just lost the desire to do *anything*. He had hit rock bottom in everything except his love for Leticia. Ron recalled a discussion he had had many years ago when his father struggled with emphysema. As a boy, Ron asked his dad, "How does somebody know they are ready to die?"

This question was very deep for just a little boy to ask, but his father gave Ron a very insightful answer. His father said, "I will be ready to die when I am no longer useful to anyone anymore."

In the subconscious part of his mind, Ron began to feel, "Is this my time to go?" His sad, dark thoughts persisted, but there was one glimmer of hope, one bright light in his depressive morass—Leticia. He further thought, *Leticia believes in me so completely. I can't let her down. I just can't quit on her.*

The months dragged on, spring and then on to summer; still he was no better. He looked at his house which now was a mess, with grass growing very high, and the porch deck needing paint badly after the hard winter that had previously occurred.

Then one day, Letty looked in the garage and saw something brand-new, a walking lawn mower, gasoline powered.

Letty asked Ron, "What's this all about?"

His reply, "I'm going to gas her up and push around the whole lawn to cut this darn grass. If I have any pain, I'll stop."

"If you have any pain, you might die. I couldn't bear losing you. Stop, don't do it!" she yelled.

"I'll just do a little bit and see how it feels. Besides, the mower does all the work and runs and powers itself. All I do is hold on to it as I walk around, just like physical therapy," Ron insisted.

Leticia remained reluctant and worried, but Ron had made up his mind. As he pulled the rope to start the mower which roared to life, Leticia stayed glued to the window intently watching Ron. Ron held the mower, plowing through the high, heavy grass, leaving a neat low furrow about an inch high across the front of the yard. Back and forth, right to left, up and down the small hill he went. As a neighbor called Letty, to the phone to ask about the noise, suddenly, the sound of the mower stopped!

Leticia panicked. Dropping the phone, she ran to the garage door which was completely open.

Where is he? Is he lying on the ground? Is he alright?

Letty looked frantically everywhere in the completely mowed front yard, calling to Ron, but Ron was nowhere to be seen and did not answer! She then ran to the back of the house. Casually sitting on one of the steps was Ron, gulping down water from a gallon jug.

He turned to Letty and simply said, "I got a little thirsty. Everything is fine. How about rustling up a big bowl of soup with a lot of salt. I'm getting hungry."

"You son of a gun, you scared the wits out of me. I thought you had had another MI when the mower went silent!" Letty said with a great deal of relief showing on her face.

She then fired off question after question at Ron as he just smiled and shook his head softly saying, "Nag, nag, nag."

For now, Ron was okay, but something *major* had happened! After working, he cleaned up by getting into a nice hot bath, laid down in the water, and just relaxed. Because Ron was so quiet, Leticia was still wary with concern.

She kept repeatedly asking, "Are you okay?"

"Yes, I am, and you know what," with water pouring down his head and into his face to remove the soap suds, he said, "I feel better. The PVCs are weaker, and I don't feel them as much now."

Leticia gave Ron a light lunch, and Ron sat in his favorite couch and slowly fell asleep sitting up after what he had done. She left him alone in the only restful sleep he had had for a long, long time.

That night, Ron wasn't sleepy and decided to watch a movie. He was determined to purposely stay awake and wait for what he knew was coming. He waited, but nothing happened! He waited longer, then the PVC's started up again, but this time, their duration was less, and surprisingly, their intensity was less. Although the PVCs remained, a definite change had taken place, for the better!

Ron thought, *I wonder what would happen if I did more yard work?* He turned to ask Letty, but she was already fast asleep so he didn't wake her. He just thought, *Hmm, the porch deck needs paint.*

Ron continued to do light work, any little project that he could help Letty with, and *she* loved it! Leticia came up with all kinds of little, easy honey-do projects. The activity made him feel better, but at night, the PVCs recurred, however, he was getting accustomed to them, and a lot of his fear had lessened.

Weeks passed. Then one night, as watching movies all the time was getting a little boring, Leticia asked Ron, "How is your heart feeling tonight?"

Ron thought for a moment and said. "You know, it didn't bother me last night."

"Are you sure?" Letty probed further.

"Yes," he replied.

However, once again, the pounding in his chest returned, but much weaker. Night after night they returned, but now, they had become intermittent, sometimes not recurring *perceptively* at all for several nights before the bouncing "basketball dance" would begin. There was no question that he felt better, but during his cardiogram tracing sessions, his doctor stated that although he didn't feel these ectopic beats, sometimes not at all, they were still always there and likely would be permanent.

After one of his usual trips to the doctor, Ron asked Letty to sit down with her and talk. He confessed to her that, "I think that this is all that I will ever be. I can't be a Mr. Mom and honey-do lists anymore. I'm worried about how I will be able to support us and what will happen when my disability insurance runs out."

Leticia saw Ron's old depression coming back. "We'll work things out," she said. "Don't worry so much."

That, however, was a lot easier said than done.

"Letty," Ron said, "you don't understand, I've lost my identity and ability. I don't know who I am anymore. I just can't sit around watching movies all day, eating potato chips, doing nothing, and just collecting a paycheck, just mooching on you and the government all the time. I don't know who I am anymore, but I do know that what I've been doing isn't me."

Uh-oh, she thought. Leticia immediately picked up the flashing red sign of *pity* right away, and she knew she had to stop it fast. The last thing in the world that she ever wanted to do was hurt her Ron, but maybe it might be necessary to snap him out of what could be potentially devastating. Leticia decided to do something different.

What she did do was to change their life again and begin an incredible journey that was to take them from the depths of despair to heights she had never dreamed of.

Sometimes a Bee Can Move an Ox

I hate to do this, my love, but I have to hurt you in order to help you, I'm so very, very sorry, Leticia thought, her thoughts being difficult for them to act on.

Leticia continued to try to form her plan and finally came to the conclusion that if she couldn't defeat Ron's depression, then let her battle be total and risk everything. Leticia was now determined, resolving that, "Let it be standing on our feet, staring into our fate, *not* crouched in a corner, hiding from our faces, as cowards!"

They sat down and quietly talked to each other about "little things" with Leticia just trying to relax Ron as much as possible. Then Leticia said to Ron, "You once said that the greatest gift God had given to you was the ability to solve any problem, and you thought that God gave you this gift because a long time ago, you prayed and asked God for only one thing: *wisdom*. Isn't it true that you told me this?"

"Yes," Ron answered.

Letty then pressed the issue further. "If that's all true, then only God can take your gift away, right, so maybe it's now just dormant in you, but it's still there?"

And still pressing even harder she insisted, "Show me that you didn't commit a great sin by throwing your gift into God's face by your actions that you are demonstrating to him, that his gift to you wasn't good enough. Because that's what you're doing, aren't vou? *Not* using that gift is the same thing as *rejecting* God's gift to you." Then Leticia loudly and dramatically shouted out, "*Who are you to reject God?*"

Then silence. Neither spoke.

Ron looked shocked at how and what Leticia had said. His face turned to a look of very deep thought, with his brow now furrowed, and his eyes getting smaller and more narrow as he began to squint. Leticia had smacked Ron in the face, not with her hand, but with what she had so bluntly said.

Then, with a still pensive look on his face Ron said, "*You're r-right.*" His words seemed to come out of his mouth in slow motion, with progressive crescendo louder and louder. At last, a small crack in this beast of depression that Ron was fighting within!

Don't stop, Leticia thought as she could feel and see the light in Ron's face and eyes. *I'm going to push and kick that dad-blamed crack wide open!*

When Ron now asked Letty in earnest, "What do you think I can do?"

She now knew that she had him. She also knew *now* is the time to play dumb but act smart, so she said in a very naive way, "How the heck do I know? You're the one with all the brains,. Fix something!"

"What? Who?" Ron asked as he was now getting interested.

Letty could almost see the wheels of his mind turning. She thought, *Well, I guess it's now time to cast some bread on the waters and hope to get something other than just a lot of soggy bread.*

She then kept pushing Ron forward, "Okay, let's start. Here's a pad and pencil. Let's go, but take your time and write down all the things that you can do, nothing in particular, anything that comes to your mind, and just start writing," Letty encouraged.

To give Ron some time to think, Letty stated, "I think I need a short potty-break," and left the room. Upon returning, she happily remarked, "My, your list is prodigious," as she scanned everything that Ron was still writing."

When he finally finished, Letty said, "Okay, think simple. Pick only one thing that you know and would *really* want to do."

Ron kept turning his ideas in his mind and said, "I want to fix people. After all, I'm still a doctor, aren't I?"

Letty threw her arms around Ron. "Yes, you are, my love, Yes, you are!"

She then passionately kissed him over and over again. In that exact moment, Leticia now knew that she had won their battle,

She had slain the beast!

Through the Eyes of Leticia

Leticia was so happy that her Ron was interested in life again, that she didn't care what he wanted to do. It was enough that she saw Ron doing *something* again, but to "fix people," was indeed a daunting task. Leticia wondered, *What and who to fix?*

Then she got an idea. "Why don't you go to the Hastings Bookstore and browse around. You might come up with some ideas," she said to Ron. "And regardless, even if you don't, you can always pick up the newest good movie."

"Okay, I think I'll do that, but I'm staying away from all medical type books, I don't want to have any constrained thinking. I'd rather wing it and get my own ideas," Ron declared. "*This* is where ideas really come from. Most of the best ideas usually come from simply wandering around, focusing on a clear mind, and *not* thinking of anything in particular."

One day, Ron saw Letty fidgeting with her shoulders.

"Hey, babe, what's wrong?" he inquired.

"Oh, it's just my darn bra straps. They're hurting me and feel like cheese slicers," Letty declared.

Now, Leticia was petite and not exceptionally buxom, so Ron asked, "Why does this happen?"

Leticia responded, "I don't know, but other girls I know that have large breasts are always complaining of shoulder pain and many have their hands going numb in addition. If these poor girls get pregnant, they really go into misery. Their shoulder discomfort can be so bad that they have breast reduction procedures done for relief."

Ron zeroed in on the problem and the dilemma: the girls liked the big breasts because men paid attention to them, but they didn't like the pain and hand numbness that came along with the large breasts. They also didn't like the thought of a surgical procedure that came with scarring, and it was expensive and could have complications from the procedure.

Leticia then questioned, "Can't you do something to fix the problem and help them?"

"Well, I've got a lot of time to think about it. I'll put it at the top of my honey-do list, okay?" Ron promised.

To Ron, this was a *real problem*, not a casual superficial request. Besides, he wanted to do something for Letty and thought, *Let me think about it some more later*.

Several days went by, and the problem nagged at him more and more.

One day, he happened to spot an old book on engineering dynamics that he had in his library. As he scanned through the old book, Leticia asked, "What are you looking at so intently?"

"Oh, it's just one of my ancient books on dynamics," Ron replied.

"What's it all about," she asked?

"It has to do with forces and their distribution," he said.

Leticia queried further, "Do you mean that it could help with my shoulder problem?"

"Maybe," he said.

Ron bookmarked a section of the book and put the book in his very large library. "I'll sleep on it," he told Leticia. Then both went to sleep.

Something had happened to Ron after the electric shocks, his myocardial infarction, and personal trauma, not only to his body, but to his mind. Quite unexpectedly, it was wonderful!

Leticia knew that Ron was always a terrific husband and man, but his mind had become intriguing, a beautiful thing that Letty loved even more and could not even begin to understand. However, she did realize that after she had jolted him to consciousness with her little "bee sting," everything was directed to eliminating pain for everyone, and that made him very special.

Leticia thought, *What do you call a man like that who is all about relieving pain, completely loving and loyal, and who has abilities I can't even come close to being able to understand? I don't know, but I do know that God gave Ron a great gift, and he gave me the greatest gift that I have ever gotten: God gave me back to my Ron!*

Leticia spoke to Ron many times about anything and everything, but when she would ask about specifics, he would seem to go off to a dream world as he was speaking.

He was always very bright but *after October 13, 1996, somehow his brain had gone into overdrive, not* slowdown, and seemed to do everything opposite.

Leticia said, "You do everything in convoluted and opposite ways, yet you always are successful. Please tell me how you do that."

Ron replied, "I can't, but I'll try to tell you." He thought deeply and, after a long pause, said to Leticia, "Sometimes things happen to me when I am just relaxing and not thinking about anything; other times when I am pressed about an issue. For example, I might be just sitting on the toilet seat and staring at the rug on the floor. If the rug has some sort of random design in the weave, I begin to actually see faces in the weave as if someone had drawn with a pencil, a non-animated picture of the face. If I look to a different part of the rug, I see another different face, never animated, but I see other different faces, that appear in succession. The rug may be in color or black and white, and depends on what color the rug might be. These faces never speak. They are rather still-frame, but they may or may not have expressions, can be male or female, old or young, not racially discerned but are rather abstract.

"Other times, I can see images of just about anything, but mostly I see abstract, ill-defined structures that seem to have no meaning, then other times, the structures are *relational* like seeing the graceful lines of a sleek sailboat deck with smooth up-sloping line. Then, I see the eyes of a beautiful young girl with up-tilted eyes from a horizontal line through her two pupils, and the relation becomes the sailboat and the eyes are both the same, *uplifting*. The idea then becomes to my mind that older people have down-sloping eyes at the lateral canthi from the horizontal. Therefore, in my mind, I see that to make women much younger, just raise the eyes of both lateral canthi equally and symmetrically above the horizontal, so you can fix this problem.

"There are many *relationals* occurring, but the most I see are *patterns*. There is always a pattern ever-present, but their meanings are most often unclear. I can't just sit and write something. These images just appear spontaneously. I can't just say that I'm going to be brilliant today, it doesn't happen that way."

Leticia then asked Ron, "How do you feel when this stuff is going on?"

Ron answered, "Sometimes my mind is blank, sort of just recharging my batteries. Other times, it comes with a sudden flash or idea and away I go. When it comes, I just don't want to stop whatever it is that I'm doing, and I don't stop until I feel totally wrung out, with nothing left to give. I'm sorry, but I can't explain what happens. Sometimes, I just wake up at all hours of the night and start doing crude sketches and can't let go of them. Again, I get totally exhausted, then crash, sometimes going to sleep restfully for a full day as you've seen me do."

"Yes, my love, I've seen you do this on many occasions, and I always worry whether you're okay, but always you wake me up asking me to make something to eat," Letty said. "I've noticed something that always happens, and that is that you can take your ideas and thoughts whatever they may be, and make them into something *real*, actually physically *produce them* yourself, and direct others with the layouts, pictures, and text being all your own creations to a concrete result. Then you just sort of move on and say, okay, what's next?"

"My god, Ron!" Letty exclaimed, "Do you realize that from 1997 to 2000, you have been *issued six patents* from the United States Government, and in addition have written *five more patents*, all are called *patent pending? All in the space of three years*, and what's even more amazing, *you did all this after your heart attack in 1996!* Who are you? Who is this man that I so dearly love."

Yes, it was all true!

- a thermally active force diffuser to relieve pain from the shoulders of women, especially those with large breasts
- for soldiers with severe injuries who had lost genitals, an artificial penis that would allow sexual relations with a female and even insemination of the woman, all with ability to prevent infections if one of the partners was already infected.
- for soldiers injured in combat, a Super Sling that could be cut to pieces yet could still give support—float—allow stabilization of steel pins right through the sling without losing its integrity and still be used as a litter between two poles to carry the injured.

Then when Leticia herself had pain because of arthritis preventing her ability to bowl, Leticia cried because of not only the pain, but she had lost the ability to do a sport that she truly loved and asked, "Ron is there anything that can help my hands and relieve my pain?"

Letty's pleading resulted in the following:

- an elastomeric glove with silicone coating that came apart to separate into a tennis elbow section *and* glove

- section that would not slip, helped decrease swelling and pain because of allowing the wearer (Leticia) to hold the bowling ball with less force
- anatomically created soft silicone bowling ball inserts that could accept deformed fingers and function to relieve pain
- bowling ball finger inserts that could be "popped out" and exchanged to allow the fingers to be used comfortably as the deformed fingers allowed swelling to relieve pain.

Leticia had become a project in herself, and Ron was only too eager and happy to "fix Letty." It seemed as if there was no end in sight. Then, for several months, Ron was very quiet. He worked only in the wee hours each day, trying not to awaken Leticia, but as things would occur, some days, Leticia would wake up and Ron would hear the often asked from her, "Are you okay? Is anything wrong?"

"No, I'm just fine," Ron responded with a rather wistful gaze, appearing as though he had a lot on his mind. Then a week later, Ron said, "I have to go to Indiana for a day or two, so how would you like a little road trip?"

"That sounds great," Letty said, "but why are we going there?"

Ron replied, "Well, you know, I've been fiddling around with a few things, and I've invented a few surgical instruments to fix bone fractures and after speaking with the company, DePuy has invited me to present what I've done."

Leticia was very excited and gleefully applauded, then shouted out, "What did you make?"

Ron told Letty the following:

- a special gun barrel trephine that allows a surgeon to fix hips without having to use big incisions (percutaneously) using either or all methods of steel pins, bone grafts, bone cement separately or all together

- instruments that allow a surgeon to fix ankle and elbow fractures directly through the skin to avoid incisions
- one-hand control power forceps to control long bone fractures like femurs and tibias.

"Sounds like fun. I can't wait," Leticia said excitedly. She then added, "I guess we're *really* on our way now, aren't we?"

Ron just casually replied, "Could be."

The trip was a wonderful experience. Everyone was very cordial and Leticia (who always had held engineers in very high esteem) had never seen so many engineers in one place before, and the engineers also had never seen Leticia before. She was absolutely resplendent and stunning in her beautiful green sequined gown when they danced at the night time after meeting soiree. She totally lit up the room, and Ron was so happy and honored that she was his!

She thought her chest would burst with pride because her Ron was conducting the meeting, showing these inventions, explaining how they all worked, but most of all, he was actually helping to save lives!

When he was introduced at the meeting, a copy of Ron's Curriculum Vitae was given to the participants so that all the other engineers and assorted medical people would know who he was.

Everything seemed too be going extremely well, so well in fact, that Leticia and Ron started their own company called Comfortable Lifestyles, LLC—*and Leticia became its president*. A website was created by outsourced contractor, and Letty was ecstatic.

"Look!" she shouted to Ron. "We're getting lots of hits, and not only that, they're agreeing to preopening discounts. This is great! Even better,"—she scanned the inventory—"the prepays are across the board of the entire product line, not just a lot of one type of item."

It looked like Ron and Leticia were on their way!

Then—

The Nasdaq crash of 2000!

Leticia and Ron did not have any money in the Stock Market at the time because they were totally invested in themselves and their own company. Nevertheless, trillions of dollars were lost as the Nasdaq plunged 80 percent of its value. The indirect collateral damage for Letty, and Ron was immense!

Suddenly, everything about their website went eerily silent. Orders were cancelled by private individuals. Previous to show product requests by large bowling concerns became unreachable. Venture capital investors dried up and took flight because of fear.

Everything relative to all the surgical inventions were put on hold by DePuy. Then after a few months went by, DePuy stated they were going to concentrate on their line of artificial joint replacements and therefore would not be going forward on any fracture instrumentations indefinitely.

Everyone was very courteous and polite in the matter, but the fact was, *they* were put on a shelf for an undetermined period of time.

This was devastating!

As all the events regarding the economy, and all their other private affairs continued to unravel, Leticia asked Ron, "Are we both completely back to square one again?"

Looking back at her, Ron glumly said, "Yup."

The Struggle

Ron sat down in his comfortable chair, saying nothing, just thinking. He tried to wrap his mind around the kaleidoscopic events that had occurred.

Leticia said, "It's okay, honey. You'll figure something out. You always do. That's who you are," and she gave him a long loving kiss. Then he said wistfully to Letty, "But there is so much that I don't know, and we're older now."

Leticia responded, "That doesn't matter. I know you'll come through."

But Ron did not feel so sure, although he did not verbalize these thoughts to Letty. He further mused, *Somehow, I've always been able to pull a rabbit out of a hat, but how many rabbits can I still find?*

He struggled mightily with the problems he saw coming at present and in the future. Since he was not able to perform his profession, and being older, who would want him? He was just an "old has been." More deeply and always on his mind, *What happens when the disability insurance runs out or one or both of us get sick?*

He was now just an old man with a lot of problems and not very many options. Ron sadly then confided to Leticia, "Time has passed me by."

But Leticia, always the optimist, responded, "What are you saying?"

She further said with emphasis, "Since when are good ideas not good anymore, and who says *your* ideas are going to stop coming like a shut-off water spigot? Give me a break, the only thing that will happen is since you are older, your ideas will become better because they will be more mature with less throwaways."

Then Ron said, "But, Letty, I'm so far behind the times that I don't know anything about computers and—"

Leticia stopped him in midsentence. "Why can't you learn? I see children taking to computers like ducks to water. Are you telling me that you're not smarter than a duck?"

Both laughed.

"Okay, I'll look around," Ron agreed.

However, everywhere Ron looked, *it seemed that people were only interested in selling something.* So Ron decided to go to a good seminar in St. Louis, a three-hour drive one way!

He did this for two trips and then stopped cold! Leticia questioningly said, "This is not like you to give up on *anything*. What's wrong, my love?"

Ron then answered, "They laughed at me!"

Leticia was shocked and said, "What?"

"That's right. They laughed at me," Ron repeated.

"I don't believe it!" she said. "I agree that you're my husband, but you're one of the smartest guys that I know for real, so how can anybody laugh at you?"

"You don't understand," Ron explained. "These kids eat, sleep, and drink computers since birth. They're light years above me. Every time I ask a simple question, I sound like a real *dolt*. It went from them looking at me from amazement and disbelief like I don't belong, to answering my questions abruptly with their faces appearing bored, to not responding to me at all, and just smirking or outright laughing. It's hard for me to accept kids with baggy clothes, purposefully made holes over their knees, ringy-thingys in their noses like they belong in a stockyard, and with wild hair that looks like some idiot spilled blue, green, and red ink on their hair and over their heads. This just isn't going to work for me."

But after regaling Leticia with all his failed attempts to try to learn, again, something had happened to Ron.

They had laughed at him! This was something intolerable to Ron and would never be allowed!

On the very last of the trips to St. Louis, Ron was fuming inside. He was not a violent man and would never hurt anyone intentionally, but he was really mad. Ron stopped at a restaurant about halfway home, ordered a burger and fries, and just sat in the corner of the room. Because he was now older, his handsome face had developed brow ptosis, giving him an appearance of always being angry anyway, especially when he was deep in thought.

As he ate, his facial expression began to worry the waiters and outright scare the waitresses. It wasn't until he ordered some ice cream and coffee and that he began talking to the servers, that everyone relaxed and realized what a teddy bear he really was.

After that episode, Ron related to Leticia something startling, "I'm going to use a computer even if I don't understand how to use one!"

Leticia just said, "Huh?"

"I've made up my mind that I'm going to do a Henry Ford!"

"I don't understand," she said.

"Don't worry about it. I know what to do now," he said confidently.

"Oh, thank God, thank God," Letty said quietly in a whisper, almost inaudible.

Ron then went to the store and bought a new desktop computer, and Leticia knew immediately what this meant—that when others had laughed at Ron, a genie had been let loose, never to be put into the bottle again!

Questioningly, Leticia then asked Ron, "What did you mean that you're going to do a Henry Ford?"

Ron then regaled Leticia with a poignant and delightful story. "Once, Henry Ford thought about running for office. In an attempt to discredit Ford, his opponents asked him many questions in a debate that Ford could not answer. Thinking that Ford had been made to look ignorant of factual information, gloating, and beginning to ridicule and laugh at him, Ford then made a dramatic statement, paraphrasing: Gentlemen, there are many things that I do not know, but I have this panel on my desk with a lot of buttons in my office, and when I don't know something, I simply push one of those many buttons and a very smart knowledgeable man whom I employ and associated with one of those buttons, immediately hurries into my office and then proceeds to tell me all that I need to know about what I want. These men are called advisors and I usually heed their advice because, gentlemen, I may be ignorant of so many things. I'm smart enough to learn what I don't know."

Leticia stood up, applauding.

"That's my Ron!" she shouted in great glee. "If you can't figure out the program, then build your own. You're Ronald, the cream always floats to the top!"

How wonderful, Ron thought, *that I have Leticia who loves and believes in me that much. I must not fail.*

With all that was going on in Ron's little world, the big world was going relentlessly forward. *Fear* engulfed everyone involved with the investment world; you could almost smell it and taste it as Ron read about the disasters befalling many people who also saw their savings vaporizing before their eyes. And yet strangely, at the same time, there were other Americans who seemed to be oblivious to all this trouble surrounding them. These people were just average people and not wealthy, who just seemed to party-on as if someone else was going to save the day.

And so, within this weird dichotomy of those who were really worried and those who either didn't care, or really didn't have a clue, Leticia and Ron faced the future. On top of everything, they had laughed at him. It gnawed at him deep to the bone. Day after day, he couldn't let his anger and humiliation go away.

Then what happened was unreal—even for Leticia to see.

She saw Ron not shaving for days and writing. The writing was everywhere in Ron's private, quiet man cave, as he called it. Leticia saw that Ron had lots of stickup notes everywhere, like he once put up years ago when he had worked on something involved in his inventions.

He bought more electrical equipment and a second large drafting board, complete with the largest T-Square she had ever seen, the ensemble filling half the small room. Letty thought, *He's writing so much and so fast, that if I stay put in one place, he's going to plaster all these darn stick-ups on me everywhere too, eyeglasses and all.*

Leticia remembered that a long time ago she had used a bee. This time, Ron's anger for being laughed at had unleashed a whole hive of bees, and it was a beautiful thing to behold! She could not keep up with him, and Leticia did everything she could *not* to obstruct anything Ron did.

Leticia thought, *He looks grungy a lot, but I know what's happening and I don't care. I love him all the more for what he's doing for us.* Sometimes, Leticia would be talking to Ron, then suddenly say to her, "Stop!"

Then Ron would start scribbling on any piece of paper that he could get his hands on, then resume the prior conversation almost at the exact last word he had said.

But I don't care, Leticia thought. *I know that all he's doing, he's doing for us.*

Later, Letty asked Ron, "How's the computer stuff working out?"

His reply, "At least I can start the darn thing, and I've figured out how to shut it off now."

Both heartily laughed. New words began to creep into Ron's lexicon—futures, trailing stops, exponential moving averages.

"What's that?" Leticia inquired.

"I don't have a clue yet, but when I figure it all out, I'll explain it to you," Ron replied. He then opened a brand-new book that he had just received. As he read it, his interest grew and grew. It was a manual on money!

Nobody had explained the topic in this way.

Money

After reading the book on money manual, Ron sat down with Leticia and then said, "We are at a huge crossroad."

Letty looked at Ron, her face showing intense interest, her beautiful eyes now opening even wider. She was completely tuned in on the tell-me channel.

"Everything about me has been about solving problems, fixing things, and trying to find something better," Ron explained, "but to accomplish anything that survives—including us—there always has to be the ability to make all these things happen. This great Nasdaq Stock Market Crash and the present situation that we're in has shown me in living, vivid, no nonsense color, that the prime mover of everything is *money*"

Leticia then said, "But, Ron, money isn't everything."

Ron replied, "That's true, but just try to do something without it!"

Leticia was silent and did not respond. She knew that that statement was right. After pausing and thinking for a while, she finally questioned, "But how do we *square things* with what we believe in God and money?"

"It *squares things* very well, and they *do not* conflict," stated Ron confidently.

Leticia was from Missouri and countered, "I don't understand. Show me!"

"Okay, the first thing that you have to understand is that money is not evil," Ron posited.

"Excuse me?" Letty said in shock and disbelief.

"That's right. What is evil is the lust for money at all costs. After all, if money were evil, then why would the Church be constantly asking for money donations, and always passing the plate around on Sundays, and in addition to all this, saying you must do tithing to the Church?" Ron asked.

Leticia was now totally silent and thinking.

"Here's the bottom line," Ron declared. "Money is a *neutral*. Nothing more and nothing less. If someone uses money to help others or buy food for them, then money is good, but if someone uses money to buy a contract to kill a person, then money is bad because of evil intent. Again, it isn't the money that is bad—it's the individual's evil intent within their heart that is evil or bad."

Letty deeply thought and said, "So you mean that a knife or gun is neutral, if the knife is used to prepare food for a family, or a gun to protect that family's life, then that's good. But to use a knife or gun to wantonly kill someone is evil."

"Now you've got it," Ron assured her.

"So how does all this work with what you've been doing?" Letty questioned Ron.

"In a nutshell, the problem that many American people including you and I have is that no matter what we do, we are always dependent on somebody else controlling our money, specifically, whether we will be allowed to have money we need or not. What we have to do is to take out of the equation the necessity of always being dependent on anyone to determine the money for us to live on and prosper. In other words, we have to fix things ourselves so that we are able to produce money independently and not hurt others in the process. In that sense, if we are able to do this, then we will have been truly able to *fix something* as a very smart girl once said to me a long time ago," Ron stated and declared. They both smiled as their recollections came to mind.

Leticia then said, "Okay, how can we fix *our* money problems?"

Ron simply said, "I'm working on it!"

As days passed, Ron finished reading the money manual book *three* times!

He remarked to Letty, "I never knew anything about futures before, but this author explains things so simply that even I can understand it. It's kind of trading like you did many years ago with both the Japanese and Americans when you were just a little girl. In reality, the *Commodity Warehouses* are the same thing as *your stashes* that you protected and hid so your family could stay alive."

"So what do we do now?" Leticia asked.

"I'm going to open a *very small* futures account to see what's going on, but trade very infrequently to limit any losses. Once I have a feel of it and understand better trade mechanisms, maybe I can *fix us*," Ron said.

And so he soldiered on. After his experience with the St. Louis computer seminar, it was obvious that he needed a computer, but in order to get anywhere, he decided to concentrate his efforts rather than try to learn *everything* which was, for sure, definitely an impossible task. After researching the field, Ron said, "I think that I've found a good software package. It has beautiful graphics, so I think I'll buy this one for us."

Letty just said, "Okeydoke," with a very laissez-faire attitude.

As the weeks passed, Leticia mused out loud, "Gee, he must like this software a lot. He's spending hours all day and night with it, and he's not complaining."

But there was something else on Ron's mind.

One day, Ron was having lunch with Leticia, and he said, "As beautiful and good as this program is, all the graphics with the formulas they give are 100 percent correct up to the point when the data service gives the up to date numbers. But the problem is that they always give the 100 percent correct answers *too late to act on because their data has already been recorded.* One always has the immediate problem of deciding exactly what one should do at the precise next day and leaves the precision of the program in limbo. They do estimated projection analysis but their accuracy is fifty-fifty at best leaving the trader with just a guess. What we need is a way to figure out a reliable method that has, not just a super fast program, but to have the ability of the method to project forward into the future, so that in any time-frame what ever futures contract of any commodity of choice is elected, it will be already set up, waiting to actually bump into whatever trade we have to execute, sort of a spider saying come into my parlor little fly and being ready to grab the fly. *Therefore, no matter how fast the computer is, it can be beaten if the method reliably can project what is anticipated in the future."*

Leticia's eyes glazed over and tried to understand what he was talking about, but she felt like she was hopelessly confused and lost at sea. After finishing lunch, Letty said, "Do you think you can figure this stuff out? I'm lost."

Ron replied, "Don't know. I'm going to keep trying."

However, Ron was certain that he was right about what had to be done but doing and getting was a long way to *gotcha*! He knew that there were lots of traders who got things right and became extraordinarily successful like W. D. Gann and Jesse Livermore. Neither ever gave away their secrets. Livermore was consumed by thoughts of numbers and time, as was an inventor named Nichola Tesla. The same was true of Gann who was a very religious man and was always quoting scripture referring to time and the sky-filled universe and would frequently reiterate that there was nothing new under the sun and that, that which has been done before, will be again, and that even those who said things were new, were things that were done before.

Leticia saw that Ron was fascinated and, for hours, could not let things go.

Then one day as they were relaxing and watching the movies, Leticia was channel surfing and suddenly Ron said, "Stop for a moment!" His face seemed glued to the TV screen.

"Don't turn off the TV," Ron exclaimed.

Ron was transfixed onto an educational program which was discussing the topic of *magnetism*. He quickly put a tape into the VCR and recorded the program in its entirety and would not let Letty move the channel, even when the commercials came on.

Leticia then asked Ron, "Why are you suddenly so fascinated by this program?"

Ron answered, "I don't know, but there's *something* there."

When the program was over, Leticia carefully put the tape on his desk. Both resumed channel surfing and later settled on the movie *New Moon* with Jeanette MacDonald and Nelson Eddy.

Little did Leticia know then that the tape she had preserved for Ron would again change her life!

LETICIA'S GREAT GAMBLE—
THE WOW FINALE

Although Leticia's great gamble was about to begin, she did not as yet come to grips with what was happening.

On a quiet day, as Ron toiled in his man cave, Letty became startled as she heard him shouting, *"I've got it! I've got it!"* he kept repeating in ever-increasing volume; *it's as old as time itself!*

Letty ran into his room to see if Ron was okay. "What are you yelling about?" she asked.

Ron, then in a triumphant air about him and with a totally self-satisfied look on his face confidently exclaimed. "I've solved the enigma of the tape!"

"Think moving bacteria, pigeons with magnetic hats, brain soup," Ron excitedly exclaimed.

Leticia thought, *Oh god, he has flipped out! The poor guy has been trying so hard that he's gone over the edge!*

Ron excitedly said to Letty, "It was right in front of me all the time, but I couldn't see it!"

Leticia tried to calm Ron down as she hugged and kissed him, but he was oblivious. She then said, "That's great, but I have no idea what you're talking about. Let's sit down over a cup of coffee so you can explain what it is that you're so excited about."

"Okay," Ron replied.

Letty then said, "Let's go very slowly and—"

Ron was still excited and cut her off abruptly in midsentence. *"What is connected is magnetism and the universe!"*

"Oh really," she responded, "so what does that have to do with the price of tea in China?"

"Literally and figuratively, *everything* that you can think of," Ron declared.

"Now, I really don't know what you're talking about, so tell me very slowly, all the gory details in terms that all of us little mortals can understand. What the heck are you talking about?" Leticia said.

"It all starts with pond scum," Ron began, but Letty thought that Ron was having fun with her, and she got up from the table and began to walk away.

"No, really, sit down, I'll try to explain," Ron pleaded.

"Okay, but if you start talking about little green men, I'm out of here," Leticia sternly said.

"It's a very hard thing to try to simplify, but I'll try. Just keep an open mind, listen, and I'll try very hard not to put you to sleep," Ron stated.

"Okay, here goes," he continued.

"Everything and all of us are connected, starting with the very smallest of things to the largest, and all is in constant motion," he posited.

"By who or what?" Leticia queried.

"By magnetism," Ron stated and declared.

"Stay with me now," Ron told her.

Again, from the smallest to the largest:

- Bacteria in pond scum *move* in relation to the north and south poles of a magnet and can be seen with an electron microscope also paramecia can be seen in magnetic structures that line up similarly.
- Lobsters in migration can navigate regardless of how murky the water is, even in the pitch-black night, being guided by the magnetic lines of the earth.
- The same thing is true for fish like salmon and birds of flight.

- Homing pigeons know how to find their way regardless of the weather conditions, but as experiments have been shown, if a homing pigeon is strapped to a small magnet on its head, the pigeon gets hopelessly lost and can't find its way home.
- Regarding *man*, if brain tissue from cadavers is turned into a brain soup with a mixer. Magnetic properties can be found, however, small.
- The earth itself, and all planets plus the sun are all huge *bar magnets*, therefore. All things in the universe are essentially inter relationally connected with everything else.

"Are you still with me?" Ron asked Letty.

"So far, so good," she replied. "Please continue this stuff is getting fascinating."

Ron then explained, "People are influenced by magnetism, some more than others, depending on how their internal poles line up when exposed to the variations of the magnetic fields that fluctuate. The internal poles of people are connected with human emotions, and human emotions and feelings are influenced by the universe and its magnetic fluctuating properties, which reach people through space and time. Traders and investors all have, anatomically, the same kinds of internal magnetic poles that must have different amounts and variation. Since people perform in a society and are interconnected with the markets, the movement of the markets can be seen and represented as graphic charts using stocks and futures. Therefore, *all markets move with magnetism*. Some more than others depending on how many and where the planetary bar magnets are located at any point in time. *This is why markets fluctuate up and down*."

Leticia had now become extremely interested, and she thought, *My god, nobody can explain things that are so complicated and make them understandable to me like my Ron can.*

She wanted to continue, but Ron said, "Let's take a short break, make some more coffee, and take a breather, a potty break might be a good idea at this point."

A little while later, they sat down at the table again. Leticia then said, "Well, I've thought about what you said, and I think I'm beginning to get it."

"That's good," Ron responded, "because it gets a little more complicated. I'll go very slowly, so if I lose you, I'll try to explain better, okay?"

Letty nodded yes in agreement.

"Here we go," he said and began. "The sun is the biggest bar magnet in our universe. It gives off the heat and light that gets to earth as electromagnetic waves that scientists have shown can be represented as *sine waves* in graphic form. That means that these sine waves can be quantified and qualified."

Ron then drew some of the different sine wave representations for Letty to see, and she immediately verbalized that what she saw was that. "There were tall ones and short ones, had a snake-like form that tended to writhe either quickly or slowly, that they changed with great frequency, and were wide or narrow."

"Boy, you're sharp." Ron applauded Letty, encouraging her. "That's exactly what you're supposed to see."

"But it's a lot more complicated in that what you're seeing and describing is in two dimensions," Ron explained.

"What really happens is the sine waves travel in three dimensions, and there's a fourth dimension of time while all this is going on, all at the same time."

Leticia then remarked, "I'm starting to feel dumb again."

"Don't," Ron said, "it's not easy to understand. You're doing fine."

"But here it gets a little *hairy*," he stated, trying to reassure her.

"By looking at the graphics of stocks or commodities like precious metals," Ron posited, "it's possible for a trader or any other person to actually see the emotions of people as these graphics move. They possess and *create footprints, which you can see and are independent of manipulation.* Understanding this allows someone to *project these footprints into the future."*

"Are you kidding me?" Leticia asked in disbelief.

"Nope," Ron confirmed.

"As a matter of fact," Ron declared, "understanding what we've been talking about allows someone who is expecting a footprint event and projecting it forward, to simply wait for the *critical point* in time anticipating the footprint—regardless of computer speed—thus simply placing an expected trade at the point in time where *time will be up*. The trade then actually triggers itself. In this sense, a knowledgeable person can render a super fast computer less effective by knowing when time is up, and a reversal has the greatest probability that that reversal will take place. And so placing an actual trade becomes almost incidental as the graphic footprint literally moves to the critical *time is up* and trips the trade itself."

Leticia couldn't believe what Ron had said. "Is this really the way to work the market?" she asked.

"I think so," he answered, "and further than that, I believe that Jesse Livermore once stated that he had made most of his money on the big moves by just sitting and waiting for them, and *not* trading frequently, and in addition to that, Ron noted that Gann had said that there is nothing new under the sun. *He may have believed that all things repeat by universal magnetic design in the same way."*

Leticia sat almost dumbfounded and didn't move a muscle. When she finally spoke, she said, "With all the problems we're facing, can this really be the path that we should take to achieve the independence that we've been looking for?"

"I believe that it is, but I have to firm up a plan for us first and try it out because I don't want to do a ready-fire-aim situation just because we're excited," Ron declared.

"I think so too," Leticia agreed.

About two months passed, ever slowly. Ron was now unusually quiet. Leticia was constantly thinking about all the things Ron had said, thinking about all the bills, thinking about failure which could then lead to absolute ruin and poverty, thinking, thinking.

But for Ron, not only was failure not an option, but it did not seem to exist for him; there were just problems that had to be solved. He was always steady and the same.

In his world, "nervous" meant "concern." In Leticia's world, *fear* was beginning to rule the day. She became increasingly jumpy. She would jump at everyone—salespeople, repair people, friends, even Ron, who would just get a cup of coffee and disappear into his man cave when Letty would be unusually wound up.

Dishes were nervously broken, the house needed cleaning but was left undone because of pain in her hands (perceived or otherwise), and sleep became less and less possible with "wee" hour bouts of coffee drinking, worsening her ability to sleep. Sometimes, she would see more hair than normal in her brush and comb in the morning. The tension was growing progressively. The tension was becoming unbearable!

And then, *nothing*. The usual "man cave" noises had stopped. The TV was off. Leticia could hear the ticking of the clock on the wall; it seemed to get louder and louder. Then she looked for Ron. He wasn't there. Leticia's nerves were on high alert, which magnified her worry. She looked frantically all around the house. Was he lying on the floor somewhere? Then, Letty heard the front door close. She hurriedly went toward the sound and found Ron beginning to make a pot of coffee.

"Hi, babe," he said.

With a questioning face, Letty said nothing, waiting for Ron to begin a conversation first. Both sat down in the kitchen and began drinking coffee, just looking at each other, Letty with a quizzical face, Ron with a satisfied expression like a cat that had just eaten the canary.

Leticia couldn't stand it any more and finally said, "Okay, what's going on?"

Ron simply said, "*We're ready!*"

The words she had been waiting for, longing for, *they had come!* Leticia's face instantly lit up.

Before she could say anything, Ron declared "Silver, that's what we'll use. I've completed our plan, and I think I know how to make it all work. We're going to use the futures market and do something futures traders usually don't do: we're going to take delivery of silver bars and force the COMEX to give it to us."

"What?" Leticia shouted.

"You heard me right," he said and repeated what he had just said.

"You're wacky," Leticia said.

"No, I'm right," Ron insisted.

"Oh, give me some aspirins, please," she pleaded.

"No, no, no. Relax, it will work as long as I'm right about pond scum," Ron posited.

"You're crazy! Do you mean we're going to put all the money we have in pond scum?" Leticia screamed. "I've waited all this time for you to come up with a good plan and you come up with pond scum?"

Leticia had been so anxious for so long that she had zeroed in on pond scum and completely tuned out what Ron had said about silver and futures. It was obviously time to stop the conversation, get her calmed down, and begin later, much later. Ron said nothing to Leticia for the rest of the day. Just before the evening supper, Letty set the table and began to cry.

"Why are you crying?" Ron asked.

Letty said nothing.

"The Mahi-Mahi looks great. I'll have a big piece, please," Ron requested, but he did not press any issues.

After supper, Leticia relaxed.

Ron looked into her eyes and asked, "Feel better now?"

"Yes," she responded.

"Can I tell you about my plan now?" he asked. "All I want is for you to sleep on it tonight. Just relax, nothing is set in cement."

"Okay," she replied.

Ron began to unfold his ideas slowly, explaining all the details and answering all her questions. As Leticia actually listened this time, she thought, *You know, this might not be so crazy after all.*

After saying all he could say, Ron declared, "Just sleep on this tonight, and we'll talk again tomorrow."

The soft, rays of sunlight gently seeped into the morning room following with it, the smell of bacon, eggs, and coffee. Bleary-eyed, Leticia slowly shuffled her way to the kitchen table.

"Good morning," Ron greeted her and kissed her. "A good breakfast will get you going."

As they ate, Leticia queried, "Do you think your plan will really work? Do you think that little people like us can really force the COMEX to fork over the silver?"

"Yes, I do. They have to," Ron replied.

"Tell me *why* again," she asked.

"The key is this: *by law* if you have bought a futures contract, and *hold it until it expires* then at expiration, the person holding the expired contract *must take physical possession of the commodity, in this case, the silver. That person must take delivery and the COMEX must deliver it.* That means, as long as you can pay for it, the silver bars are yours at expiry *and the COMEX will even warehouse it for you! Therefore, US Law forces this issue to be done: i.e., delivery forces the COMEX transaction.* The only fly in the ointment is if the price of the silver drops below the level you bought it. In that case, you have to offset the futures contract and sell, taking a loss, but releasing the delivery mandate. If I am correct regarding my magnetic resonance theory, the risk of loss should be low and gain could be great," Ron explained.

Letty pressed the question, "How sure are you?"

"Nothing is 100 percent or *always*, but the probability of success is very high," Ron asserted.

"Your ideas have *always* been good. Let's take a chance. Let's do it!" she said in a now determined fashion.

Ron explained carefully to Leticia what initial margin and maintenance margin were. Also, he told her that he would be backing the trade with some of his money that he had saved.

Leticia asked, "Are you *that* certain?"

"*Yes!*" he responded.

Leticia was now really excited; her mind was in a whirl! She thought, *How can I help what Ron is going to do? How can I help the two of us?* Her mind felt like it was going to explode.

Then, it came to her: *plastic!*

Leticia decided to attempt a great gamble and came up with the idea that she would get the necessary money and, at the same time, backup the trade, so if the trade fell sour, they wouldn't lose everything. Recently, Letty remembered a bit of advertisement mail that stated a credit card was giving terms which included a 0 percent APR for six months. She also recalled that Ron had stressed using an *intermediate* term for his theory of magnetic resonance. Leticia spoke with the credit card company and obtained information on the maximum amount of loan allowable that she could get based on the 0 percent APR credit card.

The credit card company was quite *anxious* to give her the loan, so Leticia was a little hesitant and thought, maybe rethinking the whole thing wouldn't be such a bad idea, so she casually stated, "I'll get back to you."

That evening, Letty said to Ron, "I have an idea that might help us a lot and also put a safety net under our plan."

Ron replied, "That's great. Let's hear it."

"Okay, goes like this," she said. "You've told me that it takes time for your plan to be successful, somewhere in the range of months, correct?"

"Yes," Ron agreed.

Leticia then explained her thoughts. "I've already checked the numbers, and I'm thinking that if I use *my* credit card—that is clean without any money owed—that I can get a 0 percent APR loan with the maximum amount of my credit card limit for six months, and that I can buy the one futures contract of silver and give us the time to allow the magnetic wave to work its magic on the silver market and, at the same time, put a loss protection floor under the contract to protect our savings. The day the six months loan period is over, I'll pay it all off completely. I will *not* have to pay any interest on the 0 percent APR, which will mean the credit card company will have been loaning the silver to us for free! We will then pay the cost of the delivery from the COMEX taking it from our savings, and the difference will be *our profit in the form of appreciation of the silver, not dollars,* from time contract bought to time of delivery, since we have never touched our silver, *no sale of the silver* has ever been done. If things go badly, I will pay off the six months loan STAT, which will be a wash, and we'll still have the bulk of our savings to recover. What do you think?"

Immediately, Ron understood.

"I think my wife is a genius!" he applauded.

"If you keep coming up with ideas like that, we're really going to do great!" Ron said.

Leticia's first gamble began in 2002 when silver was cheap at a little over $4 per ounce. About six months later, her appreciated silver bars were stored in a vault after delivery for safe keeping.

She had done it! Leticia was so excited, she couldn't contain herself!

"Let's do it again! Let's do it again," she enthusiastically cried out. Both of them carefully reviewed the magnetic charts, looked at each other, and with big smiles on their faces, Ron said, "You betcha!"

Leticia did it again, but this time, she increased the loan amount on the credit card. *It was the same result,* but this time, the appreciation profit was much bigger for the second transaction. Leticia had now taken full delivery of two silver contracts, paid for them in full, then placed the stored bars vaulted for safekeeping. The value of *each* of the initial two contracts had gone up, plus each of the two appreciations on top of that were growing significantly.

"Oh my god!" Leticia screamed in complete jubilation. "Let's do it again!"

Ron again reviewed his magnetic projections and said to Leticia, "Go for it!"

However, on the third attempt, the credit card company somehow decided to discontinue the 0 percent APR deal after Leticia kept increasing her maximum line of credit.

Leticia then said, "Oh no, I'm not going to be able to get this *free* trade anymore, even though they're giving me all kinds of other offers. They're just not free trades."

Ron replied, "I guess they have finally caught on."

"Guess so," Letty agreed.

"I was wondering how long it was going to take them," Ron said.

Ron saw Letty's face getting droopy and sad and said, "Why are you so sad?"

Leticia replied, "I can't help you anymore."

"Are you kidding me?" he said. "Do you have any idea what you accomplished?"

At that time, it didn't really sink in yet, but in truth, Leticia had taken a great gamble, the result of which she had never dreamed to be able to accomplish.

She had ridden the magnetic wave to glory *ten times* all the way through 2010 and beyond, taught others how to do it, and remembered something locked in her mind from the time when she was just seven years old—and that was *to be successful, all anyone has to do is to find out what people need and want, get it for them, and then get paid as much as she deserves for her efforts.*

For Ron and Leticia, *destiny had led them by the hand!*
So it was written, so it was done, and the rest, as they say, is history!

Epilogue

To all of you wonderful people who so graciously took the time to read my book, I would like to leave you with a warm thought:

If you open the cage of a beautiful, magnificent bird and release it
to its freedom as it soars to the sky, but does not return,
then he was never your bird in the first place,
but if he returns to you of his own free will,
then he is yours forever.
Never, never, ever just give him away, ever!

God bless you all.

—Leticia